# PAST TO PRESENT

*A Reporter's Story of War, Spies, People, and Politics*

## WILLIAM STEVENSON

LYONS PRESS
Guilford, Connecticut

*An imprint of Globe Pequot Press*

Lyons Press is an imprint of Globe Pequot Press.

All photos courtesy of the author.
Layout artist: Sue Murray
Project editors: Kristen Mellitt and Meredith Dias

Library of Congress Cataloging-in-Publication Data

Stevenson, William, 1925-
  Past to present : a reporter's story of war, spies, people, and politics / William Stevenson.
    p. cm.
  Includes index.
  ISBN 978-0-7627-7370-1
  1. Stevenson, William, 1925-  2. Authors, Canadian—20th century—Biography.  3. Journalists—Canada—Biography.  4. Air pilots—Great Britain—Biography.  5. Great Britain. Royal Navy—Biography.  6. World War, 1939-1945—Personal narratives, British.
  I. Title.
  PR9199.3.S7876Z46 2012
  813'.54—dc23
  [B]
                                                                            2012018726

Printed in the United States of America

10 9 8 7 6 5 4 3 2 1

*To Monika and Alexandra with all my love.*

# Contents

# A Note from the Author

A TIRADE AGAINST TYRANNY WAS SPOKEN BY VICTOR HUGO. HE SAID that back in the mid-1700s, "the suppression of autocratic regimes and the limitation of armaments were debated and dismissed . . . Is this a reason for abandoning hope that at long last men will learn wisdom?" The question troubled Helene Berr, a young Parisienne. In the first two years of Nazi occupation, she pursued a love of life, music, and literature. Then she was made to wear a yellow star. She continued to study at the Sorbonne, celebrated classical music with fellow musicians, and extracted from libraries and bookshops the dog-eared remains of classical English literature. Germans indulged such behavior among the privileged young: It earmarked future victims. Helene kept a diary. She strolls through the Paris of old. She quotes great philosophers. Bit by bit, she also notes where she is heading as the enemy clears out one Jewish quarter after another. In 1944, she writes that she is selected to board a cattle-wagon. Here her diary ends. Helene died five days before American troops reached the death camp where she was caged. Her notes survive.* And once again I hear my French mother reading aloud, at the start of the Nazi Blitz on London, the very same question posed by Victor Hugo. This girl in Paris might as well have been on Mars, so sharply did war separate us from Continental Europe. Yet she, too, wondered: "Is this a reason for abandoning hope that at long last men will learn wisdom?"

I grew up clinging to such a hope. Yet I served in a fighting navy. There was no contradiction here. I had grown up in the dockside area where as a boy I learned to deal with harsh realities with compassion. I

---

* *Journal d'Helene Berr* was finally published in 2008 by Editions Tallandier, Paris.

belonged to a Boy Scout troop where Sunday morning "Divisions" was a tradition of weekly prayers, calling our Eternal Father to "hear us when we cry to thee / For those in peril on the sea." Our warships fought the crucial Battle of the Atlantic. If it were lost, said Winston Churchill, all would be lost. Torn between hope and reality, I learned about those dragons of Greek mythology that soared, as I soared as an aviator. The dragons looked down upon us from dizzy heights. These little monsters now come up from below with old forgotten notes for me to piece together. They remind me of a boy, young as Helene, torn between hope and looming realities. "To survive past and present ills," the little monsters tell me, "accept Helene's early vision of a future in which hope is all that ensures survival." The little Parisienne did not survive. Yet her love of life emerges, more than half a century later, to teach us never to forget. She taught me about the real dragons haunting us and forever teaching us to be wary and never take things at face value, sometimes wearing masks of good intentions never straight forward, teaching us to be always on guard: the dragons of everyday life, offering us lessons we sometimes read wrongly. These were the dragons which fooled Helene while she lived among them, fooling her in her early days under the Nazi occupation so that she lived a normal, happy life as a student, never suspecting the dragons were plotting a time when she could be scooped up more easily later. For the purpose of all dragons is never easy to divine.

# CHAPTER 1

# Not Posh

I knew him in my schooldays as The Boxing Parson of London's East End. Now he tells me, "You worked out of North America. After such a snuggery, you're bound to feel down-hearted."

"I just got back from Africa," I correct him. I skip in pace with his goblin-like figure. "And I'm not downhearted."

"I heard it in your voice at lunch."

"I miss clear skies and open spaces," I concede. We are walking along Pall Mall. Tall gray buildings hem us in. The pavement underfoot is unyielding, the road is foggy with fumes from trucks and double-deck buses and boxy black taxis. Delivery vans dart between gaps in the muttering traffic. Africa this is not, with its soft, warm, natural red dirt soil.

He swerves into St. James's Street and flourishes a gold-knobbed cane in the direction of Buckingham Palace. "I preach there now." He could be a salesman pointing out the store where he works. His current title is Chaplain to Queen Elizabeth the Second, so it's pretty obvious where he works, but he never lost his taste for comedy since he taught me, a skinny urchin, how to punch out the classroom bully.

"We're far from the slums now," he says. "Been back, have you?"

"No. Too full of—" I stumble.

"Full of dragons? Little monsters of the mind." He squints at me from under his flat broad-brimmed clerical hat. I see the broken nose in a leathery face. It hasn't changed much since we spoke a different slang.

"Can we stop for a tick?" I ask while we advance to Piccadilly. "I need to pop into my bank."

"Short of the needful? Pop along, dear boy! Gather ye spondoolicks while ye may." He follows me into the Westminster Bank, fated to be gobbled up by NatWest, whose nearby local branch hums with new wealth.

Inside my cozy old bank, the queen's chaplain settles on a bench. During lunch he had said I was the right chap to manage biodiversity on the farms of the Duchy of Cornwall. There, Prince Charles, more far-sighted than he is given credit for at this time, challenges "the bastions of conventional thinking" and laments publicly that he is "dismissed as a dreamer in a modern world that clearly thinks itself too sophisticated for 'obsolete' ideas. But if we ignore Nature, everything starts to unravel." I think Charles's chances of becoming king are remote and so he confronts new realities. He writes: "China, once seen as dirt-poor, will run roughshod over our old imperialist snobbery. Our former colonies in India and Africa always understood biological diversity . . . None of us will survive if the underlying well-being of the planet is destroyed."*

I tell the chaplain that His Royal Highness voices my boyhood dream of taking better care of Nature, but for the likes of me, the Duchy of Cornwall is a challenge that sounds—well, a bit too posh.

He must have been mulling this over because now he says, "Did you know 'posh' comes from Port-Outward, Starboard Home? In days of empire, *burra memsahibs* sailing out to the colonies booked cabins according to where the sun would shine, port-side on the voyage out, starboard home." He natters on, relishing a sudden tension among bank clerks corralled behind a black grid that discourages bank robbers. A couple of new clerks whisper. They clearly think he is too flamboyant to be true. He enjoys the stir and twitters away, chin resting on his walking stick. I approach my favorite teller and tell her I need to withdraw one hundred pounds.

Her gaze slides over my shoulder. She takes in the clerical hat with purple band and the royal blue cape with golden clasps. I can almost hear the words "con artist" jog through her mind.

---

* His Royal Highness Charles, Prince of Wales, later summarized these ideas in his book *Harmony: A New Way of Looking at Our World*, published in 2010 by AG Garrick Ltd.

"May I see your identity card?" she asks me. She looks properly embarrassed. She has known me forever. My battered old naval officer's sea trunk is in the bowels of the bank, deposited there for safekeeping long ago. All I want now is to discreetly withdraw some cash to cover my share of lunch.

The manager appears. "Good afternoon, rev!" he calls out. "Another day at the palace?"

It's a little joke they share, usually when nobody is around. The reverend bangs his cane on the polished wood floor in appreciation. The teller looks suitably abashed and produces my money.

Outside, my companion says, "I'm taking tea with committee members at the Royal Overseas Club." He gestures across the street.

"I know it well," I reply. "Each time I returned with my family from some wilderness, we lived there."

"That's when the club took care of visitors from 'backward countries,'" he murmurs. "Today those we once called colonials have risen far above our assumption of smug authority."

"And I can no longer afford to rent rooms there," I respond.

He smiles. "A good reason to reflect upon this opportunity. If you have more questions about the Duchy, give me a tinkle later."

"One thing I need to get straight now." I tug his arm. "What did you mean by dragons?"

His battered old face turns up to me. "Everyone keeps 'em somewhere below. Dragons in the basement of the mind. They jump you across time-lines. Only humans follow them with our invented calendars."

I give him a "tinkle" on the telephone later. "Come stay at the rectory," he says. "Enjoy Prince Charles's clear skies and open spaces." Some days later, he picks me up with my wife and four children at Portsmouth rail station and drives us in a battered old car through winding leafy lanes. "Here's my village. It was the benchmark for the Domesday Book. William the Conqueror ordered the survey in 1085. Name is from Old English *dom* meaning Judgment Day. It records all landholdings in England from the time of Edward the Confessor." He says this for the benefit of the children. Next morning, before the Sunday sermon, the grown-ups sip sherry and he explains the dragons. "They pop up higgledy-piggledy. They link one event here to another event there, in notional proximity. Schoolboy dreams of adventure linked you to the king of Bhutan years later when you ask him about the Royal Index of National Happiness. Dragons link today with yesterday, sooner or later."

My old friend raises questions my dragons might ask. How did I see Aung San Sun Kyi as a girl in Bhutan before she defies Burma's tyrants? How did I release North Americans trapped in Tito's Yugoslavia and get an account of Tito's guerrilla tactics translated by the king of Thailand? Who sent me to a Soviet mountaintop to watch Red China's atomic bomb tests? Why did China's Zhou Enlai tell me not to board an airliner to Indonesia for an Afro-Asian conference? What made Zhou take a different route and secretly pause in Singapore to ask Royal Navy divers to search for bits of the bomb that sabotaged that airliner? What childhood memories made me report from the Afro-Asian conference: "For the first time, I feel part of a white-faced minority?"

The Boxing Parson shows me Prince Charles's environmentally friendly crops. I protest that overseeing their seasonal rotation would stop me from continuing to explore the world. He responds, "Dragons in Greek mythology soared to see distant dangers. Perhaps you still need to soar."

Dangers erupt in Malaysia a few days later. My friend Dick Haddow, a "white Gurkha," is killed in a so-called "war of confrontation against the neocolonial Malay Federation" launched by Indonesian forces, armed by the Soviet Union, and backed by Red China. I am asked by someone code-named Adelaide to return to this region I know so well and asks my wife Glenys to keep to herself my involvement with secret intelligence. We all go: my wife, Glenys, and our four children. Glenys remains "semiconscious" about a secret agency for which I work as a newsman. In Kuala Lumpur we live in a house on Jalan Kenny Timor, near "The Bashed Tin Shop" that sells us groceries. Our three older children go to a British Army school. I slip in and out of the enemy camp by way of neutral Thailand. No income tax, no paperwork to cover expenses. And no more worry about pensions: I am promised one for the first time in my life.

4

My dragons drag me forward and back across a world where calendars are ignored. Notional proximity prevails. Perspectives change and often revise earlier conclusions. These dragons make me view past events in a new light. I remember the queen's chaplain conjoining me with boyhood days when my mother read aloud Greek myths about dragons soaring high enough to view a panorama of events, both forward and back.

I never did grow healthy food for the Duchy of Cornwall. I had worked too long out of North America, where anyone may rise to the top. In Britain, an empire is transformed into a commonwealth of good intentions. "I remain working class," I tell The Boxing Parson. He understands my need to investigate worldly mysteries and justify my survival after friends died for freedom. He gives me his blessing. We both retain a schoolboy sense of fun and nonconformity.

It was his love of pranks that inspired his impersonation of a con artist at my dear old stuffy bank.

## CHAPTER 2

# Back to the Lowest Form of Marine Life

"I NEED MEN OF THE WORLD," COMMANDER IAN FLEMING TELLS ME, before he invents James Bond, and after my life as a Royal Navy fighter pilot ends. I no longer wear a World War II uniform that makes girls swoon. Silver-haired old ladies no longer brush my wings of gold and murmur, "God bless you, son."

I'm back to "the lowest form of marine life." Chief Petty Officer Pony Moore called us that while we trained to become Ordinary Seamen before we could advance any further: a quaint echo of ancient ritual. My last ship is home from the Pacific. I wear a baggy "austerity suit" dished out to cash-poor veterans. This is not America, where I glimpsed the generous welcome given to vets, regardless of social status. This is Merry Olde England, once more divided into upper and lower classes. Winston Churchill is back in the wilderness. Visions of a brave new world are shattered. Britain is broke.

I have been sent to Fleming by a fellow pilot, Terence Horsley, high enough on the social ladder to become postwar editor of *Empire News*, which trumpets glad tidings about an empire already falling apart. *Empire News* is part of Lord Kemsley's newspaper chain, serviced by *Mercury News*, which also reports to British intelligence. Fleming is no longer 17F of Naval Intelligence. He runs *Mercury News* instead.

He tells me, "You're here because you saved Horsley's life."

I am distracted for a moment by the recollection of Horsley piloting a Tiger Moth, a flimsy biplane first designed more than twenty years ago. Normally, he piloted a carrier-borne Stringbag which was not much of an

6

improvement, although now built to drop torpedoes and sea mines and armed with a gunner in open cockpit to protect my rear if attacking modern German fighters, sleek Me-109s, the Nazi monoplanes that caught Poland by surprise when Hitler attacked its ragged defenses in 1939.

My mind returns to dealing with Ian Fleming. "My Stringbag saved him. I happened to be in the c-cockpit," I stammer.

"*Who* matters. Not *what*." He waves a carved ivory holder and watches the smoke rings from his gold-banded cigarette rise to the ceiling. Alone in a cockpit, I could hide boyhood twitches. Here and now, childish stutters and blushes plague me again. But I need a job. I ask straight out: "How do I become a man of the world?"

"You've been offered a permanent commission as Lieutenant, Fleet Air Arm. That's one way."

"One way to a fast fare-thee-well. No thanks."

"Very wise. You chaps lost more lives in accidents than in combat."

I bristle. I have heard that Fleming spent the war cooking up dirty tricks for others to carry out. "His schemes were mad," wrote the embittered Operational Research scientist Freeman Dyson. He proved that RAF fliers took heavy casualties because Lancaster bombers were burdened with useless gun turrets and escape hatches too narrow for stricken crews to squeeze through. Secrecy forced Dyson to send his reports exclusively through one Whitehall government official whose only worry was to win a knighthood by never contradicting his commander-in-chief. Thousands of fliers thus met a fiery death. Dyson could not write this publicly until he moved to the United States. In the British navy, no wartime scientists investigated casualties. Our aircraft were killers of our own crews.

I have heard all the scuttlebutt about Ian Fleming's derring-do never extending beyond storytelling in Boodles and other cozy Whitehall clubs. Now he sends up more smoke rings while he says, "Go somewhere exotic, dear boy. Go—ah—go to . . . Canada."

I don't tell him I've been there already. I am muzzled by another code of silence. I won my wings near Camp X in Canada. It trained "hyphenated Americans" to become secret agents in their Nazi-occupied homelands.

They crossed Lake Ontario to avoid border controls. Camp X also taught guerrilla warfare. Later, in the twenty-first century, an infamously delayed Freedom of Information Act permits Sir Charles Wheeler, the BBC's best-known foreign correspondent, to reveal on TV that he was parachuted behind Nazi lines before D-Day, and to add: "Ian Fleming's dirty tricks were as daft as his Bond plots."

The BBC's star reporter was never allowed to know that Fleming also worked with British Security Coordination (BSC) run from New York by the man called Intrepid, a Canadian. Fleming's advice that I move to "exotic" Canada was no joke. Camp X still functioned in postwar secrecy. I was already part of a super secret postwar British secret agency, Security Intelligence Department (SID), whose existence was never officially disclosed until more than twenty years later.

# CHAPTER 3

# Foul Storms Ahead

THESE DAYS, I WRITE IN OUR ATTIC. MY DRAGONS RISE UP TO DEMAND attention. The problem with my dragons is that they bring up events out of chronological order. When they bring up family matters that can be confusing because I have two families. To clarify: I married my first wife, Glenys, in 1944. We separated in the late seventies when our four children, Andrew, Kevin (now deceased), Jackie, and Sally, were grown. All of us shared many of the adventures described in this book. Glenys and I remain good friends and delight in our grandchildren. I married my second wife, Monika Jensen, in 1984 and we have one daughter Alexandra, a journalist with a passion for covering many of the same places I did. Monika is downstairs trawling through forgotten logbooks, shorthand notes, rolls of film, and fading images. She has the background to research the history of our times, as she is an Emmy-winning producer of CBS TV's *60 Minutes*, winner of a New York gold medal for best TV documentary, author of nonfiction books, and editor of a cultural magazine. She stirs the dragons that dodge across linear time to haunt me with half-forgotten events. So many things I dumped in isolated singularity now come together and take on fresh meanings. A stream of unbidden dragons rise from my basement with memories I thought were long ago locked away. These are tiresome dragons, not always solid and hard to interpret: dragons of the mind floating up to puzzle me with forgotten mysteries. There is no mystery about my love for Monika when we both worked on the same story in Israel. We shared the same supportive view about tiny Israel and its superb advances in science and technology while

The author, age five, with his French grandmother and baby brother, Henri.

its innovators had to fight with limited weapons while also fighting for its life. The reader will later see how my dragons later bring me memories of how Monika Jensen worked in devoted harmony on unexpectedly challenging events in many strange places around the world.

⁓

Here comes something more solid than any dragons of my boyhood. An old wooden slingshot. I am a small boy again. I fire a pebble at a sparrow minding its own business in our lonely lilac tree. The bird falls and my heart drops. I never expected to hit it. My eyes are sharper than I knew. "Sniper's eyes," I'm later told at a US naval aviation base, a long time from now. Right this minute, I'm a ten-year-old who never wants to kill things that fly.

I can see now why I never cried. I had to shield myself while my parents shouted at each other, Mama in her native French and Dad in his Scottish burr. He is away for months at a time, sailing the seven seas. Her love is hard to cram into his brief shore leaves. Under such pressure, tensions rise. Mama raises us four children alone. Yet Dad's letters from abroad are pure poetry; his charcoal drawings of exotic places fire my imagination. I vow to escape into a world even wider than his, far from the gloom of narrow East London streets.

The detective who lives nearby sticks his head in the gas oven. Our gang wonders if we drove him to it by batting old tennis balls against the chipped brick wall on one side of his house. Black thoughts cloud my mind in this summer of 1934. Horrific tales are told by refugees from Germany, cousins of my chum Felix Wolfe. It's no longer fun to creep into the nearby Jewish cemetery to play hide-and-seek. I stop smiling to hide a crooked tooth caused by a schoolmate who punched me because I tripped him as we ran between the gravestones. I recruit The Boxing Parson to teach me to hit back. The crooked tooth is at the root of my chronic fear of smiling. I blame it for my occasional stutter. I blush at awkward moments.

Mama is one of the Deleportes of Alsace-Lorraine. Their estates were destroyed in the Great War of 1914–18, The War to End All Wars.

11

The author, center front, with his French grandparents on either side and his parents, back row center.

Alida Deleporte came to London in 1919 to learn English by working as a nanny for a viscount's progeny. Mama had seen the landed gentry in France lose everything. Then she saw England's ruling class invest its wealth to seal family loyalties within wills and trusts. Similar prudence in Alsace yielded no dividends after the Germans marched in. She expects the Germans to march again. So she never teaches us about money. Nor does Dad. Mama fell in love with him because, as a little girl, The War to End All Wars ended with the liberation of her home by brawny Scottish Highlanders wearing kilts and blowing bagpipes. Dad never wore a kilt nor played the pipes. But he did sound like a Scot. In a Lyons Corner House tearoom, near Admiral Horatio Nelson's stone column rising high above Trafalgar Square, Mama fell in love with his Scottish brogue. And his disdain for those who chase money.

A birth certificate zooms into the attic. It confirms I was born in Marylebone within sound of Bow Bells. I'm a Cockney! I'm drawn back to the sullen docklands from where Dad's ships sailed in a time when Mama reads books aloud to us. *The Shape of Things to Come* by H. G. Wells precedes his praise of Stalin, and is followed by the same author's disenchantment. Mama recites Tennyson's thoughts, "too deep for tears." She quotes Byron in his prison cell: "With spiders I had friendships made . . . seen mice by moonlight play . . . Such long communion tends to make us what we are."

I like spiders and mice. I want to escape the prison of school. I plan to be "the perfect naturalist" described in the 1855 writings of Charles Kingsley: "Strong in body; able to climb a rock, turn a boulder, walk all day . . . sail a boat . . . and if he go far abroad, be able on occasion to fight for his life." That's how I want to live.

"That'll be a miracle," says my little sister Blanche as she giggles.

"Everything is a miracle," Mama quotes Picasso. "It's a miracle one does not dissolve in one's bath like a lump of sugar." Nothing is certain, authority least of all. She does not mean the kindly authority of our local policeman who patrols on foot our crooked streets, but the bumbledom of Charles Dickens and Shakespeare's "figures drest in a little brief authority" and the "little tin gods" of Rudyard Kipling.

Mama reads aloud with a French accent. When she shops, she asks for ba-nan-nas and tomm-ma-toes. This enchants old Mr. Scroggins, the grocer. He always slips extra bananas and tomatoes into her bag. He knows how she feels, cut off from home in France. He left a leg back there, in the trenches, because he obeyed authority.

Our dad trusts the written word to spread comfort that money cannot buy. Mama has no comfort, and little money with which to raise me, my two younger brothers, and the small sister we call our "little blister." In voyages to New York, Dad is invited to join a big US comic-strip syndicate whose owner admires cartoons in newsletters which Dad prints along with "Marconigrams" from his "wireless room." Another passenger, Lord John Reith, founder of the BBC, offers a job in radio for more money. Dad declines. "Love of money is the root of all evil," he says after discovering an American religion. He persuades Mama to adopt it. Priests threaten her with hellfire. Defiantly, she reads to us at breakfast

13

the daily lesson from Mary Baker Eddy's *Science and Health with Key to the Scriptures*." Then I race helter-skelter to school. The sweetshop lady sometimes slips me a ball of bubblegum and says, "More haste, less speed!" The words lodge more firmly in my head than biblical wisdoms for breakfast. The dragons of today insist that Christian Science and the bubblegum lady left permanent imprints upon my mind.

Dragon-mail delivers a leather-bound diary, long since given to me by Mama's friend, the viscount's housekeeper. Such a massive book demanded daily scribbles. Seeing them now, I go back to boyhood. I turn the mangle to squeeze laundry from the kitchen sink where Mama hand-scrubs the daily wash. I count the bags carried by coalmen clumping through the house to refill the coal shed behind our outdoor lavatory. It always seems to rain when I scurry out to fill a bucket for our tiny fireplace. I vow to take Mama to Hong Kong, far from here. Why Hong Kong? Years later, I live there. Is this an uncanny consequence of a small boy's dream?

At night, under bedcovers, I explore a world of ideas, reading books by torchlight. Its batteries come from Mr. Scroggins. He says our local council saves money with the ancient gas lamps that light our streets. He says the council is full of Scrooges. This prompts me to shoot out all the streetlights with a slingshot while I trudge home from school one dark afternoon in winter. Reaction is swift. School is assembled. If the culprit does not own up, every boy will be caned. I figure it will take weeks to cane each boy across his bare hands, the accepted form of punishment. The time required for this collective caning equates to a single day of summer holidays. I decide not to confess to massacring the lampposts. "In any case, holidays will be ended by war," predicts Felix Wolfe. His Jewish relatives know more than officialdom or the newspapers care to tell us.

I win an East Ham Grammar School scholarship. It requires a fee of nine pounds and nine shillings a year "for use of books and the Athletic Fund." I reckon this equals Dad's monthly pay. "Billy," he writes from a P&O ocean cruise liner in Tokyo, "go to a technical school and get a trade. A carpenter is always sure of work."

Mama makes sure I take the scholarship before Dad sails home again. His forebears are sea captains who fell on hard times after so many ships

14

were sunk by German submarines in the 1914–18 war. Dad is one of Marconi's "Sparks" attached as officers to the Merchant Marine. They link ships to shore by Morse code, and they are held in reserve for "special operations" in a rekindled war anticipated by Admiral "Jackie" Fisher. I know more about Fisher's rebellious ways than I learn from schoolbooks listing the dukes, marquesses, earls, viscounts, barons, and Lords Temporal of the House of Lords who rule England. The nearby naval college also honors another hero, Nelson. Dockworkers tell me about the two admirals who began as boy seamen and later galvanized naval warfare. Admiral Fisher, "friendless and forlorn" as a lad, ended up launching HMS *Dreadnought,* the first true battleship. Nelson, age twelve when he joined the Royal Navy, was an admiral when he fought his last battle at Trafalgar at the age of forty-seven. "They have done for me at last!" he said, covering his face with a kerchief to save his crew agony while he took four hours to die on HMS *Victory.* This insider gossip from stevedores is not the stuff of school textbooks. Under cover at night, I jot down the dockside stories. After I switch off the torch, I dream about boy-sailors who rise to command warships guarding an empire on which the sun will never set.

Dad brings back model airplane kits from Japan. I assemble these tokens of Japanese ingenuity: clearly printed plans for balsa-wood air frames, rice paper to dampen and dry into taut fabric for wings held together by unfamiliar cements, elastic bands to drive propellers. I fly the small craft over Brampton Park at the end of our street. When the elastic unwinds, the planes still soar. Their beauty of form carries them into the tallest trees, where they perch out of reach until scoured to skeletons by wind and rain. I spend more time building their replacements than I devote to homework. I keep *The Theory of Flight* under my pillow. I imagine wresting command of the air from the fierce descendants of those who design my model airplanes, after Dad's letters warn that "Japs" are not the bespectacled gargoyles caricatured at school.

No history teacher tells us how Japanese warships in 1904 defeated Russia's Far Eastern fleet. It's Dad who says it marks the first use of wireless to scoop the world. The London *Times* hired a steamboat to stalk the

Japanese fleet and signal a shore station on China's east coast to telegraph the news to London. I want to write for newspapers and explore a wilderness of things as yet unseen. My schoolmates limit ambition to learning a trade, raising a family, caring for parents in old age because there are no pensions and no unemployment benefits. I want freedom to wander beyond horizons not yet explored, searching for wilderness specimens not yet understood.

On Empire Air Day, 1935, my school sends some of us to a Royal Air Force display. Airmen let us climb over a real warplane, conceived three years before I was born: the Tiger Moth. It looks as if it has four wings held together by cross-wires. I sit in an open cockpit behind a Gipsy Major piston engine. The duty RAF sergeant boasts, "It delivers sixty horsepower!" I jump. Here's a way to leap above horizons I can only imagine.

In our public library I find *Wind, Sand, and Stars* by Antoine de Saint Exupery. He writes of a comrade lost in the high Andes: "You were described as abounding in the witty sallies of the street arab, as if courage consisted in demeaning oneself to schoolboy banter in the midst of danger and the hour of death . . . It seemed to us that a hundred squadrons navigating for a hundred years would not be enough to explore that endless, cloud-piercing range . . . You never felt the need to cheapen your adversaries before confronting them. When you saw a foul storm ahead, you said to yourself, 'Here is a foul storm.' You accepted it, and you took its measure."

The translation is dedicated to "Guillaumet," which means William. Which, in a boy's imagination, means me! There is a preface: "By A French Aviator who followed the profession of Airline Pilot for Eight years (and) offers this book in homage to the Airline Pilots of America and their Dead." Antoine de Saint Exupery will die flying against Nazi Germany. But right now, he opens a schoolboy's eyes to possibilities previously undreamed.

The library spells freedom from streets where fathers leave home at dawn to work long hours, fearful of losing poorly paying jobs. It has racks with national and local newspapers. The *East Ham Echo* offers "cheap solutions to housing problems of the-Fourteen-Pounds-a-week-man" if he pays each week a fifth of the price "on the never-never system." Nobody on our street is tempted by the offer: SMALL DOWN PAYMENT ON AN ARCADIA HOME WITH SUNNY KITCHEN AND TILED BATHROOM. The seller remains the owner if payments are not kept up. Nobody even dreams of such luxury. There are simpler delights. One dad returning from work to his home on our street each evening calls "Mavis!" and waits for his one sure reward: his little girl running into his open arms. But he is robbed of her and all simple delights by the Blitz.

Blitzkrieg! Lightning-war. A German concept. London street kids pick it up fast. "The Blitz" is a distant threat when a neighboring plumber's daughter, Vera Lynn, says to me, "We've sold out to Hitler." It is September 29, 1938. Prime Minister Neville Chamberlain returns from meeting Adolf Hitler in Munich to tell cheering London crowds, "I bring you . . . *Peace in our time!*"

I reach my fourteenth year, no longer obliged to wear short pants. Vera is not much older, but she seems astronomically worldly-wise. I ask her about the Ambrose Band. She sings with them at the Hammersmith Palais, which is famous. Vera is not famous. "They let me sing my own songs," she tells me. "It's just a bit of fun."

A year later, her own song is: "We'll meet again, don't know where, don't know when / But I know we'll meet again some sunny day / Keep smiling through just like you always do / Till the blue skies drive the dark clouds far away." The Great War-to-End-All-Wars is revving up again. She becomes "the Forces' Sweetheart." And we do meet again. And again. And in the year 2010, her wartime songs will be heard again: top of the charts.

# CHAPTER 4

# Slipping the Surly Bonds of Earth

ANOTHER DOG-EARED BOOK SURFACES. *ROGET'S THESAURUS.* ORIGINATED by Peter Mark Roget. His father took care of the French Protestant Church on Threadneedle Street in the London of the 1700s. Peter investigated laughing gas, the nitrous oxide for use as an anesthetic. His curiosity took him to Geneva, where he was jailed in 1802 for breaching the Peace of Amiens. He escaped back to London and exposed the deplorable filth and alarming decline of the city's water supply; devised a calculating machine; built the slide rule; studied effects on the mind by the conformation of the skull. To confound a notion that learning is the prerogative of the elect, he founded the Society for the Diffusion of Knowledge. In 1852 he published his first thesaurus "of English Words and Phrases to Facilitate the Expression of Ideas." My mother reads to us from the 1922 edition. It records that "a dragonnade is a form of punishment" and also plants a notion that someday I shall take my own children to faraway places to learn about things never taught in regular schools.

Into my attic drifts a "dragonnade," a poem by a pilot later killed in the Battle of Britain:

> *Oh! I have slipped the surly bonds of Earth*
> *And danced the skies on laughter-silvered wings;*
> *Sunward I've climbed, and joined the tumbling mirth*
> *Of sun-split clouds,—and done a hundred things*
> *You have not dreamed of—wheeled and soared and swung*

*High in the sunlit silence. Hov'ring there,*
*I've chased the shouting wind along, and flung*
*My eager craft through footless halls of air. . . .*

*Up, up the long, delirious, burning blue*
*I've topped the windswept heights with easy grace*
*Where never lark, or even eagle flew—*
*And, while with silent, lifting mind I've trod*
*The high untrespassed sanctity of space,*
*Put out my hand, and touched the face of God.*\*

This dragonnade is not so much a punishment as a reminder that many of us need to escape old prejudices. I am old enough to wear long pants, a rite of passage to big boyhood in my part of London, but not of any social significance in the selection of prewar RAF pilots. But someday I plan to slip these surly bonds of earth.

※

On June 23, 1939, my school diary ends abruptly. Full stop. Nothing more but ink blots and blank pages, save for my final scribble: "HOMEWORK: Bismarck and The French Problem."

Why did I study this German statesman? What was the French problem? How odd, to stew over obscure events while our government predicts that Hitler will drop 700 tons of bombs every day on London, and a new graveyard ministry orders 60,000,000 tons of coffin timber to bury the dead. Still stricken by the horrors of the 1914–18 war, which is about to become the Second War to End All Wars, our tired old leaders stockpile collapsible cardboard coffins and prepare for four million immediate mental breakdowns.

My dragons remind me of The School Song: "Not buildings gray nor records hoary / Can make a school to last for aye / But souls aflame with

---

\* From "High Flight" by Canadian Spitfire pilot John G. Magee, killed in the Battle of Britain. No copyright. Widely quoted in aviation journals and war museums.

high ideals / That will not falter by the way / Nor shrink when effort most is needed / But fight, and fighting, win the day."

We roar out the school motto at morning assembly: "D-e/dee/t-e-r/ter/d-e-t-e-r/deter/m-i-n/min/a-t-i-o-n/ation/Determination!" We take heart from the old 1936 reports of German boys fiendishly drilling to win the last peacetime Olympic Games. Our athletes took nothing seriously back then, and yet they kept winning. The memory makes us sing with happy fervor on this last day of school in 1939: "Say not the struggle naught availeth. . . ."

A year later, a new prime minister, Winston Churchill, returns to Harrow to sing his own old school song. Then he roars: "Never, ever, ever, ever, ever, ever, ever give up. Never give up. Never give up. Never give up."

We would snigger on this last day if our headmaster intoned Churchill's later words: "The whole fury and might of the enemy must be turned upon us. Hitler knows he must break us in this island or lose the war."

Any sniggering ends when our arms and armies are lost at Dunkirk. "You're lucky," says Ken Boardman, who is a year older than me. "You're not old enough to fight . . . I am."

My mother signs my last school diary as "Alida Deleporte," an assertion of her own self-worth when the Hun threatens her homeland. Belgians no longer bicycle across the Channel with strings of onions, no longer gossip with Mama in the patois of Alsace; the Germans have already retaken it. She reads to us from such brilliant writers as Charles Lamb. He had no promise of a pension. Uncertainty spurred him to write while he toiled as an underpaid clerk in the East India Company, which runs our nearby docks. Lamb made ends meet by writing jokes for the *Morning Post* at sixpence a joke. I try writing for the *East Ham Echo*. I get a letter: "Submissions must be typed." I borrow an old typewriter at St. George's Church, home of my troop, the 25th East Ham Boy Scouts.

I am interrupted by Sunday parade on the third of September, 1939. I've grown from Wolf Cub to Patrol Leader to a King's Scout proficient in jungle warfare of a kind learned by Winston Churchill in the 1890s from Boer farmers. He fought them in South Africa, and he now borrows ideas from their irregular tactics as the only immediate response to Nazi Germany's blitzkrieg victories. From the Boers he learned survival in the wilderness, how to track footprints. From futile three-hundred-year British campaigns in Afghanistan, he remembered Kim's Game, to memorize disconnected objects. Hitler's boast of victory by futuristic "lightning warfare" is answered by this stop-gap adoption of crude old tactics. Boer War booby traps inspire the creation of Special Operations Executive (SOE) to sabotage the Nazi panzer divisions, which are said to be otherwise unstoppable.

## CHAPTER 5

# Spill This Secret and You Kill Your Dad

ONE SUNNY SUNDAY MORNING, WHILE CHURCHILL IS STILL A POLITICAL pariah, housewives stand in doorways and silently watch us Boy Scouts parade for the last time. At 11:30 a.m., the wail of air-raid sirens drowns out our beat of drums and blowing of bugles. We march back into church. The old vicar, shell-shocked in the First World War, says in a shaky voice: "We are again at war with Germany."

I expect waves of German bombers to strike the knockout blow that British air planners anticipate. Our fighters scramble to intercept what the RAF calls "bandits." Two RAF pilots shoot each other down by mistake. Major cities are evacuated: 827,000 schoolchildren and another 524,000 kids younger than school-age are sent to the countryside. The Minister of Health calls the evacuation "an exodus bigger than that of Moses. It is the movement of ten armies, each as big as an Expeditionary Force."

A total blackout is enforced by air-raid wardens who insist that even the faintest glimmer of light will attract enemy bombs. Daily at 4:00 a.m. I read the papers in the newsagent's shrouded shop, and then deliver them blind. I still bear a scar to remind me, more sharply than any dragon, that I walked into a lamppost rendered invisible, not by my slingshot but by the enemy. I memorize which newspaper goes into what slot in the blacked-out houses. Customers get cross if I leave the communist *Daily Worker* when they expect the conservative *Daily Telegraph*. I learn that the London *Times* reports in one way and the *News Chronicle* reports in another. The tabloid *Daily Mirror* shrinks the news and pays readers who send in usable squibs. I mail snippets about Scouts helping the war effort. For each item printed, I get a seven-shillings-and-sixpence postal order. I write fiction for the *Boy Scout Magazine.* The editor, F. Haydn Dimmock, prints my stories set in wild parts of the empire: the Khyber Pass, the Northwest Frontier . . . names destined to draw me later to a very different Afghanistan. Each story earns me five pounds sterling! Bliss! More pennies for Mama's purse. And I won't be tied to a desk like Mr. Lamb, who prayed for a decent clerk's salary so he could keep on writing. I make up tales about the Whirling Dervishes of Islam, never imagining I shall report on their reality long after Mr. Dimmock asks for more of my fantasies about faraway places, comfortingly remote from present dangers.

King George VI makes a Christmas broadcast. His brother abdicated and left him to lead us in the titanic battles ahead. He quotes, faltering here and there: "And I said to the man . . . who stood at the gate of the year . . . 'Give me a light that I may tread softly into the unknown.' And he replied, 'Go into the darkness . . . and put your hand into the hand of God. That shall be to you . . . better than a light and safer than a known way.'" This is when I first invent the notion of "dragons" as inspiring the Arabs in Afghanistan where I imagine all the Mad Mullahs plot the downfall of the West.

Using old schoolbooks, I teach my younger brothers and our sister, Blanche, at home. Mama thinks Dad won't find us if we leave with the evacuees. My dragons now find crumpled letters, written by Blanche after she joined the Women's Royal Navy. She says family history repeats itself. In the 1914–18 war, Mama was taught by her little brother, now my Uncle Henri, while both hid in treetops from the German invaders. Some twenty-one years later, the war resumes and here I am, teaching my siblings. Grandpa Deleporte died when his mills never recovered from German destruction. Mum, his little Alida, was lost forever among "the English savages."

Mama says Dad might have been at the British embassy in Paris when the Nazis seized the city. I cling to the belief that he is in America. I pray he will sail home and give up seafaring. Merchant ships are sunk by U-boats from the start of what the landlubbers call a Phony War. It is never phony for seafarers. A bold U-boat slips into Scapa Flow and sinks a famous warship after our admirals swore "the Scapa anchorage is absolutely impregnable."

The Blitz makes nonsense of the Phony War, a catchphrase that persists so long as land armies are not engaged. But our ships are sunk at a terrifying rate. Mama hoards the canvas-backed sketchbooks in which Dad drew the strange things he found abroad. She cannot think why she no longer receives his letters. She draws consolation from such old biographies as Boswell's *The Life of Dr. Sam Johnson* and the tangled loves of the Romantic generation of Shelley and Byron. She no longer prays with us each night: "Please find Dad a shore job." It used to mean he need never go away again. Now Dad must surely have a shore job—but where?

Dad never forgot that his father was a ship's captain, missing in the U-boat campaign of the First World War. Here's a sepia photo of Dad piloting a navy airship before his quick grasp of Morse Code led to his transfer to the Merchant Marine as a Marconi radio officer.

It's more venturesome than me earning a few extra pennies by pushing a four-tiered cart for our local milkman. I fail to see cracks from an overnight bomb. The cart tips over. Bottles break. Milk runs in the gutters. It all belongs to the Cooperative Wholesale Society (CWS) for families who cannot afford free-market prices. The CWS decides I'm too little to be entrusted with its milk carts.

I wonder how subsidized milk helps the poor. I get answers from a librarian with shapely legs. She shows me journals on newspaper racks, ranging from the communist *Daily Worker* to the London *Times*. "If you don't read them, you are uninformed. If you do read them, you are misinformed," she paraphrases Mark Twain. She adds, "Never stop looking for the truth." What I never stop looking for is the sight of her terrific legs.

Girls are bolder than boys. A girl my age catches me alone in the park. "Want to feel my tits?" she asks. I blush and run but she lifts my spirits in a year of great sadness. The girl grows up to become the model for "Jane," a comic-strip blonde who outwits Nazis six days a week in the *Daily Mirror*. Her real name is Christabel Leighton-Porter. As "Jane" she becomes famous for the next five years as the heroine of our fighting men, a girl shapelier, I reckon, than *Esquire* magazine's fabulous Vargas pinups.

I become a "fire-watcher" on top of East Ham police station while Nazi night bombers strike blindly around the shipyards. They hit houses more often. Some mornings, I walk home with bits of spent incendiary bombs to pile up around a cage I made out of thin branches cut from our lilac tree. Inside the cage is a black raven. It's the closest I get to becoming a naturalist. Some fool has pulled out the root feathers in its tail so it cannot fly. I make a fake tail from what remains of my Japanese model-makers' cement and balsa wood, and launch the great bird. It climbs way above the rooftops. Then the tail falls off. The raven spirals down into the open coal shed. It flew straight up so joyously and crashed with such sad finality. I am honor bound to save it from the coal dust and the foul lingering stench of man-made bombs. I collect the remains of burned-out German incendiaries and build a metal wall around the cage where my raven sits in silence, eyes moist and reproachful.

It reminds me of the Flying Flea, invented by a Frenchman to bring aviation within reach of ordinary folk. A prewar photo today takes me back to his Pou-de-Ciel, a tiny lath-and-fabric single-seater powered by a two-stroke engine. No ailerons. No elevators. Only two main-planes, one behind the other, and a rudder. The assembly kit, "available for a modest price," was beyond the means of boys on my street. Before the real air battles, we pretended to be fighter pilots and rode battered old bicycles pinched from the docklands. Crane operators told us, "Take the bikes. They were left by Hindu seamen who sailed back to India to help Gandhi fight us." Yet Dad brought home those same seamen from his ships. They shared our humble suppers, too timid to say their religion forbade them to eat the rich soup, *a la Françoise,* that Mama hastily prepared.

We used those bikes in Epping Forest, pretending to fly Great War fighters. I was Biggles, a fictional ace in the dogfights of 1914–18 when there was mutual respect between opposing fliers. This new air war sweeps away the few friends who were not evacuated. Ken Boardman's pretty sister has jet-black hair until her house is destroyed. She lives, but her hair turns white. Ken later becomes a navy pilot with me, but his hatred of Germans makes him reckless and will get him killed.

My fire-watching job is to locate explosions. I learned points of the compass as a Scout and can calculate where Nazi bombs drop. I scribble details on bits of paper lowered in tin cans from the police-station roof. The coppers below cannot afford to worry about their own families in the nightly inferno. If I stop to think of bodies going up in smoke, I'd also be no use to anyone.

Fire-watching is real, in contrast with prewar days when we launched matchsticks in rain-filled gutters and pretended to compete in the annual Oxford-Cambridge boat race. The real oarsmen in the real race were students with superior Bullingdon Club sort of backgrounds. Now the RAF gobbles them up. I see no way of joining their lofty ranks. But the smell of that Empire Day Tiger Moth haunts me, and gives me hope.

After the bombers are gone at dawn, the chirp of sparrows breaks an eerie stillness. I am going off duty when a gruff old police sergeant says: "Here's the address. Ask for Atkins. An air-raid warden. Or something." He shifts uneasily. "Okay. Off on your bike. Double-quick."

The address is in London's West End. I read in the sergeant's *Daily Worker* that the chairman of the US Senate Foreign Relations Committee, Key Pittman, says Great Britain faces certain defeat and "must capitulate." The Park Lane mansion of the Marquess of Londonderry, a former air minister who wanted an alliance with the Nazis, has been hit during the night. Also Piccadilly, Marble Arch, and Buckingham Palace. I bike behind red double-deck buses, my Boy Scout uniform opening a way through cordoned streets where rescue workers dig for survivors. Bus drivers change their routes to get around neighborhoods shattered by the night's bombing. Our neighbor is a bus driver. We only see him nowadays when he bikes in haste to the Boleyn Castle depot. "Last stop!" his ticket collector used to joke. "Boleyn! Bowl out!" Our neighbor doesn't tell the story anymore. Like other drivers, he tries bravely to keep to prewar schedules. I weave between double-deck buses, nose down in bomb craters, steaming gently like big red dragons snuffling through prehistoric ruins. A girl in the camouflaged uniform of an Air Raid Precautions ARP warden meets me at some new ministry, created after our regular army of 340,000 soldiers is gone, crushed in France by the German juggernaut. Churchill tells his improvised underground army: "Make the enemy's life an eternal torment." His order is made public in a brave but forlorn attempt to strike fear of the unknown in the hearts of Hitler and his generals.

I meet a large man in a pinstripe suit. The girl air-raid warden says, "Yes, Minister," and addresses him as "Doctor ————." She mumbles his actual name. He asks me, "You're a King's Scout?"

"Yessir." I don't actually say I can track enemies through forgotten jungles, know Kim's Game for training the memories of soldiers in Afghanistan, and know how to melt into the African bush if need be. Anything seems possible after hearing Churchill declaim, "The Battle of Britain is about to begin! Let us therefore brace ourselves to our duties, and so bear ourselves that, if the British Empire and its Commonwealth last for a thousand years, men will say, 'This was their finest hour.'"

The minister reminds me that Churchill learned guerrilla warfare from his enemies in South Africa, same way as did Lord Baden-Powell, "BP," founder of the Boy Scouts. "BP also means Be Prepared. Are you prepared?" asks the minister.

"Yes."

"You can be trusted?"

"Yes."

"Your father's safe. He'll be out of France soon. Tell your mum. But if you or she tell anyone else, he'll be dead."

My face turns red. My bare knees grow cold. Break the secret and I kill Dad. The secret is that he is to be flown out of France from under the noses of the German occupiers. "There's nothing certain about it," says the girl in the guise of an air-raid warden as she watches me get back on my bike. "But our uncertainty will beat the absolute certainties of the Nazis." She had steered me through dark corridors, up and down broad and barren stone steps, back to the street. She watches me swing a leg over my bicycle saddle and shift the gas mask across my back. I brace my other foot against the curbstone and look up. "Miss Atkins?"

She nods. Smoky eyes read my mind, with its dirty little schoolboy secrets, its cowardice, its disrespect for rules. Then she unbuttons her tunic as if escaping officialdom's stuffy rules. She has long legs that vanish high up into a short skirt. Her stockings are silk and the skirt is far from regulation length. I breathe easier. She is a rebel like me. Her lavender silk shirt has not been purchased with ration coupons. "Where's your tin helmet?" she asks.

"My head's too small. And my Scout hat blew off."

She laughs, a rich chuckle, not the tut-tut of disapproving adults. Back at East Ham police station, I ask the sergeant: "Who's in charge?" I mean the mysterious old building. He counters: "What were you told?"

"I was sworn to secrecy."

He shrugs. "There you are then. Nuffink but secrets. You met the Minister of Economic Warfare. Don't mean much. We can't even fight a regular war." I learn later that the "ARP warden" was born Maria Rosenberg, who re-invented herself as Vera Atkins to dodge anti-Semitism in Whitehall and to disguise her role in covert operations. Secrecy laws are suspended only in the twenty-first century, when I can write her biography, *Spymistress*. On the cover appears a quote from Ian Fleming: "In the real world of spies, Vera Atkins was the boss."

⌒‿⌒

In 1956 a British diplomat in Nepal asks if I'm the son of William Stevenson. I confess I am.

"Splendid chap," says the diplomat. "We got him from Marconi."

Marconi? Inventor of a spark-driven transmitter, tuned to send electromagnetic waves carrying Morse-coded messages over long distances. So that's what it was all about, when Dad on shore leave in peacetime said he had to visit "the Marconi office." It sheds light on why I never saw him in East Ham again after meeting "The Doctor," Hugh Dalton, Minister of Economic Warfare, a conventional title covering unconventional secret operations, independent of Whitehall's foreign intelligence services and career bureaucrats who were allies of King Edward VIII after he abdicated and sought an alliance with Hitler.

My dragons take me back to a childhood when Mama read aloud Victor Hugo's speech, recalling that the suppression of autocratic regimes and the limitation of arms were discussed in the 1750s. Wars still broke out. "Is this a reason," Hugo asked, "for abandoning hope that at long last men will learn wisdom?" The question implanted in my schoolboy mind endures. I believe the human race will learn such wisdom. The one small contribution I make is to introduce my own children to as much of real life as possible, and to find answers deeper and broader than lessons only taught in narrow Western corridors of the globe.

## CHAPTER 6

# Finding Answers

BY 1941, DAD IS ONE OF MANY VITAL LINKS BETWEEN WARTIME AGENTS and Bletchley's ULTRA boffins who intercept Nazi messages transmitted on German Enigma machines. Bletchley hides the greatest of secrets. Mum is told to move us to this Buckinghamshire town, far from the London Blitz. I cannot tell my former schoolboy chums why we "ran away," or that Mama teaches university students to forget classroom French and to learn the local patois of French regions into which they'll be dropped as agents.

Our family is crammed into a small apartment at 109 Bletchley Road. My room overlooks a splendid countryside. I have a dazzling view of Old Farmer Gurney's Land Girls. They replace farm laborers needed for the fighting ahead. I'm afraid the girls will look down their noses at a skinny runaway from the Blitz. But one of them, Lorna, takes me under her wing. Her academic studies are cut short. She needs to talk about things other than mangelwurzels. Words gush. In hay lofts, we jabber away about the brave new world we'll build after the war is won. Of course we'll win it! Her husband is fighting in the jungles of Burma. Her brother is a Spitfire pilot.

She bikes alongside me to Air Training Corps (ATC) evening classes, over the hills and far away, into the farming town of Leighton Buzzard. The ATC teaches the basics of aviation to boys hoping to fly. Lorna makes sure I'm ready with answers if I wangle an interview with some Admiralty Selection Board. The navy is less picky about the age or social origins of boy volunteers for the Fleet Air Arm.

Dad rejoins the family in Bletchley, but he never says how he got here, nor where he goes at night in an unmarked lorry. I later learn to call it a "truck." He comes back in time for breakfast, over which he falls asleep. On rare days when he escapes his hush-hush duties, he grows vegetables on a nearby allotment. "Dig for Victory" the government beseeches us. Today, I know about ULTRA and suspect that Dad dug to save his sanity.

Bletchley is known in peacetime as a tiny town of brick-workers and railroad men: main lines from London to Scotland conveniently intersect here with lines between Oxford and Cambridge. Now total secrecy shrouds everything. Odd-looking newcomers lodge with locals, or move into cottages scattered along narrow winding lanes between Fenny Stratford and Woburn Abbey. Men wear tweed jackets with leather patches at the elbows. Women wear the look of schoolmarms. WAAFs of the Women's Auxiliary Air Force are glamorous but untouchable. They disappear into unmarked buses rumbling along Bletchley Road to destinations unknown.

I find work as a junior reporter for the *North Bucks Times* and *Leighton Buzzard Observer* after the armed forces absorbed the editorial staff. I teach myself Pitman's shorthand. I type. This is good enough for the publisher, Mr. Midgeley. I write up the doings of the Ladies' Bright Hour. I distribute wedding forms for brides to fill out and one, previously known as Miss Smith, stands at her door while I check her completed form. I see that she is now Mrs. Flatbottom. I burst out laughing. Mrs. Flatbottom complains to Mr. Midgeley. She paid for a prenuptial announcement and wants her money back.

Mr. Midgeley calls me to his office above his stationery store.

"Open the door," he says, "and tell me what you hear."

I hear nothing.

"Listen again," says Mr. Midgeley.

"I can't hear a thing except the tinkle of the cash register."

"That is the tinkle of readers buying space in the paper or shopping for what they see in the small ads," says Mr. Midgeley. "Never forget that tinkle. It's the secret of survival."

He never knew the deepest secret of survival. A few disclosures leak in the 1970s. Not until 1993 will *The Inside Story of Bletchley Park* be told by such insiders as Sir Harry Hinsley, and the later director of Schools on British Secret Services, Alan Stripp. They tell readers that even now, much must remain secret. Seven thousand scholars worked night and day in scattered huts. It is impossible, even by the twenty-first century, to fully explain how HYDRA and 210 Turing Bombes cracked 3,000 German coded messages a day. One newspaper does finally disclose that the giant Bombe, forerunner of the modern computer, was invented by a brilliant mathematician and "shortened the Second World War by two years."

All this is hidden when I bid Midgeley farewell. The navy is dangerously short of airmen after losing so many antiquated airplanes, often flying off converted cargo ships. I am sixteen. I wangle an appointment to appear before a selection board at Oxford. On the way to the railroad station, I run into Dad. We seldom meet under open skies. He asks where I'm going.

I tell him.

He smiles. A rare event. "Ye must ha'e known I flew with the navy in the first Great War?"

I nod. I don't want to say I know nothing. He never speaks about these things, although now he says, "Keep your body in the cockpit and your mind outside." And disappears into yet another unmarked lorry.

~

Oxford seems remote from war. Dons bicycle down the Broad with strangely innocent smiles. Flush-faced freshmen stumble out of the King's Head. Bees still buzz on the Corpus Christi lawns. A crusty old Chief Petty Officer of the Royal Navy consults a clipboard and says, "So you want to become an aircraft fitter?"

"No!" I reply firmly. No blushes. No stutters. "I'm for pilot training."

"Then go thataway!" He suddenly grins and points down an anonymous corridor. It's a routine trick to save wasting time: the CPO sorts out those not absolutely sure they want to fly.

I sit before a row of gold braid. An elderly admiral asks, "You're at two thousand feet on the port side of a carrier two miles away. Your engine packs up. What do you do?"

"Ditch!"

He makes a note. His face is expressionless.

An unsmiling commander says, "You write?"

"Reports for the papers where I live."

"Bletchley?"

"Yessir!"

"You wrote stories for *Boy Scout Magazine?*"

"Yessir! I don't have much time for it now."

"Because you've been writing a children's book: 'Sarka The Seagull.'"

*Dear God! How'd they know all this?*

"Will you write about the Fleet Air Arm?"

Is he afraid I might report the needless hazards? I remember the great rebel Admiral Fisher, who wrote to the newspapers about the navy's lack of proper equipment. I take a chance.

"If it's allowed, sir. I need lots of experience first, sir."

The commander gives a half smile. "We need young'uns who can put across the navy's part in aerial warfare. The RAF gets all the glory. We get all their junk."

His smile broadens. "Churchill says we're not pulling our weight. We're not losing enough pilots, not on the scale of the RAF. That's because we lose most of 'em in accidents. And accidents happen because we mostly get the RAF's leftovers. We waited too long to admit that aircraft carriers are the capital ships of today."

I'm in! I know it! The selection board dismisses me politely but I know I'm in! The room is suddenly warm and fuzzy. Tiny smiles crease those craggy old faces.

# CHAPTER 7

# Going Solo

SAILORS WEAR BELL-BOTTOM TROUSERS. THEIR LOOSE JACKETS HAVE knotted ribbons with back-flaps divided by three stripes in honor of Nelson's three great victories at sea. On their heads are round caps ringed with ribbons: the names of their ships are blacked out.

"We're the only service to fight this war in eighteenth-century fancy dress," writes Lord Kilbracken, a navy pilot who began, as I must, by reporting to HMS St.Vincent, a barracks, not a ship. I am an Ordinary Seaman, but keep up my spirits with the thought that this was how Francis Drake started out in the 1500s, before he sailed the seven seas to be knighted by Queen Elizabeth. Now gull-winged Stukas, with sirens blaring, dive vertically to bomb us daily. Between raids, I must climb the rigging of a facsimile of Drake's tall mast, rising vertiginously out of the parade ground into a distant sky. I wonder what this has to do with flying.

I drill my class, and forget the order "About turn!" Grizzled old Chief Petty Officer Pony Moore barks: "Get them useless seamen turned around or I'll do a long-arm frigging stand on your stupid thick head!" My mates keep marching. Dumbstruck, mind blank, I flap my arms to make them reverse. This doesn't work. They march down the steps into a giant air-raid shelter. I run to the other end and confront them as they stolidly march up the exit steps. Finally I remember the correct order and squeak, "About turn!"

It's the right order at the wrong moment. They turn about, and march back into the shelter.

Can I ever learn to fly? I can't even learn elementary square-bashing.

I tell the squad to halt when they surface again. They look uneasy. It seemed funny until they remember that one mistake in deck-officer training can "dip" a makee-learn airman into a Forever Ordinary Seaman.

A Royal Marine colonel confronts me. "What's esprit-de-corps, laddie?"

"Esprit-de-corps!" I reply, imitating Mama's impeccable French. "Mutual loyalty among comrades!"

The colonel's face turns purple. He wanted to dip me. Mama's French and my Boy Scout training made me risk a response at least as good as anything in the colonel's repertoire. He finds it difficult to spit out the words, but finally orders me to rejoin my squad.

I glimpse glee in Moore's hooded eyes. He's contemptuous of Royal Marine officers strutting around the quarterdeck of his stone frigate, bullying his Naval Airmen Second Class. We transfer to nearby HMS *Daedelus*. Naval land bases are still tagged "HMS" as if we are warships at sea. We learn to tie knots . . . sheep-shanks, clove hitches, reefs, and bowlines. We file on board the nearby wooden warship HMS *Victory*. It brought home the dead body of Horatio, Viscount Lord Nelson from the Battle of Trafalgar, "pickled in a barrel of rum" says our solemn old navy guide. We hear that Nelson saw more fighting on sea, land, upriver, besieging or defending forts, and commanding more fleet actions than any other officer in naval history, his last battle fought with 27 ships against 33 of the combined fleet of the French and Spanish. We stand where he was struck by a musket ball fired from a French warship. We learn that upon each anniversary of his last battle, a toast is drunk to The Immortal Memory. After this, we trudge a bit more willingly to endless classes, always observing Official Traditions of the Navy: "Never whistle, always say 'Aye Aye Sir!' and salute with downward-facing palm."

We barely have time to eat in the canteen. We seem to live in another century until during one lunch break, a Fairey Swordfish crashes. It's the oldest warplane in action and is fondly known as the Stringbag. Wires crisscross between four wings that fold back for storage in a ship's hangar. It has a fixed undercarriage and two cavernous cockpits. A navigator and a telegraphist usually occupy the rear cockpit which, in this case, carries a big gas tank with only the navigator crammed behind it with a cork plugged into the top of the tank to prevent fuel spilling out during take-off. Once the Stringbag levels out, the navigator pulls out the cork by a piece of string.

By the time we reach the flaming wreck, the pilot's legs are folded back, trapped under his seat. His body begins to burn. It's impossible to get close with our small fire extinguishers. The pilot's Sidcot flying suit smolders. He holds his hands in front of his face. The protesting hands curl up into useless black hammers. The face burns to a crisp. If there was anyone in the rear cockpit, there is nothing of him to be seen now. None of us want to finish lunch, which is roast beef. Swordfish biplanes are nicknamed Stringbags because they look like clumsy great shopping bags held together by string. A record remains of the dialogue between a RAF squadron leader and the pilot of a Stringbag about to fly across the North Sea to drop mines in enemy waters.

"You fly with that thing full of petrol sticking up between you and the navigator?" the RAF pilot asks the navy pilot. "Isn't it dicey, carrying a bloody big magnetic mine, and that thing towering over you?"

"We're a bit conspicuous when we pass the Frisian Islands at sixty feet," admits the navy pilot. "A round-trip takes two and a half hours and limits the damage we do. But with that tank, we stay in the air for about nine hours. That pipe is an air vent to allow petrol to flow into the main supply. When we take off with a full tank, the petrol might slop out onto the navigator's head. So we stick a cork in the pipe and when we are flying straight and level, the navigator pulls the string and out comes the cork.'"*

Come Saturday evening, before Sunday "Divisions" of hymns and prayers, we nip out to a pub. Sailors gossip. The Swordfish is so slow, it outfoxes enemy gunners and sinks half the Italian fleet at Taranto, which then ceases to be a military port. In one blow, more damage is inflicted than Nelson at Trafalgar and gives the bomb-weary British the first good

---

* Commander Charles Lamb was finally able to disclose hair-raising details of Swordfish operations throughout World War II in his 1980 memoir *To War in a Stringbag*. Near the end of the Pacific War, he protested against amputation of a leg after a flight deck accident, and he was known as "that goddam Limey" at the US Navy hospital, where surgeons plastered a broomstick between his thighs to speed his recovery. He had to be tipped sideways to be carried through aircraft doorways when he flew home.

news since the war began. These mockingly nicknamed Stringbags later torpedo Germany's greatest warships. Their gunners lay off too much deflection, unwilling to believe any warplane flies so low and slow, and their gunsights lack low settings to match the Stringbag's cruising speed of 90 knots. Under her wood and fabric belly may be strung torpedoes, mines, or the bikes of sailors going on leave. If a swift German Me 109 fighter pounces, the Stringbag skims the waves in ever-decreasing circles, luring the enemy to follow in even tighter circles until he goes into a fatal high-speed stall. If our old girl hits the drink, she floats while the crew waits to be picked up. In Arctic waters, they are more likely to freeze to death: an unadvertised penalty for guarding our stealthy convoys carrying weapons for Russia.

"Mac" Samples becomes a friend after surviving a Swordfish attack on the German battle cruisers *Scharnhorst* and *Gneisenau* when they broke out from the French port of Brest in February 1942. The heavy cruiser *Prinz Eugen* accompanied this "Channel Dash" under a German fighter umbrella of swift Me 109s and FW190s, seven German destroyers, and a swarm of E-boats. Samples flew in 825 squadron with six lumbering old Swordfish. All were shot down: Each carried a pilot, an observer, and a TAG telegraphist air-gunner. Their commander, Eugene Esmonde, was awarded the Victoria Cross, the highest medal for valor, but he was dead. Most of his men died with him. The London *Times* commented: "Nothing more mortifying to the pride of our seapower has happened since the 17th century. It spells the end of the legend that in wartime no enemy battle fleet can pass through what we proudly call the English Channel." Samples was one of two survivors. Years later, in India with British intelligence, he tells me: "The navy insisted upon launching Stringbags on this doomed mission, and clung to a tradition that the navigator is captain of the ship. If a pilot was only a petty officer, he was forbidden to enter officer's quarters to share operational briefings with a lieutenant-navigator like me." Before the mission, he heard an Air Sea Rescue briefing on where to look for survivors: "Because they're all going to be shot down." The tough RAF station commander who dispatched the Stringbags stood with tears running down his cheeks as they took off.

At every stage of assessment, we makee-learn pilots are steered into different categories. If we dip but are aggressive, we'll be redirected to Motor Torpedo Boats to counter German E-boats in the channel. Others are good enough to fly torpedo-bombers. After watching that Stringbag burn like one of my Japanese model planes, I feel an urgent need to be recommended for fighters.

I am posted to Elementary Flying School (EFTS) at Elmdon, on the old Roman Road, south of Coventry, a city earlier bombed flat. EFTS will weed out sailors who lack aptitude. German bombers can hit an EFTS field but the alternative is to ship us through "U-boat Alley" to North American airfields. Putting makee-learn pilots at such risk is not cost-effective. Many will fail, or "dip" here in England. In the Tudor-style Stonebridge Hotel we sleep on the floor in what was Reception, now used for ground studies.

My companions fear a fatal crash will grieve their parents. Mama always told me, "Fear does not exist." When I climb into a Tiger Moth, it's my Empire Day fantasy come true! This machine has a green "gas patch" that changes color if the Hun chooses to spray us with chlorine gas. My biplane looks like a survivor of Great War air battles that we mimicked as boys on bikes. Its noble pedigree goes back to 1920 when Geoffrey de Havilland launched the "Humming Bird." This became a wooden "Moth" and morphed into the Tiger Moth. Thousands are now in service all over the world. "Even in Japan," says my flight instructor. He laughs when I echo "Japan!" in apparent disbelief. He's talking about changes the Tokyo warlords made, arming the Tiggy to support Japan's invasion of China. I'm thinking about my prophetic Japanese model airplane kits.

The instructor talks to me through Gosport rubber tubes. No clutter of radio, bomb racks, camera-guns here. I never blush behind goggles and under a leather helmet. I go solo after five hours' tuition. It's great to practice spins unobserved. I reduce speed a shade above stalling, pull back on the stick, apply full rudder, whip sharply over, whirl like a top, yet seem to stand still. Earth rises to greet me. I'm mesmerized. If I take too long to recover my wits, only in time to spin off a turn below five hundred feet, I'm dead. Night-flying is a piece of cake. I can't drive a car but I can ride

Author, age sixteen, in front of his elementary flying school biplane, the Tiger Moth.

a bike and now I can fly. I'm a bird. I'm part of Nature. I go solo in body and mind.

Some of us survive to go to Service Flying Training Schools (SFTS) in safer skies. Before I leave for SFTS in Canada, I get a foretaste of combat from a stocky survivor of battles with the German Luftwaffe. His first warplane looked a bit like our Tiger Moths. He flew it over Warsaw in 1939 against the most powerful machines in the world. He says, "I escaped in time for the Battle of Britain. At first, your pilots fly in polite formations. Poles tell your airmen that Germans fly to kill. No looping of loops. Your pilots say we talk funny. They do not listen until they lose many Hurricanes and Spitfires. Then they listen and learn to destroy the modern way." He does not give his name before he climbs into a Lysander whose pilot is a girl from what is called "a Ferry Pilot Pool." She snatches a moment to sip hot tea from a mug. I ask why her passenger does not pilot the Lysander himself.

"O that's Zura." She laughs. "Says he needs to warn baby-pilots you've got serious stuff ahead. He's afraid you think flying is fun and games. When he can, he has us nip him over to some kindergarten like this." She wears a Sidcot suit, so puffy that it hides her schoolgirl frame, and long enough for the bottoms to be tucked into standard flying boots. With irregular goggles pushed up over a nonregulation white leather helmet, her bright blue eyes appraise me. "His name is Jan Zurakowski. You'll hear the name often enough when this nonsense is over."

Zura is glaring at us. He's not the least bit interested in his gorgeous girl pilot. He's worried that she's talking too much. Poland, after all, is under Nazi and Soviet occupation and probably he has family there. Much, much later we become friends and I fly with him. Together we escape a fiery end while testing a new fighter plane.

## CHAPTER 8

# A Ghost Who Haunts a Lifetime

ON THE OCEAN LINER *QUEEN MARY* WE RACE ACROSS THE ATLANTIC, unescorted through U-boat Alley, beyond the protection of RAF Coastal Command warplanes. The eastern shores of the United States are brightly lit in boisterous disregard for the enemy. U-boats pick off merchant ships sailing along a coastline glittering like a Christmas tree. We rely on speed to arrive in New York for final training. We look odd in bell-bottom trousers, with gold anchors on our sleeves: Leading Naval Airmen. Our flat-topped Nelsonian caps carry white bands denoting officer-cadets but folks here must surely view us as part of a Gilbert and Sullivan comic opera.

My dragons retrieve S-NAPS AND S-CRAPS: MY LIFE IN THE NAVY. This tattered photo album covers from April to December 1943. I re-named it "Naps and Craps" and probably thought it should be dropped down the Memory Hole. But here it is, with notes and other echoes of friends who died. Here's "Spud" Murphy's picture, looking like a round-faced schoolboy when we practice night flying. I have the night off when Spud shakes me awake at 3:00 a.m. He stands at the end of our two-tier bunk and says softly, "Be a good chap and check my kit. Take out anything that might embarrass the folks back home. And keep the faith."

I'm fast asleep again in a jiff. I go to breakfast, certain that I had been dreaming. Pete Seary and Bob Scott are not looking great. It snowed during the night and they flew blind, or near enough. They mention this in a way that tells me this is the start of bad news.

"You heard about Spud?" says one.

"He crashed," says the other.

They pluck up courage. "Killed!" they chorus.

I look down at my plate of eggs and bacon, thinking irrelevantly that back in England, a breakfast like this would look like a gift from the gods. Finally I ask: "When did it happen?"

They regard me with frank curiosity. My first reaction should be: "How was Spud killed. Caught in a blizzard? Sudden engine failure? Lost his way and ran out of gas?" These are questions we normally ask first. Not: "When did it happen?"

"Last night," says Pete.

"No, I mean what time?"

"The tower said his last radio call was about zero-two-fifty-five."

"Five minutes before three o'clock." I push away my plate and grab a mug of coffee.

"You okay?" asks Pete.

I gulp some coffee. It's hot and my throat is no longer dry. "Yes, of course. Rotten luck."

We all nod our heads. There's nothing more to be said. There never is.

Later I join the padre who is packing Spud's kit bag to be sent home.

I murmur, "He'd like to make sure there aren't any letters or other items that might embarrass his parents."

The padre is an old hand at this. "Of course." He looks through a barrack-room window at the frosty tarmac. "It's a bit early for snow," he says, leaving me to tidy up Spud's gear. I never anticipate that Spud's ghost is so real that ahead of me stretches a lifetime of self-censorship. His needless death can only have meaning if I measure my behavior against the ideals by which we all secretly live when very young. That night I turn up the collar of my pajama jacket. This is more than a childhood habit inspired by my mother's Christian Science readings. I improvise on a boyish prayer, for Spud's benefit. "I'll make the world a better place to justify your sacrifice." It reminds me of things in which Spud believed: ideals he seldom voiced, a boyish innocence, a resolve that those of us who survive will strive to fight for what is right, without having to ever make war again.

We fly North American Harvards: sophisticated aircraft, compared to the dear old Tiger Moth. More like the real thing: crowded instrument panel, retractable undercart, sliding canopy, oxygen mask, a power-ful engine driving a propeller that makes a distinctive screech for any poor landlubber directly below. When I first sat in a Harvard cockpit, I thought: "I'll never find my way around all these bits and pieces." Flying the "Tiggy," the Tiger Moth, was simple by comparison. But I can't risk transfer to motor-torpedo boats. I have no wish to be assigned to torpedo bombers. So I do my best to impress my instructors with my aerobatics and try to remember that piece of advice given by Dad about parking emotions outside the cockpit.

Emotion overwhelms me during a blind-flying test when, from the back cockpit, the instructor tells me to flip back the hood. He has given me courses to steer while I'm unable to see outside, and I can navigate only by maps and instruments. He asks me where I reckon we are. "Ottawa?" I suggest hopefully.

"Flip back the hood!" he says. I got it right! I'm near-blinded by my first view of the Canadian capital, all spires and gracious old parliamen-tary buildings covered in rime icing. A frozen river winds through this fairy-tale city. Through my head runs the thought: "I'm coming back here, if I ever survive."

And a similar gasp of wonder chokes me when another navigational exercise takes me above the Adirondack Mountains. Tufts of granular ice cover their windward side. Rime icing turns the landscape into a glittering spectacle, like a twinkling promise of limitless challenges and opportunities.

Day and night I fling the Harvard around the sky: loops and spins and rolls-off-the-top, low flying over boundless fields, clipping hedges, mock dogfights, forced landings between tall pine trees when the instructor cuts the motor. He's a former bush pilot, now a Canadian air force sergeant. On the last day, we walk together across the tarmac with parachutes slung over our shoulders, and he says quietly, "It's fighters for you, old son."

In November, I telegraph home: "Wings and commission mine." I won't be collecting a sub-lieutenant's pay, six shillings and sixpence a day, until I get back to England. My dragons now make those telegrams look like bravado. They were curt in the spirit of thrift. I see now that I wrote in

Author, fifth from left, second row, with fellow pilots in operational training during WWII. Pilots with hat bands half blacked out were killed in later operations.

"Naps and Craps": "My current pay as Naval Airman, First Class, equals a Canadian dollar a week, which doesn't stretch very far."

Here's a group photograph of fellow pilots, many white hatbands blacked out to signify those killed in training.

Crosses mark others who failed to make the grade. Good blokes, all. It was worth the risks. We got to hitchhike around North America. Here are captions under USO girls who look after American servicemen and treat us strangers with such generous goodwill, laugh with us, and take us home to meet their parents, who fill us with home-baked cookies and Coke. Some girls are at Pensacola, the US air station in Florida where I learn about hurricanes and other marine uncertainties in a move that suggests I'm destined for specialized flying.

Back in Canada is the Thousand Islands Bridge. I find an aerial photograph marked with the route taken by some of us who fly under it. Anyone caught risking this is "dipped," and loses any hope of winning his wings. Most of us get away with it. One who did not is marked with a black cross pasted across a particular photograph he took while holding a camera between his knees. He had said he wanted a picture of himself as he flew under the bridge. He hit it while looking into the camera. It was fished out of Lake Ontario, the only piece of him left. I close S-NAPS with mixed feelings. Bright young faces I tried to forget and now remember. Boys not yet burdened with earthly woes, not yet fighting to survive peacetime rivalries, not yet forced to enter the money markets in what in England is known as beggar-your-neighbor. Good blokes who twitter silly jokes and would be aghast at any prophecy that "twittering" will become part of a culture where to be informed is to watch the one-graph scan of the print media online, coupled with television news scrolls. S-NAPS tells me more with its shabby little black-and-white photographs and hastily scribbled cut lines. Spud's ghost came to me in a spirit of comradeship. I envy him. He never lived to see the postwar divisions into warring enclaves of political hatreds and cutthroat financial shenanigans. The further back I look, the further forward I see. Past events appear in a fresh light when not separated by calendar time. New ghosts bring up pieces of the past to try to trap me in a cage of regret. I think of my poor raven, condemned by my small-boy foolishness to crash dive, and grounded in a cage forever in memory.

## CHAPTER 9

# Here Today and Gone Tomorrow

UP COMES AN OLD FORM 414, LABELED RAF PILOTS FLYING LOG-BOOK. Navy fliers are the RAF's poor relations, given hand-me-down log-books, overstamped with smudges of Admiralty insignia in bad grammar. Here is a record of machines swiftly designed by Americans for the rough and tumble of carrier operations: Wildcats and Hellcats and Corsairs. I fly them all after returning to England. But here, too, are hasty Royal Navy improvisations. The Swordfish, built in 1923, flies operationally until the end of the war. Britain had failed to spot the ingenuity of Japan's warlords. When I pilot a Swordfish, I wonder how our admirals ever noticed what Dad did on his voyages to Tokyo. His model airplane kits were proof of a deadly ingenuity.

My dragons bring up a stunningly brief logbook entry, dated June 1, 1945, my twenty-first birthday: "From shore base to HMS *Ravager* (Struck Barrier)."

Suddenly I'm back in a Seafire—a Spitfire never designed for ships but adapted with a tailhook and folding wings to be struck down below deck. I descend upon HMS *Ravager*, a converted cargo ship, now a training carrier, and float over the arrestor wires.

The skipper's only clue to the competence of incoming pilots is a daily list telegraphed from a stone frigate: the Royal Navy Air Station at Ayr. Ahead of me, a Wildcat pilot had spun into the sea and drowned, the speed of his final approach misjudged by "Bats," the batsman on whose visual judgment we rely.

My head was sticking out of the cockpit, as instructed. My eyes were fixed on the waggle of his bats instead of my instrument panels, as per regulations. Landing on a ship goes against all the instincts of pilots operating out of solid, steady airfields. My aircraft is flown tail down, prevented from stalling by gunning the engine until I scrape over the round down and get the "cut engine" signal from Bats. He's badly unnerved after losing the Wildcat and brings me in a shade too fast. I've never landed on a ship before but I have lots of flying experience, about which the skipper knows nothing. He raises the crash barrier for what he thinks is another inexperienced "makee-learn" pilot. I open the throttle to go round again. I clip the barrier, turn turtle, and slide into the sea. Mindlessly, I follow the drill for escaping underwater. I've no memory of being fished out by the guardian frigate.

Hoisted back on board the carrier, I'm terrified this will end my flying days. Then Bats greets me in the wardroom: "I owe you a drink." The skipper claps me on the back. "Try again tomorrow. Bottoms up!"

A longboat lands me ashore early next day. The ship's purser makes me sign for the four pennies I need to buy a workman's bus ticket back to Ayr. I'm still in flying gear. Other passengers offer me baffled sidelong nervous smiles. Ground crews at the Ayr naval land base frostily watch me trudge back across the tarmac after losing one of their new Mark III Seafires with updated Rolls-Royce Merlin engine, V-frame arrestor hook, reinforced undercarriage, catapult spool, and folding wings. It looks to these hardened old salts as if they're about to lose yet another of their lovingly groomed machines, painstakingly polished to kill at maximum speed.

"It's like when you fall off a horse," I chirrup at the chief petty officer. "Got to get on again at once, or lose your nerve."

The CPO is not fooled by my bravado. "Don't fall off this one." He pats another of the new Seafires he's obliged to give me. He looks about a hundred years old, but graciously adds, "Sir!" He's under no illusions.

Today, I find an assessment by Eric Brown, who flew every type of naval aircraft: "Carrier operations are harsh and unforgiving. Nautical environment is daunting. Shipboard aircraft seldom transcend the indifferent. Operational successes owe more to the valor of their crews."

I make eight successful deck landings and twenty-seven days later I'm flying Hellcats, replacing a lost pilot in a squadron led by Nigel

Author boarding his warplane during WWII.

Fisher, nicknamed "The Fish," descendant of the same great Admiral Fisher who, like Nelson, began as a boy seaman. Nigel has his ancestor's "damn-the-torpedoes-full-steam-ahead" disposition. He remains a lieutenant to avoid any suggestion of nepotism. Others who run an operational squadron would normally command a higher rank. Nigel says I'm lucky to switch from the offshoot of the Supermarine Spitfire, first known as the Sea-Spitfire. The clumsy name is simplified to Seafire but the aircraft remains unsuited for the rugged demands of carrier operations, although it's the fastest low-level fighter afloat, with an unsurpassed rate of climb and outstanding maneuverability. Against Jap Zeros, it can be devastating.

"But it suffers from the delay in Royal Naval operational control of aviation, after twenty-one years of RAF monopoly," says Nigel. "The Fleet Air Arm began with a handful of RAF aircrew without the backup of seagoing engineers with aviation experience. Casualties were proportionally heavy. Carrier captains had to make do with staid old ladies like the Swordfish."

Most pilots kept diaries, against orders. Dragon-mail brings up one quoting Nigel Fisher. He blasts Winston Churchill who, as First Lord of Admiralty in March 1940, nixed efforts to get Spitfires re-engineered for sea operations. "Within two weeks, our small carriers were fighting Nazi battle wagons," says Nigel. German invaders of Norway in April and June 1940 shot down all British carrier planes. The carrier *Glorious* then took on land-based Hurricane fighters by steaming at 26 knots into the 15-knot winds whipping over a short flight deck. "No problem for the Germans to sink *Glorious* and her two attendant destroyers later the same day."

The Admiralty had prized battleships more than carriers. The Japanese taught otherwise in 1941, with the air strikes against Pearl Harbor. My schoolboy admiration for Japanese model airplane kits was not so childish after all. The Sea-Spitfire was introduced, with arrestor hook and sling points, in trials before Christmas of that year. More Sea-Spitfires were landed on the carrier *Victorious* by pilots who learned the hard way that the view forward was blocked because the line of sight was below horizontal flight and pilots were unable see the deck. The solution was to fly in a continuous curve: Pilots stuck heads out to see the batsman and straightened up in the wake of the carrier.

I was afraid to confess that when I stuck my head out of the cockpit to watch "Bats," the slipstream flushed tears out of my eyes and into my goggles. Today I learn I was born minus a normal optical drainage system. I dropped onto carriers by glancing at instruments and squinting through tears. The take-off run for the Seafire consumed 280 feet of decking. Pilots often stuck wooden wedges in position to keep the flaps down. Once airborne, the disposable wedges fell out and flaps could be fully raised. RATOG, Rocket-Assisted Take-Off Gear, was tried, but casualties were too great when the rockets failed to fire evenly on either side.

The basic Spit was too elegant. Most interceptions were below 25,000 feet, where the Spit outperformed enemy planes. Higher, the enemy had the edge. A new Merlin 55 engine gave an extra 20 mph at all heights but there was a tendency to float on landing. "Pecking" was the word for a Seafire striking the deck with its propeller tips. A new Griffin VI engine with a two-stage supercharger gave 370 mph at 10,000 feet, and 383 mph at 13,500 feet. At higher speeds at greater heights the machine rolled uncontrollably, with devastating consequences.

Earlier training in ADDLES, Aerodrome Dummy Deck Landings, had prepared me for that first carrier landing when I nearly took The Last Cut, the fatal end to life, and an expression taken from having to obey Bats' signal to "Cut engine!" I had previously favored the Hurricane, true winner of the Battle of Britain.

I learned to challenge authority at levels higher than East Ham's town-council Scrooges and their love of old gas lamps. Between returning to England and my twenty-first birthday, my dragons remind me, was a mystifying interlude at an obscure RAF field in Scotland where I must recognize, within split seconds, silhouettes of enemy aircraft and warships. It's a bit like Kim's Game but I'm not at the Khyber Pass. Most nights I'm at the local pub, full of boisterous Russians in civilian clothes. They never explain why they are there. A nineteen-year-old girl in the Women's Auxiliary Air Force (WAFF) complains that I'm too ready to ask awkward questions.

"Other pilots," says the WAAF, "accept the order not to ask about things that don't concern you."

"My life as a small boy," I tell her, "taught me to be nosy."

She's happy to chat, but warns: "Keep your voice down. They speak better English than they let on."

"Who do?"

"Russkies! Do you ever see the same ones in the pub twice?"

"I suppose not. What's it mean?"

"Here today, gone tomorrow!" She shrugs. "Are you buying me another gin-and-it?"

"Yes, of course!" I feel flush with cash on a sub-lieutenant's pay, plus "danger money."

We walk back to base. "I'm on duty from midnight to dawn," she says. "You'll understand, if you go to bed like a good little boy and read a book."

I retire to my lonely cot and re-read Boswell's account of a trip to the Hebrides with Dr. Samuel Johnson. I hear aero engines and part the blackout curtains. It's a clear night, bright with stars. A shadow crosses the sky: the silhouette of a Mosquito, usually flown on solo missions into hostile territory to drop flares and guide the following RAF bombers to their targets. It makes no sense to launch a Mosquito from here, closer to Norway than Germany.

Dim lights along one side of a runway suddenly go out. Whoever flies this Mosquito is not spoiled by an abundance of technical aids. The lights re-appear when the engines open up. Their roar fades. The lights are switched off again. Not even a glimmer from the departing Mosquito. I open the cabin window and stick my head out. There's nothing in the sky except the usual constellations. I can't hear the powerful engines anymore. I remember Spud Murphy's ghost shaking my bunk.

"Well?" asks my WAAF when we meet in the pub again.

I look around. The usual boisterous Russians . . . But wait! Not the same faces.

The penny drops. Everyone on base knows about our "secret" Arctic convoys with arms for the Soviet Union. "Are those Russkies . . ." I ask, "ferrying our planes to . . . to Murmansk?"

She dips her little nose into her glass. "My goodness," she says sweetly. "It's empty again."

I wonder how many Russians complete these flights, guided to take-off for a few split seconds by a teenage girl. Russkies boozing in our pub one night, stealthily flying away the next. "Here today," as my pretty little WAAF said, "gone tomorrow." The words become embedded in my mind. They might imply a kind of fecklessness in today's world, but they shadowed my future actions.

## CHAPTER 10

# Captains at the Gate

MURMANSK SEA CONVOYS ASSEMBLE AT SCAPA FLOW IN THE ORKNEY Islands. Each convoy slips away without warning, escorted by warships and baby carriers. Scapa Flow may be closer to Nazi-occupied Norway than it is to London, but it takes many days for the slow-moving, heavily loaded cargo ships to reach Russia.

I spend an intensive period at Scapa, flying different types of aircraft in a Fleet Requirements Unit (FRU). I never speak about it while on leave, not for secrecy's sake but to save my blushes. For the name of this FRU base is Twatt. Few outsiders know about Twatt. No wonder *Ravager*'s skipper assumed I was a freshly minted Seafire pilot when I tried my first deck landing. He never heard of Twatt as a place on the map. Yet I get a lot of unadvertised experience here, piloting Hellcats, Corsairs, Blenheim bombers, Sea Hurricanes, Spitfires, Barracudas, Sea Otters, Walrus flying boats, and sturdy old Stringbags flown from gale-swept mainland Orkney, ten miles north of Scotland. The name Twatt comes from a prehistoric village, partly excavated between two world wars. We hardly notice this pre-Stone Age relic. Our tight little bunch of pilots is more puzzled by the Admiralty's mad impulse to send navy Wrens to our lonely hideaway.

Orkney Mainland is larger than all the tinier islands scattered around Scapa Flow, home of the Home Fleet, key to Britain's mastery of the seas. Way back in the 1400s, Norwegians named the deep-water anchorage Scalpaye, meaning the isthmus cleaving Orkney Mainland in two. Twatt is Norse for what they called Twotte. Before Vikings invaded and

53

left Norse names everywhere, Twatt was inhabited by dwarves. I imagine them lying in the tiny beds still outlined by stone slabs. Four Wrens with their arms outstretched can touch opposite walls of the entire village. Nobody comes near after dark.

Ugly memories haunt Scapa Flow, the worst inspired by the black upturned hull of HMS *Royal Oak,* the proudest of battle wagons before it was torpedoed by U-47, a German U-boat, only days after the declaration of war: 833 British officers and men were trapped and drowned. Steel nets drape the wreck to prevent bodies or bones drifting along shorelines to undermine civilian morale. We poke through the darkness to look for possible enemy bombers, hoping to miss the invisible cables of barrage balloons strung above other warships afloat below. None of us cares to linger over the sunken remains of what Churchill had called, "One of the Captains at the Gate."

Wrens wake us in the middle of the night when we're needed to fly between the barrage balloon cables because another audacious U-boat is thought to have penetrated the deep-sea anchorage. Then we drop antisubmarine mines from our Stringbags. Fliers sleep two in a hut. My observer-navigator suddenly refuses to fly a mission, saying, "It's a waste of time, we never find enemy subs or planes, and always someone goes down because a cable slices through a wing." I remind him that he risks a court-martial and add, "I know my way blindfold around Scapa. It's just another false alarm. We'll be back before breakfast."

He groans, "I've lost my nerve!" and goes back to sleep. He's back on form the next day.

One airman loses his nerve after flying sixty-seven operational Stringbag sorties and escorting these convoys to Murmansk. He led a squadron into action two years after training as twenty-year-old Naval Airman 2nd Class John Godley. He later becomes Lord Kilbracken. He is still John Godley when, at age twenty-four, he commands fourteen Swordfish, the youngest squadron commander of deadly Arctic operations aboard converted cargo ships. Flight decks rise and fall through dizzy heights in the unpredictable violence of furious seas. On first taking command, he is told, "One or two fucking things you'd better know.

First, the fucking Captain is crazy." Godley discovers crews "badly twitched" after flying ops without a break. He learns to live with this, and after four years, he is transferred to a conversion course on Barracudas, hailed as "modern" replacements for the Stringbags. They already have an evil reputation. Any flier sent from Twatt to train on Barracudas is asked politely by the rest of us to return borrowed books and gear because he is not expected to last long.

Wrens come alongside our cots with mugs of hot tea on quiet mornings. Other girls check and re-pack our parachutes, load torpedoes, comfort the layabouts or the injured in sick bay, or go "egging" with us when off duty. Egging is a cheerful interlude. We buy eggs from Orkney farmers, all of whom appear to have previously lived in faraway places, ranching in Australia, coffee-planting in Kenya, logging in Canada . . . Why do they come back to this isolation, where everyone is said to walk with a tilt to leeward against the constant high winds? "Ye canna forget the pleasures of solitude," says a poetic sheep farmer. "Away from here, I could always hear the cry of curlews and the sound of heavy seas pounding like drums along our fortresslike island walls."

I bicycle with a Wren companion on these egging expeditions. She's from Truro in Cornwall, where daffodils grow while the rest of us freeze. We explore the headland where Lord Kitchener went down with HMS *Hampshire* in 1916. He learned guerrilla warfare from the Boers. Times change. When on duty, my Wren stands on a tower and keeps score of dummy attacks by Sea Hurricane fighters. She never gives me the benefit of the doubt. She says her stern assessments "might someday save your—" She primly switches to "undercarriage."

One bright moonlight night, we lie on a rock near poor old Kitchener's watery grave. She loves poetry and writes a little. Tonight she recites my favorite poem, Gray's "Elegy Written in a Country Churchyard." She halts at the haunting lines: "Each in his narrow cell forever laid / The rude forefathers of the hamlet sleep."

"I never understood why our forefathers were called 'rude,'" she says. "I suppose two hundred years ago, the word meant 'good-hearted men of oak.' Like you chumps."

We disentangle our limbs. A creamy foam sizzles and froths around our rock, lit by the round-faced moon. "I'm afraid of falling in love with loonies like you. None of you will end up in some quiet country churchyard."

"Actually, I'd rather be buried at sea." Slowly I add, "I flew over a sub yesterday." I stop. I know something that perhaps is secret: that we have many more submarines than the navy publicizes. They fight a submarine war, which will never be fully reported until the twenty-first century. I steer away a few degrees. "This big sausage full of men grew fainter. I felt sick. I couldn't take my eyes off the bloody thing until the periscope sank from sight."

"Would you feel sorry for the men inside if it was a U-boat?"

"Yes!" I blurt out. "I'm not very good at hating—" I break off.

"So why'd you stooge around, dicing with death?" She speaks in the slang of our times.

"I never look that far ahead. I like flying."

"You're all the same." She stands up, a beautiful Cornish girl, too young for this kind of talk. We climb together to the cliff top. She leans on her bike. "You're in love with uncertainty. Don't you ever talk about the certainty of death?"

"What's the point? It's all around us."

"Think of a future with wife and kids." She reaches over to give me a kiss. Dear God! I don't want to burden her with facts like those about Bill Simpson's wife, who left him. She could no longer bear the sight of his distorted face, his hands badly burned. He wrote with a pencil between the stump of one hand and a bit of one finger. French villagers had treated his wounds with maggots that ate away rotting flesh, before he escaped across the Channel.

"Well, back to quarters," says my Wren, reading my mind. "I promise I won't talk such nonsense again."

Other girls ferry replacement aircraft. I find an old photograph of eight young women, all experienced prewar pilots, striding away from planes they have just delivered: civilian girls of the Air Transport Auxiliary who fly warplanes from factories to operational units. They wear standard-issue flying gear, except for goggles and leather helmets of their own choosing. One delivers a Sea Hurricane, but she first performs a series of slow rolls at low

Flight instructors with a ferry pilot in a sailplane, admired by the author and other powered-flight pilots from afar.

level. Jaws drop among mere males, lounging in deck chairs, seduced by a few rays of sunshine piercing Twatt's regular fog and cloud. We watch a tall girl climb out of the cockpit, jump nimbly to the ground, sling her parachute over one shoulder, whip off her bright helmet of non-regulation blue, shake out her golden curls, and stride straight for the den of Commander Flying, ignoring us jolly pilots. She's from a Ferry Pilot Pool: girls of a certain class, prewar fliers, addicted to one real passion, flying.

The Wrens of Twatt mollycoddle us with steaming mugs of tea and coffee and hot chocolate when we make the rounds on foul-weather days. I have a routine whenever gale-force winds make it impossible to fly. Coffee for "elevenses" in the morning at a hangar where Wrens hang our parachutes from high beams to dry and be tested, tea at mid-afternoon with girls at sick bay, and hot chocolate at five when others tackle our dirty linen in the communal laundry room. No Wrens are allowed in the wardroom. Most evenings, we crowd around the piano with drinks purchased from our shared "kitty." We sing: "O death where is thy sting, a-ding-a-ling, or grave thy victory?"

My Wren is posted to another stone frigate: St. Merryn, in her native Cornwall. She sings like Vera Lynn: "We'll meet again / Don't know where / Don't know when ..."

We do meet again, at St. Merryn. But only after Vera Lynn meets me again at Twatt. "I didn't believe my ears when they said I was coming to a place called Twatt!" she says. She's with ENSA, the Entertainments National Service Association. She's flown here in an old York transport plane with "a letter to our fighting men in words and music" says the bulletin I discover in the crew room. She's as gorgeous as ever, despite her quaint ENSA uniform. Her golden-brown curls pour rebelliously out of a military beret. She gets rapturous applause from servicemen. The next day she's off to some other far-flung outpost. I escort the departing York transport plane in a Hurricane, flying alongside while she peers through a porthole. We wave and blow kisses. And then she's gone.

In a stolen moment before we parted, she had said, "You were such an absentminded little boy, always writing stories about imaginary places. You're still hooked on uncertainty. Make plans for the future."

"My plans are to write. And explore wild places. I see the natural world as less destructive than humans. I can't let security anchor me."

I'm not under Vera's kindly scrutiny when flying solo missions. In solitary bliss, I make up stories in my head. My dragons today bring up old thoughts I wrote after a possible enemy ship is reported by a Walrus pilot, now back on his battleship catapult. Sea and fog present a difficult choice. Do I fly under the fog, and foreshorten my vision? Or fly above it, hoping to spot a ship's mast poking through?

The fog thickens. I climb higher. Few vessels have masts tall enough to stick above the fuzzy blanket. I check yet again my "Iffy"— Identification Friend or Foe. If I forget to switch it on, I'm liable to be attacked as a "bandit" by our own defenses. And I'm in easy range of German interceptors from Norway. I gamble that they are busy attacking our convoys or protecting their warships lying deep in Norwegian fjords, not yet ready to strike.

My single engine drones like a big bird, as if fully fed and forever content. I keep checking instruments. Under my wings are drop tanks. I don't need extra fuel yet. I bank from side to side to see if a mast pokes above the fog. The maneuver is hypnotic. Hugged by a Mae-West life jacket, strapped to a small seat, cushioned by a parachute, I yawn. I check my Dalton computer, strapped to one thigh. I fiddle with its plastic rings, re-setting numbers like course-to-steer, elapsed time—elapsed time?

I've flown too long and too far! I slide back the cockpit canopy. I turn through 180 degrees to aim for Twatt. No landmarks. Balls of cloud thicken like knitting wool. Did I drift sideways? I have no visible clues: no helpful church steeple, no railroad, no cliffs marking a coastline. Nothing but the froth of a rising sea. My return will take forever, even if I know what course to steer. I check again the Dalton computer: primitive when compared with later versions. Bloody hell! Am I adrift in Arctic waters? Pilots who ditch there freeze to death in seconds!

I break radio silence to ask for a fix from position-finding radio stations in Scotland. They tell me to say a few words. I recite, "Little Billy, in the best of sashes, fell in the fire and got burned to ashes. After a while the room grew chilly. Nobody liked to poke poor Willy."

"Gotcha!" The cheerful voice in my headset is enough. My position in the middle of nowhere is known. I am given a course to steer back to base. It means turning round again. I have overflown John O'Groats and Scotland. I have overflown Twatt and The Minch and the Outer Hebrides and now? Now I'm heading for America! Again I break radio silence to ask: "How much time to Twatt?"

"Adjust . . ."

I adjust between low engine revs and low fuel consumption. There's a buzzing in my ears. If eyes can pop, mine pop now. I push everything else out of mind except how to nurse myself home.

Twatt floats into view. All fuel tanks read empty. My brain comes in from the cold. Well-rehearsed drills take over. The prop stops as I hit the tarmac. My Hurricane has to be towed to dispersal.

I blush when Commander Dobson climbs on to the port wing. He's sure to wash me out.

Instead he thumps me on the shoulder. "We nearly lost our best Hurricane."

Nothing about nearly losing me. Still, he did say "Good show! You brought it back in one piece."

I am ferried later to Northern Ireland to pick up a Miles Martinet in Londonderry. I drone back to Orkney, alone in this single-engine aircraft, and follow a string of Hebridean islands with Norse names—Islay, Muck, Eigg, Rum. On my maps, they seem like Vikings on parade. Far ahead lies Skye and the Kyle of Loch-gilp-head. I cross The Little Minch, and point my nose in the direction of dear old Twatt. My engine stutters.

All these islands look from above like pointy chunks of rock. Not much space between these sharp peaks. I spot a fairly flat piece of land between two spikes on Jura. I swing over it. The engine stops dead.

I glide into the only field, which is small and full of sheep. No shepherds. I belly land, scramble out, and trigger the emergency flare pistol. It doesn't fire. No bother. There's not a soul to see a red flare anyway. I stumble down through the bracken until, without warning, a stone house appears. On a brass plate is the name of a physician.

A wee doctor opens the heavy oak door. He peers cautiously at this scruffy boy in a yellow life jacket and lumpish flying boots. I jabber. "Sorry! Forced landing! No joy on radio. Can I use your phone to call air-sea rescue at Port Ellen?"

"Port Ellen's a long-distance call," he says. Cautiously, he lets me into his tiny library.

I make my call. Now for some good old Scottish hospitality. Mebbe a wee dram of Scotch?

"Tha'll be saxpence," the good doctor tells me.

I fumble for pennies. He counts them and says, "Ye'll be back to your aireeplane, nae doot."

"Aye, I shall, nae doot!" I match his thrifty ways, and stride down to a tiny fishing village tucked into a bit of shoreline. The island's schoolmaster finds me a cot until one of my squadron mates, Sub-Lieutenant Buxton, collects me.

How careless I was about names! Dragons bring forth my log noting "Buxton" and a forced landing just before Christmas 1944. A pilot named Buxton warns me that the forced landing might result in a "red endorsement" in my logbook, meaning bad airmanship. Investigators later prove that instrument wires were crossed. When I switched to a fuel tank reading *Full*, the tank was *Empty*. My plane was serviced by Irish rebels. Bless 'em! Their action led to a "green endorsement," commendation for setting down the Martinet in one piece. Dear old Buxton! A boy, really, I now recall. Killed when our squadron flies fake attacks against Nazi-held Norway during D-Day. We fly along the Murmansk convoy routes and break radio silence with madly concocted jabber to persuade the Germans that fleets of Allied warplanes are airborne to cover a massive Allied invasion, not of Normandy but Norway.

CHAPTER 11

# Survivors in Notional Proximity

ANOTHER OLD LOGBOOK RECORDS OTHER UNCONVENTIONAL ASSIGN-
ments. I test new aircraft such as the Corsair, briefed only by a handbook
of twenty pages. Today, the handbook for a lawn mower would be a dozen
times the length. The first time I take off in the unfamiliar Corsair, I strain
to look around an unusually long engine. This forces me to lean out to
look ahead. The sudden slipstream wraps an oxygen tube and unfamiliar wires around my throat. At the most critical moment of takeoff, I'm
dragged against the back of my seat. It's too late to abort. I'm flying blind,
goggles askew, clawing with one hand to disentangle the mess. Straightened out, I stay aloft for an hour, testing the cannons, wishing I need
never land because, like flying a Corsair, setting it down is also an entirely
new procedure. This awkward American bird was designed as a test bed
for its huge engine. The US Navy only adopts it for operations after our
own navy flies it regularly from carrier decks.

These old logbook entries are often infuriatingly cryptic. "Exercise
Chutney" is all I note when we fly out of Twatt, chattering with made-up
call signs in sweeps across the North Sea, breaking radio silence so that
enemy ears get an impression of gargantuan air power. I find myself flying
a Sea Hurricane in mock attack on one of our destroyers. My wingman is
to dive from the opposite side to divide the destroyer's antiaircraft fire. I'm
heading directly for the target's funnel. I forget the drill. Should I break to
port or starboard? If I get it wrong, I collide with the other Hurricane. So
I hop over the funnel. Everything goes black. Hell! The other pilot must
have had the same thought. His plane must have hit me head-on.

Then I hear my engine's smug buzz. I feel around. My seat was lifted by heat from the destroyer's funnel. Then it dropped to the bottom of the cockpit, where I could see nothing. I have not smashed into my wing mate . . . Pheww! I'm alive. But I still have to render my A-25.

In the wardroom, we sing, "They say in the airforce a landing's okay / if the pilot gets out and then walks away. / But in the Fleet Air Arm, the prospects are grim / if the landing is bad and the pilot can't swim. / Cracking show! I'm alive! But I still have to render my A-25." It's a form. It details accidents for navy clerks. We think they should be regulating safer ways to fly instead of reinforcing old ways with old flying machines.

I fly odd missions in old machines. Their ghosts rise up with my dragons. "Routine dive bombing." Routine in a prewar Gladiator? "Photograph Skeabrae in Blenheim bomber." Why? Well, we are Fleet Requirements, at the beck and call of battle wagons escorting munition-laden merchant ships through Arctic waters to Russia.

I tug pilotless winged targets to train Russian gunners on *Archangel,* formerly the UK's *Royal Sovereign.* Russian shells burst around my nose. I break radio silence: "I'm towing the bloody target, not pushing it!" There's a Royal Navy admiral on board the battleship who nearly bursts a blood vessel, and I'm taken off such missions. He may have saved me much grief. Some pilots who work with Russian convoys come close to nervous breakdowns.

In a Stringbag, I fly seamen on leave. Five or six squeeze into the wide-open cockpit behind me. Some strap kit bags or bikes between the sturdy legs of the undercarriage. I drop near-frozen passengers at Thurso on the Pentland Firth, a narrow passage between Orkney and Scotland, considered too shallow for hostile subs until a U-boat slips through and sinks HMS *Royal Oak.* Stringbags are veterans of Russian convoys for which the only destination ports are Murmansk and Archangel, by way of the Arctic Circle and along the ice packs. Between German bases in Norway and the safety of Kola Inlet lie more than thirteen hundred miles of freezing water. A cargo ship makes a speed of eleven knots at best, within range of several hundred fast German bombers based in Norway from which awesome Nazi warships—*Tirpitz, Prinz Eugen, Hipper*—can

"Stringbag" Swordfish lands on baby carrier in dangerously heavy seas during WWII while escorting supply ships headed for Russian ports after the Soviet Union became the ally of Britain.

strike, supported by destroyers and cruisers, preceded by U-boats. Convoys are codenamed PQ. After PQ17 leaves Scapa, two-thirds of its merchantmen are sunk. Convoys are beyond range of our shore-based aircraft and our allies, the Russians, won't let us operate from Lapland. PQ17 made do with MAC-ships, Merchant Aircraft Carriers, cobbled together from grainships and tankers. MAC flight decks are 62 feet across and 420 feet long. Without hangars, only three Stringbags can be accommodated. They sit on deck. The lead Stringbag has the shortest take-off run: the other two wait astern. When gale-force winds exceed a Stringbag's forward speed while taking off, it flies backward, relative to the ship while its bows dip under water. MAC-ship pilots must enroll in the Merchant Navy and sign articles as deckhands; they are paid only a shilling a month, but they are allowed seven bottles of beer on Sundays.

By dragon-mail comes an old postwar letter from the youngest Stringbag squadron leader of them all, John Godley, now Lord Kilbracken. He says the Stringbag prototype was built in 1930 for the Greek navy. My dragons flash me forward to 1990. I ask the Russian ambassador in Thailand why the official history of the Soviet war at sea omits our Arctic convoys. The Soviet Union has collapsed. The ambassador's living expenses are meager. He appreciates free drinks, courtesy of King Bhumibol. In my Stringbag days, Bhumibol was at university in Europe and closely followed Royal Navy operations. As king, when I work with him in the 1990s, he recalls that the now-thrifty Soviet ambassador was based at Kola Inlet. Russians refused to let PQ convoys use it or any other havens except Murmansk and Archangel. The ambassador's wife is a KGB archivist. She suggests a reunion between today's Russian and UK warships to acknowledge our help. Moscow agrees. I pass this on to Lord Kilbracken.

"Tell the ambassador to get stuffed!" answers His Lordship, remembering losses inflicted on convoys because the Russians forbade use of Kola Inlet.

The notional proximity of survivors is a great social leveler. The Godley I knew is now a peer. I am a commoner. Bhumibol's mother was a Chinese nurse who gave birth to him in the United States. He is now His Majesty, known cozily within the Grand Palace as "HM." The ex-Soviet ambassador asks me how he can become a capitalist. The king's intelligence chief advises him: "Russians need mass transport, so copy our tuktuks. Three-wheel motor-driven conveyances. Cheap way to get around our 'backward countries.'"

Christmas 1944. My dragons jump across time to link me with HMS *Dipper*, a stone frigate and naval fighter school in Somerset. Here I practice ADDLES, Aerodrome Dummy Deck Landings, and here I meet a striking young redhead, Glenys Rowe. She was the draftswoman for Frank Whittle while he designed the first jet engine, despite initial opposition from the RAF. Her drawings went to America in case his workshop in Coventry was bombed. And it was bombed in 1941, flat as a pancake. Only the cathedral stood, a scolding question mark cast in stone: Why was the city not warned, if Churchill knew what was coming? Glenys is now at HMS *Dipper* as a nurse in the Women's Voluntary Services, the WVS. When I first enter Dipper's wardroom, a pilot says, "You can't be Stevenson. He was killed." Red Martin of 768 Squadron raises my spirits with a shot of rum. "This dead bloke's first name was Bill. We'll call you Steve." And so Glenys calls me Steve. This can be confusing for my dragons. At one stage I'm a dead bloke called Bill: at a later stage, I'm Steve, and this new name sticks.

# CHAPTER 12

# The Final Cut

RED MARTIN IS A NEW ZEALANDER COMMANDING 768 SQUADRON. I make a dummy deck landing one day when my Seafire's port wheel stays in the retracted position. Red begins to talk me down for a one-wheel landing. His corncrake Kiwi voice unnerves me. I unplug my radio. I can minimize the damage if I don't have to listen to Red. Ambulances inch parallel to my descent like beasts smelling blood. Hooded firemen stand ready to dive into blazing wreckage to yank out what's left of me. I gently maneuver the tip of the unsupported wing so that it comes to rest in the damp dish-rag grass beside the runway. I walk away without a scratch: the Seafire looks a bit lopsided but only the sticky undercarriage seems in need of attention.

"Red saved your life," Althea tells me later. "He's cockahoop!" Red is not much older than me. He's in love with Althea. She shares nurses' quarters with Glenys. I sometimes creep out of Glenys' room to the unforgettably beautiful dawn chorus of Somerset nightingales. When Red learns about my late nights, he tells me, "I can afford to lose pilots but Seafires cost a fortune. You need your sleep. You're worth nothing as roast meat."

I marry Glenys later, when my father returns to a liberated Paris. The war against Japan goes on. A squadron is earmarked for the Pacific, in such haste that pilots leave behind their laundry. I drop it off at Blackpool, where the owners await further orders. Pilots are at such a premium that we get away with making our own informal decisions when not in action. I borrow a small Stinson Reliant and bundle Glenys into the spare seat.

Here's my gleeful note: "Instead of thanking me, pilots ask how I wangled this joyride with a gorgeous redhead."

I join another stone frigate at Woodvale, near Liverpool, to fly Hellcats before joining a tiny assault carrier, HMS *Trouncer,* whose small-caliber Oerlikons are not much match for kamikaze suicide bombers. Six Hellcats with spy cameras in the wings belong to 889 Squadron. Each pilot will fly solo photo-reconnaissance missions over vast territories held by the Japanese. We practice ADDLES in Hellcats, and bless the Americans who quickly designed and built these rugged new shipborne aircraft to fight a new kind of naval warfare.

Our Chief Pilot is Nigel Fisher, descendant of the great Admiral Lord Fisher whom I remember as the hero of dockyard workers in my schooldays. Here's an obituary I wrote later about a fellow pilot, Bill Kempe. The Fish had ordered us to fly upside down in formation and Kempe refused.

After we land, I tell him, "You're in deep shit."

"The shit'd be deeper if I flew upside down," he confides. "I had whiskey and eggs loose in the cockpit." We had been flying from Ireland where, as The Fish knew perfectly well, pilots go to buy black-market booze and unrationed foodstuffs. He had the same prankster's impulse as The Fish's relative, the crusty old Admiral Fisher who expected sensible chaps to disobey preposterous orders.

Glenys is in the operations hut one afternoon when Nigel sees my Hellcat dive straight into the ground. On his long legs, Nigel bolts through an open window, anticipating the blood wagons. Glenys knows that for dummy deck landings, each pilot takes his turn with a white bat in each hand to signal aircraft during the final approach of a comrade who sticks his head out of the cockpit to obey signals that end with a sharp crossing of two bats to "Cut engine!" Glenys knows that if a pilot stalls and is killed, he is said to have taken "The final cut!"

My best friend, Len Hardy, is Bats this day. I'm the guinea-pig pilot. Len takes his cue from my handling of the plane. I take my cue from his signals. It's a confusion that ADDLES are meant to prevent. I stall, and bury my prop in Len's head. I slide down the Hellcat's blazingly hot carcass, which seems to be stuck vertically into the earth. There's blood everywhere. I'm sure Len is dead. But he threw himself aside at the last second. All that blood comes from his nose hitting the metal rim of one of his own bats.

We qualify for real deck landings on HMS *Trouncer*, a converted cargo vessel. Len is on the catapult ahead of me. The preparations make me think of a guillotine's deadly ballet. Men in skull caps, variously colored for different roles, cavort around Len's Hellcat. It looks enormous on the narrow deck after Woodvale's wide field. He pushes the throttle through the gate for maximum power. His aircraft strains against the catapult's leash. His left elbow digs into his stomach to stop throttle creepback when the catapult fires him over the bows. He makes his cockpit checks before his gauntleted right hand rises above his head and then flashes down. He hurriedly jams his right elbow into his stomach to stop the control column from jerking back when his Hellcat bolts from zero to flying speed in seconds. The catapult officer presses the firing button.

I roll forward onto the suddenly empty slot. Len sinks a bit as he shoots over the bows. The jolt drains a pilot's eyes for a few critical moments when elbows are jammed against stick and throttle to keep the Hellcat climbing. A freak gust of wind, or a sudden tilt if the carrier plows into a seventh wave, can make the Hellcat sink from view. It only lasts for a moment. No problem.

But Len continues to sink. His tail drags through the seas ahead.

The last we hear from Len is a laughing shout of defiance over the radio telegraph. A cry more often heard ashore when we're several sheets to the wind, staggering out of London pubs, trying to drown the cries of American servicemen competing for cabs. Len shouts his final farewell as if the ax is already falling and he has a split second to cheat the guillotine: "*T-a-x-i!*"

Helplessly, hopelessly, we plow him under.

His laughing farewell gets a laconic entry in my logbook: name, date, and one bleak word: "Killed."

We are not indifferent. We cannot afford lamentations. The Fish concentrates on breaking our own record for launch and recovery of aircraft to reduce exposure to enemy submarines. Carriers can be forced by disobliging winds to turn out of line for a convoy's collective safety during launch and recovery of warplanes. The rest of us follow each other onto the catapult. An escorting corvette is nearby to pick up unlucky pilots, but only bits of Len's Hellcat bob up astern. Last night, he is belting out the old songs with me. Silly songs of nostalgia, like "Bring back, Oh bring back / Oh bring back, bring back my Stringbag to me, to me."

I'm grateful for my Hellcat. Grumman improved the original Wildcat like the one which had spun into the sea before my first deck landing. The Hellcat is no slinky beauty like the Seafire, but it has a combat edge: a new Double Wasp engine made its debut in August 1943, after which US aerial supremacy over the Japanese is seldom in doubt. My version is a stubby-winged single-seater, normally with a range of 1,085 miles, six machine guns, and provision for six rockets or bombs under the center section. Mine has downward-facing spy cameras and can penetrate enemy skies for distances beyond the standard 1,085 miles, higher and faster than the enemy.

Up comes a long-forgotten photograph. I am in my Hellcat, pretending to smoke a pipe. It's fake. Hidden inside is a silk map, in case I'm shot down. Only one manufacturer prints this: John Waddington, licensee for the board game of Monopoly. Silk escape maps are concealed in Monopoly boards during the war with Germany because "games and pastimes" are allowed in prisoner-of-war packages. Captured airmen spot a rigged board by a red dot in the Free Parking square.

I wonder why we get these escape maps from Mr. Waddington: The Japanese behead pilots who are captured alive.

Now back in my cockpit, I follow Len onto the suddenly vacant catapult. I repeat the drill. Adjust for engine torque. Trim elevators. Left elbow in stomach. Left hand behind throttle. Check instruments one more time. A windblown figure crouches near my starboard wing, ready to signal the unseen catapult officer when I drop my raised right hand. Bang! Wallop! Blood drains from my eyes. For vital seconds I see nothing but feel blissfully free from thinking about what I must do next. I emerge from this happy state to find I'm climbing steadily. I level off at a thousand feet and enter the circuit for a practice deck landing.

Slide back the canopy on the downwind leg. Bank to port. Level out for final approach. Stick head out of cockpit. Pick up tiny fluttering figure

70

of Bats. He stays close to a safety net hanging over the side, in case I dip a wing and charge him. The Hellcat thunders at full throttle, flaps down, nose high, defying rules for land-based fighters. Bats signals me into the wind. My speed is almost nil relative to the deck. Tailhook down. Creep over the round-down. The white bats drop down sharply and cross below Bats' waist: "Cut engine!" He's brought me directly into a wind sweeping the flight deck, for'ard to aft. I stall sedately, watched by off-duty seamen in the goofers' gallery, and allow the wind to gently roll me back to disengage the tailhook.

And then I forget to raise my flaps before folding my wings. There's a horrible crunch.

I taxi onto the elevator and descend into the gloom of a crowded hangar, where maintenance crews will have to unscramble bent flaps and crooked wings. I fear Nigel Fisher's fury will be recorded on an Admiralty "flimsy" of wafer-thin paper. Or in a franker report in secret files, blotting my copybook forever?

A bent old photograph of The Fish comes up. He is laughing, black hair blowing, straps of his safety vest undone. "Good show!" he scribbled across this picture of his boyish face. "He raised his flaps before folding his wings!" Nigel is a chip of the old block: "Jacky" Fisher, the Ordinary Seaman who rose to First Lord of Admiralty and damned the old fogies who opposed change. He scrapped what he called "A miser's hoard of useless junk" to build the revolutionary battleship *Dreadnought*. He would certainly have cussed admirals who adopted the Barracudas that kill our own crews. Japan changed the nature of naval warfare, and Americans swiftly responded with big carriers and safer planes. The Fish would never blame any of us for muddled reactions while still making the speedy switch to a new weapon like the ferocious Hellcat.

But neither the admiral nor The Fish would turn a blind eye if I fail to learn my lesson.

Dragons recover an old photo of mechanics running up the engines of our tethered Hellcats before dawn, back at Woodvale. The thunder and lightning of Double Wasp engines are separated only by a fence from the terraced houses of hardworking folk whose brief sleep is shattered. Bright exhaust flames stab the departing night. I wince now at the memory of those decent neighbors who put up with that awful racket on their doorstep, knowing it was the roar of revenge for the heavy bombing of Liverpool dockyards where they worked all through the Blitz.

Glenys sees me for the last time before our Hellcats are due to depart for the Pacific from Woodvale. We fly in tight formation at low level to salute a girl who knows we defy natural laws. Dragons bring up my 889 Squadron log. Entries are terse: "S/Lt. Mackenzie, killed, 21 June 1945 . . . The Fish, killed, date uncertain."

Later, Lord Kilbracken writes furiously about the Admiralty's failure to recognize that real aircraft carriers are not cobbled together out of old cargo vessels like Catapult Armed Merchant Ships (CAMSHIPS) with no landing deck. A CAMSHIP launched its Sea Hurricane to destroy a long-range German Condor shadowing the convoy. The pilot had two choices: ditch or parachute into the sea. "Twitch" O'Neil glimpsed his assigned target in thick cloud. With mini-seconds to make a decision, he shot down a Skymaster full of top Allied officers. At his court-martial, O'Neil showed camera-gun footage of other encounters with such Skymasters. Only a privileged few knew about Skymasters, secretly flown by a fake Western airline, Canadian Pacific. O'Neil then projected combat film of a Condor. His judges saw no difference. O'Neil was exonerated. The ordeal left him with a twitch in one arm. After the war, on a London tram, I spot a similar twitch in what looks like an office boy.

"Twitch O'Neil?" I ask hesitantly.

"You remember?" His sudden grin lifts him out of his cheap civvies. The tram trundles through the grim post-Blitz streets. Our exchange of stories we never told outsiders now carries us past O'Neil's battered office among neglected bomb ruins. We speak of that fake Canadian Pacific airline flying unarmed bombers from Montreal to Britain. The "Pacific" tag was to mislead enemy watchers. Inside those bare-bone aircraft were experts in special operations. They shivered from lack of heat and oxygen, and from the tinny rattle of thin metal skins separating them from the cold Atlantic air. The first planes were built by the United States and then dismantled and trucked across the United States–Canada border to avoid attention in a time of US neutrality. American civilian pilots came by train to Montreal, disguised as regular tourists. After Pearl Harbor, hundreds of old barnstormers and bush pilots flew the airliners across the North Atlantic, minus uniforms, minus radio or navigational aids. They crept back anonymously in acute discomfort aboard cargo ships, dodging a worse fate from the waiting U-boats.

At O'Neil's court-martial, the chief of British Security Coordination in New York intervenes. Twitch could not know that real warships guarding real convoys might mistake a converted Allied bomber for a Condor. Convoy skippers know nothing about the fake Canadian Pacific airline nor its successor, Ferry Command. The unmarked planes contain such Camp X assets as General Colin Gubbins, chief of SOE, Special Operations Executive, and civilians such as Alexander Korda, the movie mogul who staged dummy UK airfields to fool the Germans before D-Day. Their BSC chief is Little Bill Stephenson: Intrepid.

Camp X was near my old Service Flying Training School. Some agents were ferried to Montreal from where Canadian Pacific flew them eastward, not westward across the Pacific. To Twitch O'Neil, I now confess that while flying Hellcat spy planes, I got stomach cramps and was sent to Mad Hatters' Castle, a name coined by pilots for a medical center with psychiatrists we called "trick-cyclists." They dealt with fliers who commanders felt might develop a nervous "twitch." After much interrogation, I am told: "We think you're mad . . ." I blush and almost miss the rest of the verdict: "Mad to do what you do. On medical grounds, we can't stop you."

Hiroshima stops me. The squadron is disbanded in September 1945. I'm transferred to a reserve squadron, to lead a double life, flying at weekends while trying to earn an honest living as a civilian in "Civvy Street."

We used to say, "There are old pilots and there are bold pilots but there are no old-bold pilots." I'm not an old-bold pilot but I pray to Spud's ghost: "Help me justify being alive." I imagine his reply: "Explore wildlife in faraway places and don't shed blood over wasted arguments." Time was wasted by army education officers talking down their noses to airmen. One asked me to name our ally in China. "Generalissimo Chiang

Kai-shek," I reply. He sneers, "You read that in some rag." I don't tell him the "rag" is the London *Times* reporting back in 1904 Japan's first victory over Western power: sinking the Russian fleet at Port Arthur, known as Dalian in China. Many years later, I search out the facts in Dalian itself, and find that an American newsman in the 1800s covered earlier Japanese conquests there. I remember myself delivering newspapers, a boy who wanted to report the news as it happened, before history could be redesigned to suit political connivances of the day.

Such schoolboy idealism is challenged after my Hellcat squadron is disbanded. In what seems like a long interval before my demobilization, I learn about Black Propaganda at Oxford, one of only three universities to which one goes "up" no matter from what direction. Other universities in London and Cambridge are linked by rail with ULTRA's code-breakers at Bletchley. Oxford has a long tradition of civilizing discourse. At Woburn Abbey, Kim Philby invented wartime lies to plant on captured Germans who were "turned" to spy for us, and after some pretense of training for intelligence work against the Nazis, were sent back by parachute. The turncoats never knew their parachutes were fixed to fail. On their bodies were misleading plans about Allied intentions. None of the UK brainwashing experts spotted Kim Philby as a turncoat serving the Soviet Union.

Oxford teaches "psychological warfare," difficult to associate with dreaming spires, scholarly presentations, and the college of Corpus Christi, which still keeps bees in memory of King Charles the First, who directed from here three honorable battles. Honorable battles? I recall our Hellcats ushering in dawn with hellish blue flashes beside the humble homes of kids like myself who mimicked the Oxford-Cambridge races by floating matchsticks down rain-filled gutters. Only the parachute slung over my shoulder had assured me that I was not playing games. I find no honor in turning truth into lies. The Final Cut severs me from my past as a half-baked warrior.

# CHAPTER 13

# Facts Are Sacred

IN PEACETIME ENGLAND, AFTER OXFORD, THE NAVY CHARITABLY CON-
tinues to pay me while I report once again for the *Leighton Buzzard Observer*
and *North Bucks Times*. On days off, I report for *Mercury News*, whose boss,
Ian Fleming, assigns me to inquire about a secret meeting in London on
October 31, 1945, between the Russian ambassador and Canadian Prime
Minister Mackenzie King. His aide asks if I am related to another William
Stephenson. I say lots of chaps have similar names, differently spelled. He
mutters what sounds like "The Corby Case." I learn later that CORBY is code
for a defector from the Soviet Union's embassy in Ottawa. Roger Hollis, chief
of UK security services, later accused of being a Soviet mole, had first flown
to Ottawa to persuade Mackenzie King to send the defector back to Moscow.
Now Hollis intercepts Mackenzie King in the UK in a further effort to neu-
tralize CORBY. Kim Philby, another Moscow-run mole, is chief of the UK
security service's anti-Soviet operations, and is thus perfectly placed to sabotage efforts to counter Stalin's operatives. But both Hollis and Philby fail to
get CORBY returned to Moscow before Sir William Stephenson intervenes.

I get Stephenson's sample of CORBY's top-secret Russian communications: "Cables numbered 18956/538 and 9482/625 TOP SECRET
URGENT: To Lavrenti P. Beria, Commissar General of State Security,
on 10 July 1945: Agent sources NKGB received data that in the USA
in July this year the first experimental explosion of the atomic bomb is
scheduled for the 10th . . . data is available about this bomb . . . first test
explosion took place at Alamogordo on 16 July 1945. . . ." Beria's spies in
the United States were run by the Soviet embassy in Canada.

Why did Mackenzie King conceal this? He believed CORBY was a Jew. This is finally disclosed on June 7, 2010, when another Prime Minister of Canada, Brian Mulroney, writes in the *Globe & Mail of Toronto:* "Before World War II, Mackenzie King met Hitler and wrote in his diary that he felt the Fuehrer was a mystic like Joan of Arc. King decreed that Canada must reject Jewish survivors of Nazi death camps." This is the one diary never released from King's other voluminous diaries that otherwise record even the most intimate details of his life. The missing diary covers his 1945 meeting in London. The Russians told him the Soviet defector is Jewish and must be returned to Moscow. King turned back a ship, the *St. Louis,* loaded with Jewish Holocaust survivors. "None is too many" was the answer to how many Jews could enter Canada. Mulroney concludes, "I continue to be deeply troubled by the insouciance of our federal government confronted by such a stark moral challenge."

Such matters are unknown to the public when Fleming tells me to go to Canada. He knows I shall be contacted by Sir William Stephenson, knighted for his intrepid wartime operations against the Nazis and their Japanese allies. His spy-training camps after 1945 reinforce US secret operations against the new enemy: Stalin. The UK Establishment, whose anti-Soviet secret service is run by Soviet moles, tries to shut down Stephenson by painting him as a loose cannon. He never swore an Oath of Secrecy. He takes the same kind of independent action he displayed as an ace fighter pilot in the 1914-18 war. Later he fought in the tough arena of commerce, inventing gadgets, building businesses, and using his German steel corporations to cover his investigations into Hitler's preparations for war. When moles in the UK try to send CORBY back to Moscow, Stephenson whisks the defector and his family into the safety of Camp X. I learn that CORBY is Igor Gouzenko. A Canadian passport and identity were faked for another Soviet agent who traveled to Mexico to kill Stalin's Jewish arch-enemy, Leon Trotsky. This is a separate mystery and a good news story. Stephenson asks me to confront the assassin with proof of his real identity.

Today's dragons bring me a signed telegram from Allen Dulles, dated January 28, 1949, praising Stephenson for "an outstanding investigation of the Soviet spy ring." Dulles proposes "here in the United States a federal agency which we might for convenience call a 'Commission of Internal

Security.'" This becomes the peacetime Central Intelligence Agency. My copy is addressed to *Washington Post* publisher, Philip L. Graham. But the campaign to discredit Stephenson continues, even into the 1980s when the National Film Board, financed by the Canadian government, staffed by an Englishman with Moscow connections, produces a film "documentary" claiming that Stephenson never was a fighter ace, based on interviews with elderly ground staff who clearly would never have known one end of a WWI German warplane from another.

I never anticipate this when I move to Canada with Glenys in 1947. I am hired as a reporter by the American-born proprietor of the *Toronto Star,* Harold Comfort Hindmarsh, known as HCH. His son Harry is a former Spitfire pilot. HCH likes to quote Shakespeare: "Rumble thy bellyful! Spit! Fire! Spout! Rain!" His son is also a Golden Gloves champion boxer and HCH proudly links him with Gene Tunney, the world heavyweight boxing champion who helped Stephenson establish British Security Coordination in New York.

I begin reporting in the local law courts. As each trial unfolds, I scribble "running copy" on cheap copy paper: each paragraph is dispatched through pneumatic tubes winding under Toronto roadways to the *Star's* city desk. Sub-editors piece together the reports, including last-minute items for afternoon editions and scooping less inventive competitors: the *Globe & Mail* and the *Toronto Telegram.*

HCH discourages bylines and columnists. Opinions belong on the editorial page. Facts belong in news reports. These must begin with: "What/When/Where/Why." He quotes the *Manchester Guardian's* C. P. Scott, who famously wrote on May 6, 1926: "A newspaper's primary duty is the gathering of news. At the peril of its soul, it must see that the supply is not tainted. Neither in what it gives, nor in what it does not give, nor in the mode of presentation, must the unclouded face of truth suffer wrong. Comment is free but facts are sacred.'"*

---

* Scott did not anticipate today's online challenge to his ethics. "Citizen reporters" feed a public appetite for free-wheeling speculation through the Internet. By 2009, the *Guardian's* pre-tax losses are the equivalent of US $93 million annually, and its income comes mostly from its website. The *Guardian's* auditors try to shut the newspaper down but are dissuaded by C.P. Scott's Trust, established in 1936 to protect its editorial independence.

# CHAPTER 14

# For Services Unofficially Rendered

IN THE LATE 1940S, I AM SOMETIMES TOLD BY CANADIANS, "GO BACK where you came from." Old French-Irish-Anglo feuds account for this. HCH's hatchet man says he loathes Englishmen, and will fire me the moment I slip up. He is Irish. I don't mention the sabotage in Ireland of my plane: it's all so long ago. I look for stories about Canada's achievements and let other reporters fret about job security and pensions. HCH pays me the lowest salary, but he is generous with expenses to chase out-of-town stories. "Expenses," he points out helpfully, "are not taxable."

Expense allowances pay for my discovery of Canada. I report events in a country bigger than any other in the world except Russia, but the population of Canada is smaller than the population of Pittsburgh. I write about huge and disproportionate contributions made by Canada in wartime: the swift creation of the free world's third largest fleet of fighting ships. Seamen from the prairies who had never seen the sea until they sailed on convoys when U-boats came close to defeating Britain. Canadian airmen, described as part of the RAF, are killed in action in disproportionate numbers. A test of German defenses prior to D-Day led to the slaughter of Canadians storming French beaches at Dieppe. I describe a peculiar nation that was first the home of Indian tribes, then organized in 1662 as a crown colony named New France with Quebec as the capital, and finally occupied by French, Irish, and Scottish settlers in a British Dominion loyal to a royal family of German blood.

Canada plays down its history of giving safe haven to black slaves fleeing US bigotry. I dig up details: The story might offend our neighbors but HCH runs it anyway. I report on bush pilots who fix damaged aircraft after Arctic winds force them down on frozen lakes. I write that the first flight by a fixed-wing aircraft was in Canada, and that Canada's longest border is with Russia, whose aerial routes run parallel to our northern frontier. I write a series on bush pilots who understand Canada's future is in the air. HCH suspends his aversion to bylines and prints the whole series. This is read into the parliamentary record by a new prime minister, Louis St. Laurent, a French-Canadian who calls for an end to quarrels between descendants of settlers of different origin. He is asked by Prime Minister Nehru if India, newly independent, should break all ties with Britain or follow Canada's example of appointing a governor-general to represent the monarchy. St. Laurent recommends India become a republic within a British Commonwealth. This creates a bond with Nehru, who trusts Canada's experience in preserving parliamentary systems based upon centuries of trial and error. Because of this, Nehru shares his anxieties with me during many subsequent crises.

Before my first assignment to India, I write about lumberjacks, isolated, but keen readers of the *Toronto Star Weekly* because it covers world affairs. The magazine gives me space to report on the world's first jet airliner, built by Avro Canada, which later produces the first "flying saucer." Avro Canada is part of a British firm whose Toronto base challenges US rivals. Before their pressure leads Ottawa to scrap Avro Canada, I fly with its test pilots in innovations such as the Jetliner, the world's first, and the CF-100 long-range fighter, designed to protect the frontier with Russia. I see the first delta-wing warplane, the Avro Arrow, take shape. All are far ahead of their time.

I seek assignments across the United States, and marvel at its eccentricities. "Groundhog Day," I write, "arrives every second day of February when Punxsutawney Phil of Gobbler's Knob in Pennsylvania emerges from his winter burrow and sees his own shadow, which foretells another six weeks of winter, according to his handler in frock coat and broad-brimmed hat. He's part of the backbone of an America much misunderstood abroad."

———

Convoys of trucks cross the US border into Canada at war's end. Herbert Rowland, who works undercover as a private businessman for Intrepid and IRD, tells me the trucks are packed with secret documents. If made public, some files would cause trouble: They expose US citizens who opposed aid to Britain before Japan attacked Pearl Harbor and identify US manufacturers who did business with the Nazis. Clearance for these trucks to cross the US border with the secret files unexamined has been arranged beforehand. Herb Rowland promises me "a good story" in New York State. I submit a cautious proposal to HCH. He sends me to Rochester, New York, to study the Gannett Newspaper Group's foundation. It yields tax benefits. The structure can be adjusted to meet Canadian regulations for the *Toronto Star.*

Rochester is where wartime US covert operations had a base on the southern shores of Lake Ontario. Agents were ferried from there to Intrepid's Camp X. Gannett executives applauded this partnership and now show me how their foundation is set up. HCH figures that sending me to Rochester is a sound business decision. But underlying this is a deeper purpose, well understood by Herb Rowland. I meet again a former RAF pilot: Squadron Leader Bill Simpson, his face disfigured by burns after the crash of his Hurricane fighter. He remembers meeting Glenys at a sailplane club in postwar England: "Do I need a shave?" he had asked her, a device to force new acquaintances to look him in the face. She stroked his cheek: "You'll do until tomorrow." She'd seen worse.

Simpson takes me to William Stephenson. Now I understand the confusion of Canadian prime minister Mackenzie King's team. This is the Canadian-born Stephenson. We are joined by an ex-fighter pilot from World War II: Roald Dahl, author of bestselling children's books. After he crashed his RAF fighter, he was sent to Washington, D.C. as an air attaché, "where I became so outspokenly critical of UK stuffed shirts," he tells me, "they ordered me back to London. Bill Stephenson said, 'Go. I'll have you back here to work for me.' Bill was Churchill's man, free to defy the UK's secret services, who seemed more at war with each other than with the enemy."

Stephenson has the narrow eyes of an old fighter pilot from the last war. We begin an enduring friendship. Roald Dahl says, in a later TV documentary that I produce: "The first time you met Stephenson, you were right there in the lion's den. There was bound to be trepidation and fear . . . a small man of immense power. Worked hard, played around with his scientific things, coupled them up, grabbed every new idea created out of what he absorbed. In BSC, he won support from Americans who mattered. In days of US neutrality, he got Roosevelt to bring fifty old US warships out of mothballs. That saved us from defeat in the Battle of the Atlantic; the only battle Churchill said could destroy Britain. Stephenson's Canadian accent didn't turn off Americans, like some Englishmen with posh, plummy voices."

In my own first meeting with Stephenson, I feel as I did when facing an Admiralty board, except that this is only one man. I also meet for the first time Gene Tunney, the world champion heavyweight boxer. Gene brought Stephenson together with the FBI's J. Edgar Hoover back in 1940, when Hoover agreed to support British Security Coordination. "This was a great victory," Stephenson tells me. "Hoover admired Gene Tunney but the FBI had been under pressure from the US State Department to strangle us at birth. My clerical staff was recruited in Canada because they talked like Americans. They called me 'Mister Williams,' and worked in separate offices so each thought she was my personal private secretary."

Gene Tunney was a longtime friend of George Bernard Shaw. Both saw the connection between physical muscularity and brain power. In 1940, senior members of the US State Department and other influential Americans, including some with pro-Nazi sympathies, opposed a foreign secret service based on their territory. Gene saw the need for ingenuity at the height of Britain's physical weakness. Canada was ideal for ingenious enterprises like Camp X. Nearby, global wireless traffic was handled by the world's most powerful network of transmitters, centered on "Hydra," named after the monster in Greek mythology: if one head was cut off, two more replaced it. Station M in Toronto forged false documents and was one of many Hydra-like activities.

During these reporting assignments for HCH, I meet General William J. Donovan, who partnered his Rochester, New York, training camp with Camp X after creating the wartime Office of Strategic Services, forerunner of the CIA. He said publicly: "Stephenson taught us all we know about foreign intelligence." Donovan knew the BSC records might be leaked with malice after the postwar downfall of Winston Churchill. He quickly advised King George VI to dub Stephenson a knight of the realm. "This," wrote Churchill, "is dear to my heart."

Intrepid was now watching Stalin's SMERSH agency: "Death To Spies." Later, Fleming wrote SMERSH into his James Bond books, initially drawing upon his IRD experience. Readers supposed SMERSH in those days was all fiction. Stephenson wanted me to go to Mexico to report on a suspected SMERSH operation. The *Star* would assign me to the story. I would also report directly to Stephenson in telegrams. Since not only my wife Glenys but all our friends now called me "Steve," I would sign cables as STEVERITE, addressed to him as INTER. He said, "Wartime mail was slow. We had girls opening envelopes but this took time. Sometimes we let mail go through with visible signs of tampering to unnerve the enemy. Today's cheap air letters, those blue sheets you fold and stick with your tongue, are too messy to be opened by counterintelligence. You can write economically in one, link up details in follow-up air letters. STEVERITE-INTER cables will go 'Press Collect' and should be written like normal news dispatches."

I deliver my Gannett report to HCH. Then a terse proposal: "Might it be worthwhile to report new disclosures about Trotsky's assassin, now in a Mexican jail?" I limit the wording to a sheet of copy paper that I roll up and pop into HCH's pigeonhole. There are pigeonholes for reporters and HCH and one or two senior editors: equally brief responses return by the same route, often no more than a "YES" or "NO."

This is when I learn about the mystery Russian defector, code-name CORBY, viewed as a threat by the UK's traditional secret services, protected against public scrutiny by secrecy laws that perversely make the Establishment agencies easier to infiltrate. He defected with details about Pavel Sudoplatov, chief of Soviet Special Tasks, who turned English cocktail communists into moles. "Such moles," Karl Marx wrote in 1865, "are worthy pioneers of the Revolution." Undetected British moles, by the 1940s, include Kim Philby, who created Section IX, a new addition to the UK Establishment's old spy agency, MI6, whose existence is never officially acknowledged until decades later. Kim betrayed the established UK secret services to his Kremlin masters. Intrepid suspected such betrayals when, during the war, he investigated the Duke of Windsor, ex-King Edward VIII, who admired Hitler and was sent by Churchill to the Bahamas as governor. Edward and his US-born wife, the Duchess of Windsor, were watched while they communicated with their Nazi friends. Details of how this ex-king and colonial governor got around wartime financial restrictions through German bankers of Hitler's Gestapo are kept secret until the twenty-first century. Stephenson was prevented from disclosing his proof of the Windsors' treachery during the war. In the aftermath of the war, Stephenson launched World Commerce, an enterprise of good intentions to help "backward" countries build strong economies to counter the new enemy, Stalin. The manufacture of high-quality cement in Jamaica is an example of such enterprises, also used to filter secret intelligence. A Cable & Wireless Press Collect card makes possible my cabling from anywhere in the world as STEVERITE to INTER via Caribbean Cement of Jamaica, a location least likely to attract unwanted attention. I can report events the way I see them, not as editors or bureaucrats of Bumbledom might. I never take a penny for this service. My reward is an unbiased audience for news that editors find too boring for a mass readership generating mass circulation.

In New York on another HCH assignment, I share a meal with Stephenson, who starts off by saying, "You saw Russian pilots take off from Scotland." I don't know how he knows. Nor do I know how he knows my father worked with ULTRA decoders. He asks me, "Do you still think of the Russians as allies?"

"Russian officials in Murmansk treated our fliers and ships' crews as if they were enemy spies."

"So you don't trust the Russians." He wants to be sure I can help CORBY, and reminds me that my Oath of Secrecy still applies. If I publish all the facts now, I can be prosecuted. He has an interest in Trotsky's murder in 1940. The killer made his way to Mexico, using a forged Canadian passport in the name of Franc Jacson. SMERSH drilled him in the art of disguising his origins. Tough training was given to all Stalin's assassins. This one drove an ice pick into the skull of Stalin's rival. It was the most historically significant assassination since the shooting of Archduke Franz Ferdinand in 1914, which led to war and a dictatorship under Leon Trotsky, Stalin's arch rival. Stalin had the resources to hunt down Trotsky and drag CORBY back to Moscow.

<hr />

In Toronto I write a variation of my earlier, unanswered suggestion: "HCH: Might it be worth confronting the killer of Leonid Trotsky in Mexico?" Now there's a quick response: "Yes. HCH"

In Mexico, I am put in touch with a banker who trawled through Spanish police files for a fraudster and stumbled onto a photograph of Caridad Mercador, a Spanish aristocrat and communist fighter in the Spanish Civil War. Caridad is the mother of Trotsky's killer, Ramon Mercador, code-named Mother.

I enter the assassin's jail cell, hold up the photograph, and ask, "Is this your mother?"

He leaps across the cell, clawing at my throat. Armed prison guards yank me out.

My published report deflates Mackenzie King's notion of Stalin as a loyal ally. The Official Secrets Act stops me from reporting three other Soviet networks in Mexico. One employs a Polish news agency correspondent I know only as "Rena." She manipulates Mexican lawmakers and gets Ramon Mercador out of jail. He becomes a SMERSH Special Tasks adviser to Fidel Castro. When Ramon dies in Cuba, his body is returned to Moscow. Dragons remind me that I later found the assassin's gravestone in Kuntsevo Cemetery, inscribed: "Ramon Ivanovich Lopez, Hero of the Soviet Union." I recognize the same "Rena" in the Moscow airport, with startling revelations that again jump me across timelines.

But, for a moment, I scratch my head when dragons remind me of a silver cigarette case, tarnished with age, embossed with the Royal Coat of Arms, engraved: "Number 48700: For Special services as Assistant Director of BSC Operations." Intrepid presented it after an assignment in Mexican waters that failed. He believed a cargo vessel was carrying "bigwigs," the German term for top Nazis. Many were escaping by sea to South America. I take a weekend near BSC's base on Lake Ontario for a quick course in swimming underwater to attach limpet mines to suspect vessels. The operation was to be a basis for questioning Trotsky's assassin about a postwar German organization to bring surviving Nazis to Latin America. The assassin's instant attack on me made disclosure impossible. "Rena" later becomes a source of such information.

Dragons speed me to the summer of 2011 and the unanticipated opening of postwar German secret intelligence files. They disclose names and locations of Nazis who fled to South America, including the mass-murderer Adolf Eichmann. I am reminded of interviews I had in 1973 with West Germany's secret service chief, Reinhard Gehlen, about the Nazi "brotherhood" escape lines. Gehlen is a former Nazi whose claim to be the expert on Stalin's secret agencies won him US support to create the "Gehlen org" and spy on the Soviet Union and its East German satellite. This made possible his protection of ex-Nazis seeking safe havens abroad. My long private talks with Gehlen are salvaged by my dragons, with disclosures made in 1973 by Dr. Otto John, a German patriot who infiltrated East Germany and gathered evidence of Gehlen's postwar recruitment of former Nazis.

No longer secret by the twenty-first century is Intrepid's list of US corporations that did business with Germany during the UK's lonely resistance to the Nazi Blitz in the first two years of World War II. Reichsleiter Martin Bormann, the financial wizard behind Hitler's rise to power, turned I.G. Farben into the largest single earner of foreign exchange for the Third Reich, trading with such major US industrial concerns as Standard Oil, the Aluminum Company of America, and Dow Chemical. Intrepid hatches a plot to blow up a cargo vessel thought to be carrying prominent ex-Nazis after the war's end. Luckily, the plot is aborted for reasons disclosed in 1949, when former Nazis move secretly to Egypt to continue their war on Jews by making Israel their target.

HCH agrees I should investigate Bormann's disappearance after Hitler's death. I write a series based on interviews in Berlin, assisted by Sefton Delmer of London's *Daily Express,* formerly a fertile plotter in the UK's Psychological Warfare Executive. Delmer is on the trail of Germans who plan to create a Fourth Reich. He has photocopies of Nazi financial dealings abroad, including a joint bank account shared between Bormann and Juan Peron in the Deutsche Bank of Argentina, when Intrepid's wartime staff included a British banker. A dinner is given in 1976 by author Arthur Hailey in the Bahamas, where the pro-Nazi ex-king Edward was once governor. The banker asks that I never disclose his identity. As part of BSC, he had worked for a foreign intelligence agency and this could blight his postwar career in the United States. The chief of Israel's Mossad secret service, Issar Harel, had already told me how West German intelligence kept details of ex-Nazis in Latin America. He caught Eichmann in Argentina in 1960 and brought him back for trial in Israel, where he was later hanged. My dragons bring up a book I later wrote, influenced by Mama's romantic readings, and the "foul storms ahead" foreseen by the aviator-writer Antoine de Saint Exupery. I never guessed what challenges lay ahead when I promised Spud Murphy "to make the world a better place" and give some meaning to his deadly crash under a night sky. In 1973, after research in South America, I write *The Bormann Brotherhood.* I postpone disclosure of certain inconvenient truths. It is difficult for newsmen to report on underground activities by ex-Nazis or the Soviet Union. CORBY eventually appears before a Royal Commission. Yet his most damning disclosures are kept secret throughout the twentieth century. Stephenson warns me: "Publish full details, you can be prosecuted under the Official Secrets Act by moles who protect England in order to betray it!" I postpone writing about CORBY. He fought Stalin, survived in Canada, but was endangered by Soviet-inspired lies. Lenin once wrote of "useful idiots" who are not known as active communists, but can be used to spread lies. Many in Canadian politics, the police services, and the media unwittingly helped Moscow by calling Igor Gouzenko a fraud. But he beat SMERSH and Stalin in the end.

## CHAPTER 15

# Nehru, Tito, and the Pigeonhole Express

BY 1950 I FEEL LIKE A YO-YO, YANKED HIGH UP INTO BRIEF VENTURES abroad, then dropped back into local reporting. By covering local events, I learn to be accurate. Reporters on domestic beats may be confronted the next day by victims of careless reporting. One moment I am flying with Jan Zurakowski in a prototype jet, the next day I'm heading for India. I remember Zura first counseling me at Elementary Flying School when he was a Battle of Britain hero. Now he is Avro Canada's chief test pilot. HCH is not much interested in Zura.

Instead, HCH responds with a terse "Yes" to my discreet suggestion that perhaps India's Prime Minister Nehru might be worth interviewing about why he took Canada's advice to make India a republic. Ironically, Nehru later becomes my adviser. He feels indebted to Canada. We meet again in China and then in Delhi. Later, I write his biography *After Nehru What?* In it, I foreshadow decades of growth in India, and China's rise to become the world's second largest economic power. I am fated to return again and again to both republics.

In my earliest conversation with Nehru, he suggests that to understand India, I should join Mahatma Gandhi's successor, Vinobe Bhava, as he walks across the subcontinent. Neither Nehru nor Bhava's supporters in Delhi know where to find him on any given day. "He goes barefoot from village to village preaching Land for the Poor," I am told. But the poor are everywhere. Modern folk tales provide verbal clues leading me to a small village in the state of Rajasthan. I meet Bhava, wrapped in white muslin. He looks mummified, walking while talking. He lies down at night in mud huts and sleeplessly reflects upon the social benefits of self-denial. He persuades landlords to donate some of their land. I cannot prove that the poor continue to own the patches of dry soil after the saintly figure moves on.

Nehru then suggests I travel through the subcontinent by bus and train. I carry a portable Olivetti manual typewriter and bash out brief dispatches on blue airmail-letter forms, an economy inherited from the British Raj. I can get a 500-word report on one, fold and seal it, then pop it into one of the red postal pillar-boxes left like tombstones in memory of the late departed empire. An unfolded air letter is the size of a sheet of the running copy I roll up into canisters fired through hydraulic tubes from Toronto criminal courts to the *Toronto Star*'s news desk. I return to this kind of local reporting after submitting my Indian expense claims. These include "two gurus for $15."

The *Star* accountant asks what this means.

"One guru costs ten," I reply airily. "I got two for fifteen bucks."

He graciously accepts the explanation, although he's clearly dying to know what a guru is. So am I.

Expense claims are an exercise in creative writing, improvised to make up the difference between an advance and what remains when I return. Back home, I ride Toronto streetcars to whatever small desk is free in the crowded newsroom of HCH's daily newspaper, denounced as the Red Star of King Street because during the war it welcomed the Soviet Union as an ally.

"HCH" I write one morning in 1949: "If Marshal Tito has broken with Stalin, is it worth seeing what happens in Yugoslavia? WS."

I never propose an assignment in the first person: never begin: "I suggest ..." My one-line proposals are rolled up in my newsroom pigeonhole to be later poked into HCH's pigeonhole. I learned this from tales of how Ernest Hemingway got fired as a reporter at the *Star* for writing to HCH on a 10-foot-long strip of teletype paper.

With matching brevity, HCH always returns his responses to my pigeonhole. If he replies "No thanks HCH" I continue with local assignments. Such exchanges leave a trail my dragons can now follow: cause and effect across time, and connections I might have forgotten. I tag my HCH-WS exchanges: The Pigeonhole Express. Dragons remind me of my old note about Tito. The response: "Yes please: HCH."

Overseas travel to unknown destinations such as Belgrade is simple, if indirect. I fly first to England with Glenys, who is recovering from a personal tragedy. Young Harry Hindmarsh, in the spirit of wartime comradeship, arranges for the *Star* to pay her expenses to fly to England, where she works with the Land Girls. She revives her good spirits, with the stoicism of the very young, by helping to beat food shortages, worse now than in wartime.

I cannot take her to Yugoslavia. The first visa issued to a non-communist correspondent is for me alone. I travel first to Paris. My father, now at the British embassy, gives me a letter of introduction to Lawrence Durrell in Belgrade. The UK foreign office nurtures writers through its Intelligence and Research Department (IRD). I assume Durrell, not yet a renowned author, is an agent. I meet him after riding the Orient Express, rejuvenated after sections of the railroad were sabotaged during years of anti-Nazi resistance.

Today's dragon brings me a document, belatedly declassified on August 7, 2009: "UK National Archives FO 371/78682/R11215." It dismisses Durrell's reports: "Far too long and discursive to be of any use." This reinforces suspicions among some later historians that Whitehall hid its mistakes under ancient draconian secrecy laws.

Durrell meets me at Belgrade's old Metropole Hotel, in a hall full of floor-to-ceiling mirrors. He is arguing in English with a local girl. Not a single sentence makes sense to me. Finally they burst into laughter. Durrell tells me, "It's a game. One person makes a statement. The other picks out one word and weaves it into another sentence that has nothing to do with the previous sentence. Then the other person picks a word from the new sentence and uses it in the next one, which is also irrelevant. Masters of the game can send an outsider like you bonkers." That is the totality of his advice. I never see him again.

My better sources are among Tito's anti-Stalinist advisers who see the Soviet world mirrored in George Orwell's *Nineteen Eighty-Four*. The novel depicts a secret class of occult power holders, an Inner Party clustered around Big Brother, recasting all languages into Newspeak, in which concepts of liberty and conscience cannot be formulated. Copies are printed on ultrathin paper in London. This is where Durrell shines, although he is never credited with arranging this version's circulation among Yugoslavs who already see Stalin as Big Brother. Many wartime communist partisans admire Tito for breaking away from the Kremlin's "occult powers," but they also fear that Tito is targeted for assassination by Yevgeni Pitovranov, the Soviet deputy minister. "His recruits get the best education before joining SMERSH," I am told by Tito's wartime translator, Mrdjn Lenka, my official minder. She says that Orwell foresees dictatorship cemented by Newspeak. Yugoslav-Canadians were asked by Tito's Soviet-trained security chief to come with all their possessions to rebuild their homeland after the war. "They flocked back," she says. "Their Canadian passports were confiscated on arrival. Now they are trapped here."

Mrdjn helps me track down one unhappy Yugo-Canadian after another: each leads me to the next. She locates call boxes, never the same one twice, from which I phone brief reports on their virtual imprisonment. My procedure reminds me of Toronto court cases when I write details as they unfold. Instead of HCH's pneumatic tubes, I use the telephone to Prague. The Czechs are still under Stalin's thumb and gladly send what they misinterpret as anti-Tito telegrams to the *Star*'s city-desk editor, Borden Spears. He wires back to Prague the cable costs. Spears, a former squadron leader in the Canadian air force, aches to return to the study of ancient Greece. The nearest he can get to such a challenge is to disentangle events of the day. He is a veteran now back in the news business. I don't need to tell him why I cable through Prague. Tito's enemies, cutthroats from SMERSH, may watch me but fear to strike while Yugoslavia moves from Soviet control to comradeship with socialist Britain.

Mrdjn Lenka was an interpreter when Winston Churchill courted Tito as a communist whose partisans slaughtered Nazi armies. His son Randolph parachuted into wartime Yugoslavia to work with Tito. Mrdjn tells me, "I adored Randolph. But as an interpreter, I had to translate from Croat-Russian to Russo-French and then from French to English and back again. It was awkward and wasted precious time. Randolph asked the RAF to send me a plain old English-Croat dictionary. A Dakota dropped it by parachute."

"Did they drop anything else?" I ask.

"Randolph knew I needed the dictionary urgently. That's what's so wonderful about him."

"RAF crews might take a different view," I point out. "Flying through miles of German flak."

"Tito killed Germans. That dictionary was worth whole cargoes of arms," says she. "You're so naive."

We talk in her tiny Croatian apartment. Her husband is an engineer in Belgrade. I sleep on an old sofa. She wakes me with ersatz coffee and slivovitz plum brandy. "Why," she asks, "do you sleep with your collar up around your ears?"

"Vampires! I protect my neck against their bites. It started when I went to Saturday afternoon movies for kids. One kid paid and then sneaked the others through a side door. After *Snow White and the Seven Dwarfs*, I hid under my seat until the screening of *The Vampire Bat*, classified For Adults Only. I saw vampires suck blood from their victims' necks. I ran all the way home with my collar turned up against the bloodsuckers. I made a promise then that I would fight all forms of evil. I still can't sleep without my pajama collar turned up tight."

Mrdjn is incredulous. "Even now, when you're grown up?"

"Yes. Honest."

"Even when you were a pilot?"

"Especially when I was a pilot. It's a compulsion now." I tell her it became a compulsion after Spud Murphy crashed. The upturned collar reminds me of values we shared when he was barely old enough to shave.

"Do you think I might bite?" she asks.

"I'm afraid of where that might lead."

She pats the top of my head. "I am afraid, too. Better we stay friends, okay?"

We meet again in another place in another time of danger. Meanwhile, Tito fired his Stalinist security chief who tried to expel me from

Yugoslavia for uncovering four thousand Yugo-Canadians held against their will. They were freed and returned by sea. A *Toronto Star* reporter, George Bryant, interviewed them in Halifax. Their leader told him, "The Canadian government did nothing to make Belgrade honor our passports and said we were communists although we had only wanted to help those who lost so much to beat the Nazis while we were safe in Canada. We got back the passports, thanks to Stevenson's reports in the *Star.*"

I am fated to be drawn back to Yugoslavia time and again. On one assignment to Belgrade, I am given a desk in their foreign office. Dragons bring shorthand notes I made from the Yugoslav files about Dom Dova (House Number Two), Moscow's security service headquarters and CHEKA, the Extraordinary Commission to Combat Counter-Revolution, later the NKVD, running slave camps and hunting enemies abroad. The files reveal why Tito still needs Western allies. He is the target of Stalin's chief of Special Tasks, Pavel Sudoplatov, who planned in 1953 to kill Tito. But the Soviet dictator died before action was taken. Tito visits London, where I meet him to plan a documentary film about his life. A Kremlin shake-up topples Pavel Sudoplatov, who drafts *Memoirs of a Soviet Spymaster: Special Tasks* in which he writes: "William Stephenson directed operations from BSC headquarters in the Empire State Building." It's the wrong address but reinforces Stephenson's claim that Stalin's spymasters got information from moles in Whitehall, where the Establishment's secret intelligence service chiefs were hostile to BSC and damned Intrepid as a loose cannon.

Between brief foreign assignments once again I go back to local news. I learn responsible legwork from reporters who cover city hall or parliamentary affairs with eagle eyes. They would know how to deal with these Belgrade files on Soviet apparatchiks. I find wartime film shot by Ted Howe of Special Operations Executive (SOE). SOE was later shut down by rivals in Whitehall, and SOE records were destroyed in a mysterious fire. The film shows communists fighting the Nazis. I use the old footage in a TV documentary on Tito, and title it *The Meaning of Courage.* This is seen in Europe by a future Asian monarch. Years later, it plunges me into a long period of Siamese intrigue.

Up to my attic come letters from Ted Howe, written after he employed me for another unconventional war. He is wary of all intelligence bureaucrats. When he parachuted into wartime Yugoslavia, he was caught in a cone of German searchlights. The UK Establishment's secret service had told him the area was clear of any such enemy units. He warns me to look out for moles. "They take advantage of bureaucratic humbuggery."

HCH has his own brand of humbug: "Keep reports brief. Just what, when, why." His reporters would prefer him to introduce pensions. I grew up among workers who never expected to retire on a pension, so I fully intend to live on royalties from books I shall write about what I see and hear. A wartime reporter, Fred Bodsworth, was fired by HCH when peace came. Fred's crippled hands barred him from serving in the armed forces but were good enough to tap on typewriters until HCH, penny-pinching after the war, was obliged to hire former staffers back from military service. Fred turns to studying birds and writes best-selling books about wildlife.

I have no illusions about HCH. I ignore the issue of pensions. HCH is easy about travel expenses: they avoid long-term financial commitments. He never increases my modest salary. Glenys manages our family on this, beginning in Toronto where she gives birth to our son Andrew, daughter Jackie, and then Kevin.

HCH's terse approval comes, by pigeonhole express, to my diplomatically brief note that perhaps a sudden war in Korea might be worth investigating. Tokyo becomes my base for reporting the Korean War: an assignment with expenses that will help Glenys pay the growing family bills.

# CHAPTER 16

# Truth and Consequences in Korea

THE *STAR* SENDS ME TO KOREA, TEN DAYS AFTER THE OUTBREAK OF THE bloodiest of wars. I am also technically a navy pilot. A letter from Admiral N. N. Zuill, Commanding Reserves, says: "I have pleasure in informing you of your appointment to the Air Branch of the Royal Navy Volunteer Reserve in rank of Lieutenant. The King's Commission will be forwarded. You are appointed to No. 1833 Squadron." In June 1950, the squadron is still on its way to counter the sudden invasion of South Korea by Soviet-equipped North Korean armies. It is agreed that I'm more useful as a war correspondent.

I move with ground forces through a region known as Death Valley because shellfire from the unseen enemy is heavy and unopposed. A colleague, Ian Morrison of the London *Times,* is killed when his jeep is blown up. He had been much influenced by Dr. Joseph Needham, an English biochemist attached to Chinese Nationalist headquarters during the war against Japan. Needham explored China, way beyond the Kunming base of Generalissimo Chiang Kai-shek, and gathered evidence of "the astonishing inventiveness of the Chinese people since the 14th century B.C." Needham dismissed Chiang as "an American lackey" in the Civil War against Mao Zedong's communists, and became an open admirer of Mao's legendary Long March to power.

Within a few months of Mao Zedong declaring: "The Chinese people have stood up. No one will insult us again," the Korean War began. After reading some of Needham's scholarly research and listening to his political views, Ian was uneasy about the timing and manner in which

94

hostilities broke out so soon after Mao's appearance in Beijing. There had been a lot of talk in Washington that Mao still did not control some regions of China, and that the West should prevent him from controlling Manchuria, historically part of China, and bordering Korea.

Ian traveled extensively in China and was in Hong Kong before war broke out. He had been concerned that the United States might use the atomic bomb to kill Red China at birth, and he spoke of this to the widow of a Nationalist Chinese general, Han Suyin. She fell in love with Ian and describes their doomed love affair in the best-selling novel *A Many-Splendored Thing*. She becomes an unofficial voice for Premier Zhou Enlai long after he mobilizes an army of "Chinese Peoples' Volunteers" to stop any US military advance through Korea into China. Ian Morrison had proposed to Clem Attlee, the UK's socialist prime minister, "Zhou might become another Tito." Attlee put this to US President Harry Truman, who rejected it out of hand.

All I know about China is gleaned from books. I report the war as a necessary United Nations action. Like other Western correspondents, I take breaks in Tokyo and attend briefings by US General Douglas MacArthur, who assumes the role of Supreme Commander with such panache that one observer, William Manchester, later calls him American Caesar in a book with that title. MacArthur's decision to cross the 38th Parallel brings about a major revision of Mao's policy after November 1950. His Peoples' Volunteers, dizzy with success in their first offensive, declare they will drive the UN barbarians into the sea. This suggests a dangerous ignorance of the outside world among leaders of the young Peoples' Republic of China.

Riding a military plane back to Tokyo, I see US infantrymen labeled LMF. "That means Lack of Moral Fiber," sneers a civilian adviser in a canvas bucket seat beside me. I remember Freeman Dyson, the UK Bomber Command scientist who wrote that when RAF fliers were pushed too far, they were retired as Lacking Moral Fiber. I remember navy pilots diagnosed with PTSD: posttraumatic stress disorder. We never labeled them as cowards.

Some US fliers, bounced by Russian pilots, are never heard of again. A Canadian pilot goes down in China. Later, through luck and opportunity,

I negotiate with Premier Zhou Enlai for the pilot's release. The Canadian ambassador in Tokyo, Herb Norman, fears that the Korean War will lead to the nuclear bombing of China. He thinks Canada has a right to put the brakes on MacArthur, since Canada helped develop the atomic bomb, and now gets precious little thanks for halting the Maoist Chinese and North Korea attempt to drive Americans out of Seoul in 1951. A small battalion of the Princess Patricia's Canadian Light Infantry, preparing for Easter Sunday services, were almost wiped out by a surprise drive by 200,000 enemy troops to capture what was then the South Korean capital. The battle lasted three days. Canadians were surrounded and almost destroyed before turning the enemy. General MacArthur had given no warning of the communist attack and Herb Norman's honest comments on this and other failures are valued by US correspondents who distrust MacArthur's manipulation of information and his noisy belligerence. These war reporters are under constant US military scrutiny. MacArthur's censors advise Norman to stick to his own specialty: Japanese culture. His closest aide tells me, "Herb lives in an ivory tower." He bemuses pilots at a private dinner by reciting ancient Japanese haiku, an unrhymed verse form. His detached criticisms of some aspects of US policy grab the attention of Senator Joe McCarthy, investigating the alleged influence on the US government by communists and fellow travelers. Dr. Joseph Needham and Ambassador Norman are brilliant scholars, steeped in ancient cultures, but schoolboyish about ugly realities of the day. Senator McCarthy tar-brushes prominent personalities and later hounds Ambassador Norman to a shocking death. The McCarthy witch-hunters denounce Dr. Needham for alleging that germ warfare is waged by the United States in Korea.

Much later, too late to save Herb Norman's life but in time to make the life of the eccentric Dr. Needham less burdened by charges of being a communist dupe, I learn that Stalin himself was fooled. The KGB wife of a Soviet diplomat in Bangkok tells me, "Russian technical advisers helped North Korea fabricate evidence of American bacteriological weapons." Her disclosure follows Stalin's gruesome death and is confirmed in Moscow's subsequent official reports, disclosing the astonishing truth. The Presidium of the Soviet Union, after vicious infighting, declares that these fabrications seriously damaged Russia's image abroad because an earlier minister for state security, Semen Ignatiev, faked information by creating "false areas of exposure to cholera bacteria in Korea" to fool investigators from the World Peace Council as long ago as 1952.

## CHAPTER 17

# From a Coronation to Auschwitz and a Lost Pilot

THE PUBLIC MEMORY OF CARNAGE ON THE KOREAN PENINSULA IS eclipsed in 1953 by the coronation of Queen Elizabeth II. It's the first ray of sunshine after England's endless postwar austerity. HCH sends me, with other *Star* reporters, to cover the June festivities. At the London School of Economics (LSE), I meet again the Polish news correspondent I first saw in Mexico and knew as "Rena." She is studying at LSE.

"I'm going back to Poland," she says defensively. "I'm only here to research why Auschwitz was never bombed by the Allies." She looks me over. "What are you researching?"

"History of the first Queen Elizabeth."

Rena is incredulous. "That's centuries ago. More important things happen today where I come from."

"I'd much rather see what's happening in Poland but I can't get a visa."

"Come to my embassy," she retorts, sounding as if I have insulted her country.

I get the first visa issued to a Western reporter. "Rena has clout," I write in notes now rediscovered. For her own security, I avoided fully identifying Rena, and took similar precautions with Jan, my minder in Poland. He also went to the London School of Economics. "A lot of us study there," he says.

"To become communists?" I ask, thinking of LSE's far-left reputation.

"No! Here is what made me a communist." Jan points to rusting railroad tracks in Old Warsaw. "That's where I last saw my parents. On cattle

98

wagons. Rena last saw her parents here too. All were sent to Auschwitz. That's why Rena went to Mexico as Poland's news correspondent. She's Jewish, like me."

"But why live under Stalin? He persecutes Jews."

"He liberated Poland. Your air forces claimed they could not bomb Auschwitz and liberate Jews because it was beyond their range. Yet they bombed the I.G. Farben chemical works next door." Later, I get photographs taken by US Air Force bombers as they struck I.G. Farben, slap up against Auschwitz, which is untouched.

Jan drives me past the ruins of I. G. Farben. A violent thunderstorm bursts overhead. He quotes a French expression for Nature in tune with horror: "The elements are shocked." Auschwitz shocks me. Work Makes Free! proclaims the cynical old Nazi sign, left to dangle outside empty blockhouses. All that remains of those who were murdered are ragged clothes, spectacles, artificial limbs . . . neatly piled outside the ovens. Jan recalls that when the Supreme Commander of the Allied Forces, General Dwight Eisenhower, saw the death camps, he ordered photographs to be taken: "Get it all on record now, get the films, get the witnesses. Or somewhere down the road of history some bastard will get up and say this never happened."

The 1948 Pulitzer Prize went to W.H. Auden for his *The Age of Anxiety* but I know of no other writers who commemorated the Holocaust by the time I see Auschwitz.

Later, in my strange encounter with Rena inside the Soviet Union, she tells me Auschwitz is now tidied up for sightseers "who gawk at big tourist signs: This way to the gas chambers."

Auschwitz in 1953 is nothing but rubble. "We leave it that way out of respect," I am told by Prime Minister Jozef Cyrankiewicz in the first interview he gives a non-communist reporter. An agent of MI6, Anthony Cavendish, under cover as a correspondent for United Press, later writes *Inside Intelligence** claiming he was the first journalist to interview

---

* After the earlier private printing by Anthony Cavendish, his book was published in 1990 by William Collins, London.

Cyrankiewicz in 1956. The MI6 man's "insider disclosures" are touted as "The Book the British Government Tried to Ban." Later, I get a cable: STEVERITE from INTER: "Here is one more reason for distrusting intelligence bureaucrats in any guise. MI6 does not officially exist." MI6, self-styled as the world's oldest foreign intelligence service, never admits it exists until decades later, in 1994.

Cyrankiewicz tells me, "The West abandoned us. Now the Soviet Union pretends to protect us." He makes it clear that his people foresee a time when Stalin will need them more than they need Stalin. "We pray for justice," he says, and suggests I go to Cracow cathedral any Saturday night. I find it overflowing with worshippers. They spill into surrounding fields and alleys. Soldiers stack their rifles before going inside to pray and mark the Assumption of the Blessed Virgin Mary into Heaven. Among worshippers is Karol Jozef Wotyla, leader of "the little family" known as Rodzinka, which conducts "philosophical discussions," helps the blind and sick, and avoids the attention of Stalinist spies. He is instrumental in ending communism in Poland, and eventually all of Europe after he becomes Pope John Paul II in 1978, later acclaimed as one of the most influential leaders of the twentieth century. My dragons now remind me of another case of notional proximity: My housekeeper in later years is invited to a small dinner for him and only then tells me that she was his housekeeper long ago.

During my first venture into Poland, I wonder if Rena became a Polish communist agent in Mexico because she was bitter about the West's short memory. Poland played a huge role in defeating Hitler, beginning with the prewar dispatch to Britain of German Enigma encoding machines that led to ULTRA. In the early columns I write for HCH, reprinted in the *London Daily Express*, I disguise sources like Rena and Jan out of a well-founded fear of incriminating them during the era of Soviet oversight. My columns prompt Intrepid to send me a shocking report on Jan Karski, the underground courier who repeatedly crossed Nazi-occupied Europe to bring intelligence both to London and the Polish government-in-exile. Poland's underground army was Europe's largest, with 350,000 fighters. Karski sought support from the UK's foreign secretary, Anthony Eden, who dismissed his reports as imaginative nonsense. Karski appealed to the US Supreme Court associate justice, Felix Frankfurter, himself a Jew, who refused to believe Germany was capable of genocide. Franklin Roosevelt, as US president, dismissed Karski's reports. Later, Karski made public his despair: "After the Soviet Union turned from enemy to ally of the West, people asked where did the Polish sacrifice rank next to the immeasurable heroism of the Russians." A Jewish member of the Polish government-in-exile, Szmuel Zygelbojm, had committed suicide in 1943 in despair over the indifference to the Holocaust. Karski commented, "Of all the deaths that have taken place in this war, surely Zygelbojm's is one of the most frightening, the sharpest revelation of the extent to which the world has become cold and unfriendly . . . separated by immense gulfs of indifference."

Dragons disinter details in an INTER-STEVERITE exchange, adding that I am right to hide Rena's identity. I remember this when Rena unburdens herself to me in Russia, in China, and in communist North Vietnam.

---

HCH dislikes "think pieces." My *Daily Express* and *Toronto Star* reports are brief. I telegraph tougher and fuller reports to INTER. Specific details follow by mail. It's a rewarding way of letting off steam for which no other form of compensation is offered. HCH gives his readers the impression of worldwide coverage by having me hop in and out of trouble spots: war in Korea, revolution in French Indochine, uprisings in Malaya and Indonesia. His formula is "Get the dateline and get out." I want to do my hopping from a base in what is still a British Crown Colony. Up comes a crumpled reminder of a typically cautious message: "HCH: Is Hong Kong best springboard for new conflicts brewing in Asia and Mideast? WS."

This is prompted by a flight out of Vietnam in late 1953. Air France in Saigon suddenly cancels all services without explanation. A cheerful Australian hears me curse and says, "I'm going to Hong Kong. Wanna lift? I've got a PBY flying boat. Yes? Okay, mate. See you, dawn tomorrow."

101

I track down the plane, a Catalina with four piston engines. Inside are two casually clothed Australians, and a big cargo of wooden crates. I squat on the biggest crate and peer through a blister side window. We fly low over the South China Sea along the rugged coast that in a far-distant future will conceal China's nuclear submarines. We drop even lower to circle Macau and the façade of the cathedral of St. Paul, standing like a huge cardboard cutout with nothing but broken stones behind it, a hollow token of Catholicism in the oldest European outpost on the China coast, occupied by the Portuguese in 1557. To this place, now known as the heart of evil, I am fated to bring Ian Fleming to meet the model for one of James Bond's most terrifying fictional enemies.

We land in a spray of seawater, among anchored junks. A Portuguese police boat chugs out to meet us. Coolies help the Aussies transfer the crates.

The pilot says to me, "Bet you never guessed what's in 'em."

"They looked kind of heavy."

"Too bludy right they were heavy. Full of gold. Don't ask why. I just deliver the cargo." He straps himself in again. "There's an old saying in Oz: 'I signed nothing, you can prove nothing.'"

The gold is transferred from the French Bank of Indochina to Macau's drug barons, who ship the gold up the Pearl River into the Chinese interior. Chairman Mao licenses them to pick the pockets of rich "foreign devils" who swarm here by ferry from Hong Kong, lured by tales of lurid sex and "foreign mud"—opium. Fortunes are made in gambling dens. For three hundred years of tenure under lease, the Portuguese were never allowed to enter China from Macau. I am about to discover that Chairman Mao is smarter than his Manchu predecessors, Lords of the World and Dispensers of Light.

We take off again, heading between small islands and fleets of big junks that leap out of some ancient Chinese work of art. The bat-winged junks turn with the changing winds. Hulls lean to one side in unison like gigantic brown moths gliding between rocklike islands along this coast of mainland China. It's a breathtaking approach to a colony where, from 1941, Japanese troops imposed such a reign of terror upon Chinese residents that they were glad to see the British colonizers return in 1945.

The deep-sea junks infect me with their display of boundless ambition. "Boat people" spend all their lives on the huge wooden vessels. Their predecessors mapped the oceans, centuries before Columbus. I view this as a challenge. I want to live here. With the zest of the very young, Glenys and I intend to explore the entire world with our children, for we feel untouchable. Hong Kong seems the right place to start.

HCH signals that he will base me in Hong Kong if I can get into Red China. And he will cover household expenses. This will cost him less than a boost in salary or a pension. All I care about is the prospect of writing books about distant shores. There will be plenty to write about. Red Chinese armies and Stalin's Red Air Force combined to stop the Korean "police action." Communist uprisings in other parts of Asia are easy to foresee. HCH does not expect readers to care about such "small wars." His newspaper circulation is not boosted by reports of Dutch intrigue to recover colonial power in Indonesia. Advertising is not boosted by British campaigns against communist Chinese guerrillas in Malaysia. The conflict is called "The Emergency" to discourage any supposition that this is a war to hang on to British rubber, the Raffles Hotel, and the Singapore Cricket Club. How many of our readers care? All HCH wants is that I get an exotic deadline cable a brief report on the turmoil, and get out fast.

I receive a message from INTER. I have won an American Aviation Writers Award. I make the mistake of assuming it is for *Exercise Eagle*, asserting sovereignty in the Arctic against the Soviet Union's claims.

～➤～

Old notes jump me back to *Exercise Eagle*. Arthur F. Hailey, a former RAF pilot, returns to Toronto with me in the bucket seats of a four-engine transport modified from a Second World War bomber.

Hailey asks, "Could we fly this thing if all the crew got food poisoning?" This inspires him to write his first TV drama, "Flight into Danger." He is with a magazine called *Bus and Truck* and not amused when I call it "Truss and Buck." His revenge will be to churn out best-selling novels and movies. He reaps a fortune but never forgets a gross indignity at the start of his wartime service in the RAF. He was corporal adjutant to a lofty wing commander, and corrected his superior's spelling mistakes in Orders of the Day.

"You're a clever sort of chap," sneers the wingco, "in a night-school sort of way."

Hailey goes on to serve as a pilot when a shortage of aircrews forces the RAF to let lower-class boys fly. Years later in London, Hailey signs copies of his latest bestseller. The former wing commander stands in line until he reaches Hailey and asks humbly: "Would you sign this over to myself? You do remember me?" Hailey says, "I've never forgotten." He adds with a gracious smile, "I do hope I spell your name correctly, old cock!"

Hailey's father was a humble English hatmaker. As a girl, his wife Sheila lived above an East London garage. Sheer guts took them to the top. Sheila was in the typing pool of *Bus and Truck* and other magazines. I'm jealous of Hailey because he is what I want to be: free to write books. He envies me in days when he glues himself to his desk in a Toronto house. My foreign adventures fuel his resolve to reach the heights.

My dragons retrieve an old telegram. Hailey hears I am to be one of the first three bona fide Western newsmen to enter Red China. He wants to write a magazine piece about me because "if you drop into a cannibal's cook pot, you see the cannibal's point of view."

The cook pot is Mao's China. In the tradition of China's emperors, Mao is Lord of the World. He has the reputation of a cannibal in the United States. And Mao is paranoid about the West after US General Douglas MacArthur, Supreme Commander in Tokyo, talks about dropping atom bombs on China a short time after Mao mounts the gate of Tiananmen on October 1, 1949, in the famous proclamation: "The Chinese people have stood up. No one will insult us again." Mao's adviser on foreign relations, Zhou Enlai, means to get the point across by issuing a visa for me. It certainly means that HCH has to keep his promise to base me and my family in Hong Kong.

I fly to Berne to see Mao's consul. He hands me a rice-paper visa. He explains carefully how I should fold it away, somewhere safe. Nothing will be stamped in my passport. "Then you shall not suffer inconvenience after passing back from China into the capitalist world," he tells me, as if I shall descend from a Red Heaven back into Capitalist Hell. It is a period when most Western governments prefer diplomatic relations with Chiang Kai-shek's China, now parked on the island of Taiwan. Mao's diplomats abroad have to work out of Switzerland.

Mao's man in Berne lets me believe I shall be the first Western reporter allowed into the Peoples' Republic. I meet two other "firsts" at Lo Wu, where I have to walk across the bridge between sections of the railroad that once linked Hong Kong to Canton. My unheralded companions are a French aristocrat who reports for *Le Monde,* and a seasoned correspondent for Agence France-Presse. They have no more idea than I have about why, out of thousands of journalists maneuvering for visas, we are the first to enter Mao's Heaven.

It is late 1954, three years after Soviet Ambassador Jakob Malik first conveyed the willingness of the Chinese People's Volunteers in Korea to discuss a cease-fire. Squadron Leader Andy MacKenzie of the Royal Canadian Air Force, piloting an F-86 Sabre jet fighter, had been shot down on December 5, 1952, and parachuted into Manchuria, recovered by China as its biggest industrial base after those fourteen years of Japanese exploitation under the cloak of the fantasy emperor, Pu-yi. Manchuria, once more a Chinese province, had become a platform for intervention in the Korean War. China feared American intrusion from Korea. Russia wanted to re-establish control over Manchuria before it became a base for US operations.

# CHAPTER 18

# An Absentminded Fool Puts a Foot Wrong in Mongolia

SQUADRON LEADER ANDY MACKENZIE'S WIFE JOYCE HEARS I WILL BE the first non-communist newsman in Red China. She is alone with their four young children in Montreal. She has no news about the fate of this thirty-two-year-old veteran fighter pilot who won a Distinguished Flying Cross for shooting down Germans. Now she hears he was shot down by Russian MiG-15s in Manchurian skies. Is there any way I can locate him?

My chance comes in September 1954 in Beijing's Hall of Magnanimity when I come face-to-face with Mao.

Dragons retrieve notes and an old letter signed: "Mister Four-Five-Six." He is the Canadian consul in Hong Kong: real name, Forsythe Smith. He wishes he was a journalist: "My dispatches are ignored, forestalled by press reports." I reply that most journalists are also ignored. I don't add that my frustrations are eased by STEVERITE in-depth reports to an attentive INTER.

Before entering Red China for the first time, I lay plans for my family to join me later in Hong Kong. Four-Five-Six finds me a rentable apartment. These are hard times for more than four million mainland Chinese who seek safety from the new regime by moving to Hong Kong. Most feel like slave labor in their early struggles, but many reach high levels of entrepreneurial success in this tiny place of less than five hundred square miles. Its British governors call China's capital Peking until a rain-sodden evening on the Hong Kong waterfront when the Union Jack is lowered for good on June 30, 1997, ending more than a century and a half of British governance. China's new rulers achieve a significant moral victory when their capital is once again known as Beijing.

Hong Kong attracts more capital investment from Red China than from the United States. While it lays these golden eggs, Mao has no wish to kill the goose. Soon after Mao takes over in 1949 he sends Madame Kung Peng to Hong Kong to run the Xinhua News Agency with her husband, Chiao Kuanhua. She returns alone to become chief of foreign intelligence under Zhou Enlai. She also becomes my most useful contact after I persuade the Security Liaison Office (SLO) to let Xinhua enjoy the same facilities as other news agencies. The SLO is cover for the UK foreign intelligence service, and it reads the cables of all news reports anyway, so everyone benefits.

Still acutely aware of Joyce MacKenzie's distress, I press for news of Squadron Leader MacKenzie when I enter Manchuria, land of the Manchus, who conquered China some four hundred years before. I ask about "a Canadian flier who crashed here." I get blank looks. In Shenyang, once called Mukden, I fear MacKenzie might be shut away in the block-houses built for The People's Workers. No building has windows. Each blockhouse has one number painted across several floors: the only address for inhabitants is a combination of Soviet-style Cyrillic characters: for instance SJ: 109. The massive blocks rise like memorial stones to Stalin's effort to enforce Russian control.

With me is James Cameron, a brilliant essayist and reporter for London's *News Chronicle.* Our minder is a solemn Chinese whom we dub "Chairman Chan" because his chubby face resembles a young Mao Tse-tung. Zhou Enlai has told him that Manchuria is always part of China. Zhou, as a poverty-stricken teenager, lived here on coarse millet buns while attending one of the "new learning" schools. They taught that China was beaten to its knees by Western powers in 1898, the year Zhou was born; that Chinese reformists launched the Boxer Rebellion, "the uprising of righteous fists," two years later; and that Japan and the West then marched into Beijing to loot, rape, and kill. Japan, entrenched in Korea, occupied Manchuria until Zhou Enlai returned with Mao's forces in

1945, not yet equipped to govern all China. Stalin declared war on Japan in the last moments of World War II, grabbing the Manchu provinces and Japanese-built industrial equipment worth sums far beyond the reckoning of Mao's penny-pinchers.

Madame Kung Peng is now Zhou Enlai's sleeping partner as well as political adviser. Both need Western support for the recovery of China's Manchurian possessions. I tell her that one way to win this support is to release MacKenzie. The Peoples Liberation Army, the PLA, does not see it this way: thousands of its "volunteers" died during the Korean conflict. I run afoul of the PLA when Cameron and I travel to the Great Wall. There I see traders astride enormous horses with bulging saddlebags and follow them along a muddy trail through an ancient stone archway into Mongolia. I know China destroyed the Mongols' unique record of this land that revolutionized the medieval battlefield, including *The Secret History*, written by a Russian scholar-priest, Archimandrite Palladius. As a boy, I read that in 1866 Palladius described Genghis Khan overturning the entire world west of Mongolia. His bowmen fired arrows greater distances than those covered by the English longbow. He introduced "rolling fire" to soften up enemies before releasing mobile catapults as devastating as heavy artillery. I imagine those so-called Mongol Hordes as I peer through my 16 mm movie camera at the mounted hawkers.

My arrest is low-key. Chairman Chan says "our car has broken down." He leaves us from time to time to speak by radio to Beijing. Night falls. High cirrus clouds drift out of Mongolia and catch the first streaks of dawn. "Silver fish-belly" Chan calls this spectral sight when he finally announces, "the car is fixed."

We head back to Beijing. Chan says to me, "Remember I told you it is forbidden to enter Mongolia?"

"No!" I reply each time he repeats this, until he falls back, eyes closed, body rigid.

Cameron says under his breath, "Poor chap's catatonic. He's in trouble for not stopping you."

"Wasn't thinking," I whisper. "I only walked into Mongolia by a couple of steps."

"Enough to convince the army you're a spy."

The truth is that Chan never expected me to wander off along the trail. It occurs to me now that Mao fears descendants of marauding Mongols who once held a large part of Europe for close to three hundred years. They swept through China, forcing what Mao calls "national minorities" to leave their places of origin on the Burma Road and migrate into the Golden Peninsula. I later travel often along the Burma Road. It becomes, in my mind, the true symbol of China's intention to revive its dominance from Tibet to the Gulf of Siam.

In Beijing I am summoned to meet six comrades in blue uniforms with tiny Mao badges.

"Did I take pictures of Mongolia?"

"Yes. You can process the film." I offer a roll of Kodak 16 mm color movie film.

"Were you told not to go through hole in Great Wall?"

"No!"

Their leader studies the mystery can of film. The comrades talk among themselves and disperse.

The next day, I take a bicycle-rickshaw to Madame Kung Peng's modest office at the Temple of Political Diligence. She tells me. "The army wanted to arrest you as a spy. The foreign office stopped them."

I hide my astonishment. Zhou Enlai can overrule the army?

Suddenly, Kung Peng smiles. "Come for dinner at The Three Tables tonight?" It's not really a question.

Chairman Chan joins us. He is no longer in a state of rigor mortis, and stuns me by saying my wife met him on a transatlantic ocean liner and told him where to make the best of his time in London on his way back to China. Chan does not forget that she treated him as an equal, when the Chinese in Canada were still only remembered as slave labor on the railroads. My dragons remind me of this fresh example of notional proximity, leaping across time, rejoining people and events. Glenys had shown Chan good inexpensive restaurants in London. No wonder Madame Kung Peng tells me where to find the best dumplings in all of China, on the sidewalks of Chungking.

Author, center, with Soviet agent masquerading as an official Soviet Tass News Agency correspondent. On left is China's "Chairman Chan," which is the author's nickname for a Beijing (then spelled Peking) source who confides his concern about Soviet policy toward China. Author had previously helped "Chairman Chan" find his way around England, and Chan trusted him with inside information on Beijing policies. They are traveling on a road beneath the Tibetan foothills. 1960.

The Three Tables is literally a three-table restaurant. Only Peking's top people get in. Its specialty is "Peking Duck." I eat with Madame Kung Peng and another dignitary. Their faces reveal nothing when I bring up the case of the missing Canadian pilot. "My newspaper will publish on the front page a tribute to the great kindness of New China in helping to find our distinguished airman," I improvise wildly, "if you find him." Kung Peng repeats that she knows nothing of the case. Then she says sharply: "We developed your film. It only shows ancient stone camels along the road to the Great Wall. Why not project the progress we make in New China?"

I dissemble. "I felt the whole world should see how New China preserves centuries of culture."

"You never got permission to bring in cameras," she snaps.

"Nobody asked about cameras when I entered China. If nothing much is happening when I travel, I film rare spectacles." I add helpfully, "I also make notes in the Pitman shorthand I taught myself long ago."

The Peoples Liberation Army must have stolen a quick squint at my notebook, and saw my squiggles as secret code. Luckily, before entering China, I burned a notebook chemically treated to render invisible anything I might write for the enlightenment of British military intelligence, which mostly wants to know where railroad signals are sited along China's tracks, and similar loony-bin items. The army is unlikely to transcribe Pitman's inscrutable dots and slashes. But to be on the safe side, I memorize what I see, using tricks Baden-Powell learned from his Boer War enemies, and passed down to us Boy Scouts.

We leave The Three Tables after many toasts in the fierce mao-tai liquor that Jim Cameron had once dubbed "Manchurian locomotive vodka." It was in Manchuria where we first saw these liquor bottles with labels eccentrically decorated with puffing railroad steam engines.

I have a warm feeling that Kung Peng is going to find the missing pilot in the same spirit of expedient goodwill which inspired me to argue the case for filming ancient stone camels near the Great Wall. A front-page *Toronto Star* report acknowledges China's readiness to cooperate in locating the missing pilot. And on December 5, 1954, two years to the day after Squadron Leader Andy MacKenzie was shot down, he walks alone across the old Lo-Wu bridge into Hong Kong. I remind HCH of our other bargain: "My base Hong Kong?" It reads like Pidgin English. His response follows the drill of abrupt newsroom pigeonhole exchanges. "OK: HCH."

Notional proximity suddenly jumps me from my close call with Maoist forces at the Great Wall to the year 2009 when Alexandra, my daughter with Monika, freely strolls into Mongolia and runs a marathon on the same Great Wall. She enters The Temple of Heaven and finds photographs of earlier visitors, including myself. "Aha!" I can hear her

The author with wife Monika and daughter Alexandra in front of the Temple of Heaven in 2009. The Temple of Heaven was renamed the Temple of Political Diligence by Mao and was where the author covered the young Dalai Lama's first visit to Beijing and Nehru's meeting with Mao.

thinking. "Dad really did meet Mao here when it was The Temple of Political Diligence."

Back in those hairier days, I had switched my footage of the Mongol traders for a can of film showing camel statues. This bridged the gap between the army and Kung Peng. She is closer to Zhou Enlai than her title might suggest as adviser on intelligence and foreign affairs. She prompts Zhou to give China a genial mask. I see him declare in Nepal, "For thousands of years, China and India had little direct contact. We share a 3,500 kilometer border along the Himalayan Mountains. Down all these centuries, we stared in opposite directions. We must change this." Zhou's proposal is reversed by Mao in the official version. This bolsters reports of rivalry between Mao and Zhou. The army is regimented by Mao. I removed my Mongolia footage to pacify the PLA.

Author's photograph of Red China's Premier Zhou Enlai with Nepal's Prime Minister on the Chinese leader's visit to Nepal. 1958.

# Chapter 19

# Meeting Mao and the Dalai Lama

MAO DISPLAYS A FRIENDLY FACE WHEN IT SUITS HIS PURPOSE. BEFORE the Mongolia misunderstanding, his round cheeks floated into my viewfinder. PLA soldiers first hammered at my door in a dormitory-hotel, then escorted me to the circular Temple of Political Diligence. I had time to grab a new movie camera. I had used it once only, shooting footage in Toronto for Glenys to develop and cable the results, which were good.

In the Temple of Political Diligence, I fiddled with a newfangled light meter, peered through an unfamiliar viewfinder, and measured the dawn light filtering through the rotunda. Men line the temple walls, standing rigid as toy soldiers in blue tunics. I wonder if, for other occasions, the temple turns into a palace. Crimson banners and bold ideograms cover the walls like movable stage props.

Someone blocks my view. Blindly, I wave aside the intruder. I feel a sudden drop in temperature. The silence is deafening. I lower the camera and see Mao Zedong. His face floats at the level of mine. No mistaking the black tufts of hair on either side of the famously broad forehead. If this really is the Chairman, shouldn't he be accoutered in robes of some grandeous style, Napoleonic or monarchical? Instead, he stands there like a clay figure in plain gray jacket and gray pants.

Mouth dry, face red, I attempt a stiff little bow. What's the protocol in a situation like this? I know his history of ruthlessly destroying anyone who got in his way on the Long March to communist victory. I can only stutter in awkward Mandarin, "I am an Englishman."

Mao smiles. "And I am Chinese," he replies politely in English.

He pats my arm and turns to greet a new arrival: India's Prime Minister Nehru. All the comrades move like mechanical dolls. In a well-rehearsed drill, they close around us. We are conjoined, Mao, Nehru, and me, as if figures in a Chinese opera, except there is no squeal of instruments, no wail of operatic voices. I imagine a roll of drums, a blast of trumpets. In reality all is silent until Mao's multilingual interpreter, Huang Hua, gives me a toothy smile and says softly in fluent English, "You are welcome to spend the day with us."

This sounds more like an order than an invitation. Huang is Mao's closest aide, known as Yellow Flower, a pseudonym he adopted when he joined the communist party while studying at the UK-US Christian missionary university of Yanjing in Hubei, a province that surrounds Beijing. One of his teachers was the American journalist Edgar Snow, author of *Red Star Over China*, a 1937 best-seller. I had read Snow's book and recognized the description of Yellow Flower as the student who rebelled against poverty under the name of Wang Rumei. I become well acquainted with him later as Huang Hua, who tries to build bridges with the West. Right now, he reflects Mao's amiability and my day unfolds in even more unexpected ways.[*]

I have a blurred recollection of being steered in and out of black limousines. We are in another temple called, presumably for the occasion, the Sea Palace. In some other part of the Forbidden City, Jim Cameron joins me and murmurs, "We're here to show Nehru that China is open to the Western press." There are no other free world reporters in sight. Premier Zhou Enlai arrives while we are ushered into the presence of the young man I know as the fourteenth Dalai Lama of Tibet, reincarnation of Lotus Thunderbolt, patron deity and founder of the Yellow Hat Lamas: "The Great and Precious Prince of the Faith, Noble One of the Soft Voice, Powerful Ruler of Three Worlds here and above and below the Oceans." The Chinese know the word "lama" as Mongolian for "ocean," and regard this reincarnation of the spiritual head of Lamaism as belonging to ancient times when China's power spanned all the oceans and ruled Tibet.

[*] When Yellow Flower died in December 2010, the *London Financial Times* published a tribute to him under the headline "The Yellow Flower who became China's Heart and Soul" and described him as "China's most influential diplomat best known as Huang Hua: b. 1913, d. Nov.–Dec. 2010."

Beside him is an even younger man, a boy really: the Panchen Lama, officially named Leader of The Red Sect in Rear Tibet, groomed to replace the Dalai Lama and become Mao's puppet, with or without violence.

Zhou Enlai moves smoothly among Western ambassadors normally denied access to China's leaders. The British ambassador has never been recognized before by any Chinese leader. Representatives of non-communist countries have been summoned, without preamble, to assemble here as silent props, hemmed in by dramatically uniformed Red Army officers drilled by an unofficial "Chinese Governor of Tibet" and his Political Commissar. Tibet claims independence but already it is wanted as part of China by Heroes of the Long March, who proclaimed in 1949 the People's Republic when Mao the Chairman finally stood above Tiananmen Square.

Cameron is maneuvered with me into a privileged position near Nehru, who is aware of the charade and later tells me so, during one of our private conversations in New Delhi at the Indian Prime Minister's official home; a modest bungalow in contrast to Mao's spread of ancient temples and displays of raw power.

Cameron nudges me and mutters, "I've never done this before!" He pulls out an old envelope. "May I have your autographs?" he asks both the Dalai and Panchen Lamas. The Dalai Lama scribbles his spidery signature across the envelope and hands it to the Panchen Lama, who glances at Yellow Flower to get his approval before adding his name. The Dalai Lama points to his own signature, and says in English, "Dalai Lama on top."

He could be innocently identifying his name. The two separate lines of scribbled characters are inscrutable to foreign "long-noses" like Cameron and me. The surrounding Red Army generals miss the signal. In all the years after he murmured those four words, the Dalai Lama never modifies his claim to be "on top" of a free Tibet. The next time we meet, he is forced to flee Tibet and arrives in Nepal with a dusty but colorful entourage.

By now Hong Kong has become a springboard to places far apart: Arabia, Siberia, India, and mainland China. My old notes predict that here must explode future economic and militant challenges. Today into my attic comes an old photograph of myself at the residence of the Indian

Author with India's Prime Minister Nehru during one of many informal discussions with him when the author was news correspondent for Southeast Asia.

prime minister. We sit in his garden, watched only by Lady Mountbatten. A messenger hands Nehru a telegram. He scans it, leaning back in his wooden cane chair. "Our man in Lhasa reports the Dalai Lama has run away. Nonsense! He's forced out at gunpoint by the Chinese. He's making the long trek to Nepal. He faces weeks of danger."

In 1957 I am warned about the crisis by Boris Lyssanovich, a White Russian who fled to Manchuria, ran a circus in Shanghai, moved to Calcutta, and finally built a new life in Nepal. I first met him when Chinese army surveyors were planning highways and railroads from Tibet into Nepal.

That's how I meet the Dalai Lama for a second time. "Boisterous Boris" runs the ramshackle Royal Hotel in Kathmandu. He tells me the Tibetan reincarnation of past lamas "is on his way here with two hundred fighters disguised as porters carrying trunks crammed with Tibetan salt, more valuable to the Nepalese than gold." Boris became suspicious when a former Chinese Red Army guerrilla warfare expert, General Yuan

Chung-hsien, acting as Mao's representative to India, suddenly took rooms at the inn as ambassador to Nepal.

King Mahendra of Nepal is favored by India as a different reincarnation: that of the Hindu god, Lord Vishnu. Nepal's Prime Minister, Acharya Tanka Prasad, doubts Chinese troops will penetrate his land: it resembles a spiked steel doormat: twenty-two of the spikes are mountains more than 25,000 feet high. Prasad is a genial old man with a passion for English literature. His library expands seamlessly throughout his home with books he orders from London. Whenever I need to research some topic, he obliges by skimming up and down his avenues of books on a wheeled ladder, instantly picking out the best books for my projects.

His place is taken later by a frightened king playing host to Zhou Enlai who makes a speech recognizing India as Nepal's "big brother." Zhou has the backing now of China's top general, who asks me to explain a march-past by Nepalese soldiers wearing kilts and blowing bagpipes. "They're Gurkhas," I explain. "Recruited in Nepal to serve in the British army." He hides his bafflement behind a smile and steers me to the back of an old Kathmandu temple. Here he and Zhou plunge into rice paddies to show new ways to transplant rice shoots with simple equipment invented in China. I ask why this demonstration is kept hidden from other Western observers.

"They would call us peasants," says Zhou, "teaching other poor peasants." He speaks with the bitterness he felt as a youth of the early 1920s, searching for knowledge in Japan, Britain, and France, resenting the way his people are looked down upon as cheap labor, and haunted by the memory of China, among nations who defeated Germany in the First World War, being the only country excluded from the Paris peace talks. In Nepal, he wants to avoid any head-on collision with the British, who still exercise influence in Indian Nepal. But Zhou's conciliatory speeches are reversed in official versions broadcast from Beijing, dictated by Mao. His revisions insist that British imperialists seized regions from Nepal to Tibet that must return to Chinese rule. Puzzled by this upside-down version of what Zhou actually said, I consult Boris, who seems to know everything about Zhou's mandarin background: his schoolboy studies of

Author with Nepalese guide on an unpaved road to Tibet during several treks to Tibet borders.

English and French literature; and how he turned to Russian communism as a way to lift the Chinese people out of enslavement. Chairman Mao distrusts Zhou as a rival for power. Boris says Mao will never soften his resolve to control Tibet and strengthen oversight of Nepal. "Softly, softly, catchee monkey." Boris drains his glass of whiskey. "That's Mao's way. First broaden ancient trade links with Nepal and then . . ." He shrugs.

The longest mountain frontier in the world divides China and India. I go back often to Nepal while it is still regarded as part of India. Now China seeks to dominate. Who will win? Zhou Enlai's flexibility, or Mao's iron fist? I get no clear answer from my friend King Mahendra. He no longer behaves like a king but continues to scoot through his alleyways of books. He wishes Britain still had the power to assert its imperial obligation to protect Nepal. All he foresees now is China rising to Mount Everest and dominating Nepal and neighboring regions, all the way from tiny Bhutan to the heights of Tibet. His one joy comes from his adjoining valley of brave Gurkhas, still at the heart of British military actions abroad.

# CHAPTER 20

# Making Enemies by Dropping Allies

HCH IS NOT INTERESTED IN REMOTE ISSUES, SUCH AS MAO'S DETERMI-nation to seize Tibet, the highest platform from which China might project power. HCH wants startling *Star* datelines above snappy reports, the shorter the better. I travel from Hong Kong in all directions, armed with cameras. The most photogenic of threatened neighborhoods is Vietnam, once embraced by China, still known as French Indochina. I stay at a fort commanded by a French colonel. During the daylight hours, he drives with his pretty French secretary around the surrounding terrain where he only sees villagers peacefully transplanting rice in the paddies. I travel one day with a French soldier, just the two of us. He stops our ancient Citroen to walk down the muddy trail to a village. Sudden banging of tin pots! Tiny men rise out of rice paddies. A ragged headman confronts me with what looks like a rusty pistol. Tension rises in the hot, sticky air better suited for a lobster waiting to be boiled alive, which is how I feel.

"Reds!" warns my French army driver. He shouts to the farmers in their dialect. The drumming stops. The figures in black sink back into the paddies. "This is all that our colonel sees on his daylight rounds: exotic straw hats among pretty little green rice shoots," my driver confides later. "He's Napoleon and I'm just an old soldier. But with my comrades at night, I wear the black pajamas of these communist Vietminh. We fight an enemy that my old-fashioned colonel says we can find, fix and strike by daylight. He really believes he's another Napoleon. We ignorant *poilus* take matters into our own hands and fight primitively like the enemy."

Author inspects communist damage to a French fort in North French Indochina during his fifth trip there.

A few nights later the fort is attacked. I photograph the scarred battlements. The Vietminh have weapons, crudely improvised along with munitions smuggled across the China border. Communist peasants use booby traps and other tricks, more advanced than "primitive," although our local Napoleon still scorns them.

In Saigon, through "Mister Four-Five-Six," I listen to Jean-Paul Claude of the Direction Generale de la Securite Exterieuere. "I must move to Canada where they speak French—Quebec, yes? The situation here is hopeless. US intelligence teams interfere. They hire Vietnamese spies who are my double agents. I use them to feed false information to the communists. The Americans don't want to hear this. They say, 'Don't tell us how to win our war. You lost yours.'"

He opens his files. They go back to Ho Chi Minh's cooperation with the United States against Japan. "Uncle Ho," says Jean-Paul, "was an ally who wanted to end colonialism. We could have negotiated a settlement. Now Ho gets help and advisers from the Soviet bloc and the US reaction will be suicidal—a fatal full-scale invasion."

I learn that Ho worked his passage to France as a ship's deckhand when he was a boy. Under other names, he took the most poorly paid jobs in France, England, Ireland, and the United States, or so he claims in his autobiography. My own research shows that, with other young poverty-stricken rebels against Western imperialism, he turns to communism. He writes passionate poetry and articles about Vietnam. Zhou Enlai befriends him. The scholar and the self-educated peasant look to the Soviet Union for help. By the Second World War, Ho Chi Minh, under yet another pseudonym, is a seasoned guerrilla.

On July 16, 1945, while Japan still occupies French Indochina, an American OSS intelligence officer and two enlisted men parachute into Tonkin where a landing zone is prepared by a Chinese-American, Lieutenant Frank Tan. Together, under the code name of The Deer Team, they assist a Vietnamese independence movement: the "Viet Minh" led by Ho, using another nom-de-guerre: Nguyen Ai Quoc. He tackles a formidable trek through jungle and mountains, and over what was then known as "The Burma Hump," to reach Kunming, the Chinese headquarters of US-backed Nationalists led by General Chiang Kai-shek, who confines him to filthy Nationalist jails. Major General Clair Chennault of the famous Flying Tigers liberates "Uncle Ho" and arms him with a sack of pistols. Ho walks back to Tonkin with his sack of guns, while suffering from malaria and dengue fever. His

Author (right) with a French commando and his communist prisoners in North Vietnam. 1956.

life is saved by the Deer Team's chief, Major Allison Thomas, and his medical orderly.

The so-called "Burma Hump" is the seemingly endless, winding ribbon of dirt road pioneered by US soldiers. When I live in Washington, D.C., many years later with my second wife, Monika Jensen, I meet one of the soldiers. "We were all black," he tells us. "And we never got credit for building what's now known as the Burma Road. It's China's most important highway into regions where the communists hope to dominate."

With a premonition that I shall explore the Burma Road many times in the future, I decide I must interview Ho. Dragons bring up my old notes describing Ho as a will-o'-the-wisp who won the West's admiration when his Viet Minh forces were trained by US military officers to fight the Japanese. His chief aide was "Comrade Vo," who was identified by his French colonial white suit and black fedora when he helped rescue American fliers. After Japan's defeat, Ho led a Viet Minh victory parade that honored the US Deer Team. But the team was then disbanded and ordered home. Comrade Vo put away his black fedora and became General Vo Nguyen Giap, the supreme military commander who inflicted the final French defeat at Dien Bien Phu in 1954, and overwhelms US forces twenty-eight years later.

I use guile to organize a private meeting with Ho. My dragons remember that I thought it might not yet be too late to get him to imitate Tito. "Uncle Ho needs Soviet munitions smuggled across the border with China," I cable INTER. "His broader vision is narrowed by a fanatical Politburo. It anticipates American 'aggression' and forces Ho to lean on Russia and China." Sir William Stephenson responds this time by airmail. "You might think it useful to try for another Tito. But Whitehall civil servants fear losing pensions if they contradict the flavor of the day." His caustic words are in this old letter delivered to Vietnam by "safe hand" from World Commerce. INTER's enterprise is now tucked out of sight in Bermuda. Unless there is any urgency, we prefer letters to cables for reasons of security. I reply: "When French reporters catalogue the pileup of disastrous miscalculations in French Indochina, colonial authorities get them recalled to Paris. French reporters familiar with Mao's tactics in

China foresee the pattern being repeated here. But the colonizers stick to old habits, imposing their imperial will on 'ignorant' peasants to turn them into French cannon fodder."

This contempt for the locally hired help is dramatized when I fly with Aigle Azure, a small military-funded airline. I board one of its battered old Dakotas with Jim Cameron to fly to Laos, a landlocked French colony threatened by communist uprisings. The Dakota is adapted for dropping paratroopers recruited from Hmong tribesmen. The plane's rear doors are removed for quick and easy exit. The mercenaries sit in single file on the oily floor, parachutes within reach. Cameron and I squat with three Hmong behind and several more ahead. The pilot makes a lazy climbing turn, feeling his way through heavy rain curtaining the airstrip. The Hmong slide toward the tail. I am grabbed by Cameron, squatting behind me. The men behind him are falling helplessly through open doors. He groans, "The men don't have their 'chutes and I don't have a lifeline!"

The plane levels out in time to save Cameron from sliding out with the luckless trio. The French crew seems undismayed. The Hmong are disposable. Their leader is Vang Pao. Later, his anti-communist forces are funded by the CIA, whose chief, William Colby, calls Vang Pao "the biggest hero of the Vietnamese war." But right now, Cameron wires his column to London and the *News Chronicle,* lamenting this indifference to the tribesmen's fate. His editors spike the column. This is not the first time by a long shot that Cameron has been silenced. From Korea, he reported the spectacle of communist suspects, stripped of their clothing and strapped to the front of US army jeeps in the bitter cold. *Picture Post,* London's answer to *Life* magazine, had an edition ready to go, with a front-page photo of frozen prisoners. The UK government ordered the editor, Tom Hopkinson, to scrap it. Much later, in South Africa, the still-rebellious Hopkinson tells me, "Whitehall shrank from offending the Yanks."

My report on the accidental dropping of Hmong paratroops without their parachutes is tossed aside, but not for diplomatic reasons. Any story about the Hmong would require lengthy explanations and merely make readers yawn. And so I write detailed accounts to INTER, as usual my own escape hatch and private lifeline.

# CHAPTER 21

# Enter the Dragon Lady

I REDISCOVER RENA, THE POLISH NEWS AGENCY GIRL I FIRST MET IN
Mexico when I cornered Trotsky's assassin. I find my notes on her, written
while I puzzled over an old bronze plaque from my past. It records the
North American Aviation Writers' Association award of 1954 for "Outstanding Reporting." My editor-in-chief, Jim Kingsbury, accepts it "on
behalf of Mister Stevenson who is... ah! ... somewhere between Tokyo
and Cairo."

In fact, I am flying a trimotor Junkers, one of Nazi Germany's warplanes, later commandeered by the French Air Force. The tough old
bombers now look as ramshackle as their French crews who used them
in the battle of Dien Bien Phu, which ended colonial rule in French
Indo-China. I find a link between Rena and the French politician Pierre
Mendes-France, who spent years demanding that France withdraw from
Indo-China. As a Free French Air Force pilot, he delivered to French
Resistance armies the improvised devices later copied by France's enemies
in its Asian colonial outpost. Rena is a source of further intelligence during Mendes-France's premiership in 1954. Her disclosures influence the
French leader to hold secret talks with Zhou Enlai, who proposes a truce
between France and the Viet Minh. Rena conjoins events across time. I
remember her anger at the West's wartime failure to help Jan Karski and
the Polish underground. I still wonder about her true motives and beliefs.

Rena now leads a Polish team of peacekeepers in Hanoi. Canada,
India, and Poland form an International Control Commission (ICC) that
monitors the truce. Rena undermines the ICC by helping Ho smuggle

Soviet and Chinese military aid across the northern border. She is called The Dragon Lady by frustrated ICC colleagues. Some pieces of this puzzle I know as Rena begin to fall together when my dragons whiz me back to the final defeat of the French in March 1954. Deaf to alarms sounded by the Paris press, the French army concentrated 11,000 soldiers in the deep valley surrounded by jungle known as Dien Bien Phu. I fly over this echo of the old Beau-Geste fort mentality and it reminds me of the mind-set of the colonel I saw happily cruise by daylight out of his fort and into territory controlled by night by the Viet Minh. The valley is a gigantic version of the fort that bottled up battle-hardened French Legionnaires. Many are former German prisoners of war captured during the Second World War by the French, who offered them freedom in the Foreign Legion. The ex-POWs fight on. Other German POWs were sent home long ago.

Dien Bien Phu is attacked by the Viet Minh with improvised weapons, backed by Russian mortars and rocket launchers and howitzers smuggled in from China. Within moments of the battle's commencement, Colonel Christian de Castries loses the first of his nine fortified strong points. The rest collapse, one by one. Within weeks, he signals "The end is near. I am blowing up all our installations. . . . Adieu! Vive la France!"

This eerie finale to French rule is recalled when dragons recover my old 100 mm rolls of film shot on Friday, May 13, 1955. I walk with a Canadian ICC observer alongside Vietminh forces who tolerate us on the last stretch through the port city of Haiphong. The first sweat of the day trickles down our faces: early mists dissolve above brilliant squares of paddy, or linger in villages behind flimsy-looking bamboo fences. Russian trucks driven by Chinese Red Army soldiers hang back to leave the rest of the day to tiny Vietminh soldiers in jungle green, slipping silently on sandals re-fashioned from bits of tires stripped from the French army's abandoned vehicles. French soldiers walk backward, surrendering one street after another in impressively disciplined submission to the armistice accord. The streets are lined with neatly spaced poplar trees like those that flanked the refugee-clogged roads after Hitler invaded France. Now the French point their weapons at ragged Viet Minh guerrillas who slip forward from tree to tree. The French slow-march backward, weapons aimed but never fired, oddly symbolic of the war run from forts where I stayed with French colonels who scorned the threadbare foe. My Canadian ICC companion says, "This is worse than watching your best friend's funeral." General Rene Cogny is burying seventy years of French rule and memories of 71,500 soldiers killed in eight years of fighting Ho. At the end of this set-piece withdrawal, the last French soldiers board French warships. Eight buglers sound *descente des couleurs.* Garde Republicaine troops disappear into the supply ship *Jules Verne.* The last lament comes from a Moroccan Legionnaire guarding abandoned knapsacks, scattered bedrolls, and notched rifles. He plays *"Malbrooke s'en va-t-en guerre"* on a mouth organ: A requiem to the French Empire in Asia.

The Vietminh flow forward. There is no crash of boots, no thunder of tanks, no shouted orders. Several thousand more peasant soldiers move softly through houses, shops, and bistros where bottles of Pernod gather dust and whorehouse signs fade. "Re-education" begins with a version of Chairman Mao's Three Cardinal Rules of Discipline and Eight Reminders, formulated for the Chinese Workers and Peasant Red Army. The rules copy those of Hung Hsu-ch'uan, leader of the Taiping uprisings a century ago. Like Ho Chi Minh today, old Hung ordered his peasant army to befriend citizens, pay for everything used, avoid damaging crops, and use persuasion, not force.

And now, here in North Vietnam, clocks are turned back one hour to conform to Beijing time.

———

Before this final French exit, I fly in a converted German Ju-52 bomber. The last of the French commanders in the north lets me observe a final effort to hit Ho Chi Minh's jungle hideout around Thai Nguyen. Intelligence on Ho's location always proves wrong. Ho's moles planted in the French intelligence service warn Ho with details of where the Junker trimotors will strike next. Ho fades into some other bit of jungle. It all looks the same from above. The French dump bombs on a featureless green canopy. The captain invites me to fly the Junker back to Hanoi. He and

Author about to fly French Air Force Ju-52 seized from the German Air Force after WWII for their operations against the communists in North Indochina.

his crew curl up in the metal cavern astern and fall asleep. I'm so intent on handling the unfamiliar wooden steering wheel that I'm startled when the captain, rubbing his eyes, croaks that we seem to have overshot Hanoi, overshot Haiphong, and appear to be above Baie d'Along, the Bay of Dragons. I was down there once, with a wearily disillusioned French news correspondent, Lucien Bodard. We were with cynical French soldiers in an old landing-barge wallowing between conelike islands in a fore-doomed hunt for Vietminh guerrillas who cut throats quicker than the eye can see. I tell the bomber pilot I have no wish to ditch among them now. He laughs good-naturedly. We turn back to Hanoi. There we quaff rough red Algerian wine from big wicker caskets. The crew has flown so many fruitless missions, they don't care anymore about anything much except going home to a vineyard, or buying a small bistro with pay they accumulated during years mucking about in a senseless war.

I never report my unprofessional conduct in piloting a French bomber, so this cannot explain the Aviation Writers Award. Nor do I report this attempt to bomb Ho's hideout. I don't want to ruin my chances of inter-viewing any communist leaders during the subsequent truce. In Hanoi is Wilfred Burchett, a London newsman who moved to the Soviet side. I had seen him earlier in New Delhi, desperate to return to his native Aus-tralia, where he was banned as a Red. Once again, past distractions link up with later opportunities. I had seen in Delhi a new British governor-general who fought with General Orde Wingate in Burma. Burchett also served in Wingate's Chindit lone rangers with the governor-general when they fought alongside communist guerrillas against Japan. I bring him together with Burchett, who later tells me: "'What-ho!' says the guv. 'Been up to some mischief since we last met, eh?' And he fixed it for me to enter Australia and visit my sick daughter."

So Burchett owes me. He now occupies the former Hanoi residence of the departed British consul, Denis Duncanson, who has told me that Burchett is respected in North Vietnam as an adviser on foreign relations. Duncanson, before he left, reinforced a suggestion that I place before Ho Chi Minh: a British offer to follow Tito's example and escape Soviet control. Did Burchett put in a good word for me? Or did it come from the Polish agent I knew as Rena in Mexico, now damned as The Dragon Lady in Hanoi? I learn of her hatred of Russia during a journey with her across the Soviet Union to Red China. She grew up in a Catholic Polish community. What inner conflict torments her now, when thousands of Catholics flee south to escape Ho Chi Minh?

I meet a French priest, bicycling the other way, back to his flock in the Red River Delta.

"You face torture and death," I tell him.

"I have no choice," he replies. "What's left of my parishioners need me." He bikes off. In his own way, he represents the resolve of his enemy, Ho Chi Minh, who was born to Catholic parents.

Dragons again leap across timelines to remind me of events separated on the calendar. Heavily guarded doors open for me to enter what was once the Emperor Bao Dai's palace, re-christened in 1955 by President Ho as "The Palace of the People."

# CHAPTER 22

# Who Is Ho?

UNDER A MOSQUITO NET IN MY ROOM AT THE METROPOLE HOTEL, I AM suffocating from the heat and wondering: Is it a lichee bird crying plaintively outside, or another Vietminh patrol leader whistling in code to his scouts? Dawn in Hanoi always begins with the screech of cicadas, making me think of a million steel blades held against the iron wheels of artillery dragged by an army of converted knife sharpeners.

"Mister William Seemen!" The familiar voice pierces the competing racket. Comrade Duc bangs on my door. I can tell he is in a flap. We went through this same procedure yesterday when his panicky voice led me to a pair of tame monks who gabbled on about Uncle Ho's enlightened policy on Buddhism.

This time I detect a truly astronomic hysteria. It rises above the ear-splitting noise from the cicadas. If I pretend not to hear Duc, he will report to the bar boy who used to reel home on the dregs of French officers' drinks. He found redemption in the wine cellars, persuaded by Vietminh brain-washing experts. Now he keeps tabs on my exits and entrances. Where French colonels once sat with their ladies, the stools are empty and the counters are bare. The boy wipes them over and over, eager to prove his salvation, along with whatever tales he can make up about the hotel's new generation of guests: the ICC's Poles and Indians and Canadians. And me.

"Mister William! You are ten minutes late already!" Comrade Duc is in a panic.

If only to save the bar boy's neck, I grope for my clothes while the first heavy sweat of the day trickles down my back. I wriggle into an old Viyella shirt, too solid for the tropics but least likely to fall apart in this heat. Shove feet into sandals. Pull on scuffed chinos. No belt! O Lor', where is it? Grab necktie to hold up pants. Stagger to door. Confront Duc in one of those threadbare blue tunics that always remind me of patched school uniforms.

"Late!" he manages to cluck.

"Late for what?"

"The president!"

So it's really happening! I hold onto the door frame. "I can't go like this!"

"President is waiting. No time! No time!"

In emperor Bao Dai's palace in 1956 at Hué before it was taken over by Ho Chi Minh and later briefly by American Forces during the Vietnam War.

I fear Comrade Duc is about to enter a catatonic state like the one into which Chairman Chang fell when I drifted into Mongolia. I'd better not keep Uncle Ho waiting. For Duc's sake, I necktie my trousers.

We rush through what was once the manicured courtyard of the last emperor's palace. The Vietminh have caught the Maoist Chinese infection. Even temples become palaces of political diligence. But the vast entry hall boasts only two rusty chairs, two chipped enamel washbasins, and two empty camp beds. Comrade Duc is poised in front of enormous studded doors. Can he open them?

A soft voice behind me says in English, hesitant, almost apologetic, "We got you up early."

I turn to confront a thin man with a gaunt face, a straggly beard, and a head of stringy gray hair. His narrow eyes study me through smudged spectacles taped across the bridge of his nose. His khaki tunic is buttoned at the neck. Bleached pants reach halfway down thin legs. Black sandals are cut from old French army truck tires.

I fumble a reply, "C'est-moi, Uncle H-Ho. Who got you up early."

My sudden nervous twitch hits the right note. Ho Chi Minh chuckles, rests a hand on my shoulder. The studded doors swing open. Ho propels me to a wooden table at the very center of a vast rotunda. I glimpse two small men in blue uniforms closing the doors again. I'm alone with this man who looks older than his calendar years. I should call him "President." Yet "Ho" springs to mind after so much research on this former ally of US Special Forces. His facial skin is still the yellowish color of the victim of malaria and dengue fever who was saved in 1944 by the clandestine US Deer Team. This is the poverty-stricken lad who washed dishes in the galley of a French ocean liner to get to Europe. Who wrote about his time in the United States during the Great War of 1914–18. Who was spokesman for Vietnam at the 1919 Versailles peace conference when the victors refused to assign a seat for China or Vietnam. Who in despair met with Lenin and Trotsky at a Comintern congress in Moscow. Who was sentenced to death in French Indochina after starting a peasant revolution in 1930 under another name. Who publicly quoted Abraham Lincoln on freedom. No wonder I think "Who?" and call him "Ho." Who is Ho? So many conflicting sides to his story! Can he be won over, like Tito, as a tough communist guerrilla fighter willing to work with the West to loosen Moscow's grip?

Two sturdy mugs appear, steaming with a local tea whose leaves form a solid black base. The brew is heavily, pleasantly scented. I sit on a chair facing Ho across the table. Both chairs have pink cushions. Pink! Is this the sole surviving trace of French self-indulgence? No hint here of cognac or the rough Algerian wine the colonizers imported. Certainly no champagne. Uncle Ho's sole addiction seems to be hand-rolled cigarettes. He snaps open a crude lighter. Looks like an assembly of bits cut from discarded cans of French corned beef. Must have been improvised by his inventors of booby traps. It reflects a golden sheen from the early sunshine creeping through the rotunda's glass roof. He offers me lumpy brown biscuits that materialize out of nowhere. Perhaps delivered by the skinny comrades lurking in the shadows? They look like veterans of clandestine operations. Are they ready to refill the mugs? Or shoot me?

Ho lights up and says, "You smoke a pipe."

He has seen photographs of me standing in front of a French conversion of a German bomber. I looked slightly idiotic, with a droopy moustache, a pipe sticking out of my mouth. He says, "Please smoke."

"I gave up smoking," I reply. "It—well—you know, I found a pipe made me sleepy."

He nods pleasantly. I dip my face into my mug. He says, "The tea is from my native province of Nghe An between the north and south of our country."

"It is good tea. Good for export to England."

"You drink much tea in England. I remember."

"You were a long time in England." I mean to make it a question but it comes out flat.

"You have done your homework. The English at home are good. As colonizers, not so good."

"They are no longer colonizers, Mister President." I try not to see him as Uncle Ho. He is, after all, titular head of the Democratic Republic of Vietnam, the DRV.

"England's empire still spans all continents and oceans," he replies drily.

"Old colonies are now part of a new Commonwealth."

"Still run from London."

"A matter of convenience. The Commonwealth brings together new leaders in a Colombo Plan for economic aid to old colonies." I add helpfully, "A plan born in Colombo—in Ceylon."

"All decisions come from London, the old imperial capital."

"Not really. Although all decisions do rely on historical data stored in London. All Commonwealth leaders meet there to discuss how best we can work together."

"And sometimes the Queen Elizabeth flies into the other capitals to watch the natives in costume, sing and dance in native rites." He stubs the cigarette in the lid of another old tin can that also materializes miraculously on the table. His smile reflects some inner amusement. He knows why I'm here.

"I am asked to offer you an invitation to join the Colombo Plan as a partner in mutual aid."

"So we depend less on our foreign comrades." He's ahead of me.

"You can continue economic cooperation with other communist states, separately."

He says, with the quick ferocious emphasis of the pitiless victor at Dienbienphu, "We did not push the imperialists out through the front door only to have them return through the window."

This is the end. Full stop! I tell myself. Uncle Ho's been told I'm on a specific mission.

The mission had originated with Malcolm Macdonald, son of Britain's first Labour Prime Minister, Ramsey MacDonald, and former governor-general in Canada, now Britain's High Commissioner in Malaya. Malcolm had befriended Zhou Enlai and hoped to build bridges, form alliances with South Asian leaders, and raise barriers against Soviet domination. But Ho is hemmed in by opponents within his Politburo. They view any conciliatory proposal as a cunning feint. "Uncle Ho" is now a puppet whose strings are pulled by comrades dazzled by what they admire as China's huge military victories in Korea against the mighty US war machine.

I am wrong about Ho being ineffective. He murmurs an order. A young helper springs out of the woodwork. I remember being escorted to Ho's old underground headquarters at Thai Nguyen. There was no evidence of human habitation in that forested hillside. Ho's men emerged as if by magic. Here in the presidential palace, I wonder if he communicates by mental telepathy, which is, of course, absurd.

"I was in the jungle a long time," he tells me now. "You speak of mutual aid. Our mutual aid came in the form of French paratroops. At Dienbienphu, we captured them and used their parachutes for shelter—"

This is an unexpected chance to learn more about Ho's final victory. "How?"

He responds with a clucking of the tongue. The sound can be mistaken for one of a multitude of noises made by strange insects in the jungle. Or by Hanoi's cicadas. An orderly appears with the battered old sun helmet I have seen on Ho's head in Jean-Paul's French intelligence photographs.

He inverts the helmet on the table and points into the crown. "Down here the French put all ground forces. We surround them along the rim. Imperialists underestimate the resourcefulness of our people."

"You had heavy weapons from the Soviet Union. Artillery, mortars, anti-aircraft guns." I quote General Chu Van Tan, president of the Executive Committee of the First Inter-Zone. "He got angry when I said this was more than unconventional weapons improvised by the people."

"He is right to be angry. All these many years, by our own ingenuity, we fight and capture weapons from the enemy. You have seen what served as our headquarters, a hole we kept changing in the jungle. The French kept bombing, always claiming to have killed me. They used napalm. Such atrocities harden the resolve of the people."

I quote words Ho is said to have spoken after he arrived from Paris to campaign for communism: "Overthrow tyrannical government in Siam . . . Unite under the struggle against the king of Siam."

He responds smoothly that things were different then. "Siam got rid of its king. It became Thailand. It is our neighbor. It was an obstacle to Asian revolution but . . ." He shrugs. "It brought back the monarchy and a new young king who makes changes in a new Siam, land reform, barefoot doctors."

"But part of Siam is Laos . . ."

"It is independent but landlocked."

"Your guerrilla forces were able to take it to defeat the French at Dienbienphu."

"General Giap won the victory. His wife was jailed by French colonialists. They killed his sister. He had every reason to win. The French put all their military power here!" Ho points again into the bowl of his old helmet. "The French have no more fight in them once they see they have no future here. They already lost all support back home. In Paris, nobody wants to hear any more about this old French Indochine."

General Vo Nguyen Giap is twenty-two years younger than Uncle Ho, and he is now the supreme military leader, commanding a legendary adoration among the masses. Exactly one month after this interview, Ho is received in Moscow and Beijing. China grants him the equivalent of 300 million dollars in aid, an enormous sum at the time. The Soviets offer aid worth more than 90 million dollars and an immediate shipment to North Vietnam of 150,000 tons of rice from Burma. That's the Sino-Soviet answer to our penny-pinching Colombo Plan.

I write a profile of Ho Chi Minh for the *Sunday Times* of London. A Vietnamese school textbook produces an edited version, printed on cheap paper improvised from wilderness fibers. The text leaves out my references to the Party's acceptance of Soviet dictates and does not quote my questions about touchy issues, but it does include a comparison of Ho to Tito. This little book, reprinted with a cover that calls me a "Literary Hero," gets me out of a jam many years later when I re-visit Vietnam with Dana Delaney, star of the TV series *China Beach*. By then, the country has survived its costly war with the United States with heavy casualties on both sides and a final hurried exit by American forces. A new Vietnam absorbs the damage from US aerial bombings and the reduction to wasteland by chemicals showered from the air. It wins a subsequent brisk but savage frontier war initiated by Maoist China that challenges the conventional wisdom of Western intelligence analyses that Beijing's communist warlords are obedient servants of the Soviet Union in its conspiracy to control the world. Vietnam remains a communist state, now unified and refusing to blindly obey the dictates of the Kremlin or the Forbidden City. Its people prove to be resilient and inventive. Vietnam's peasants are on their way to building a moderately successful economic power by drawing upon their own mental and physical skills and their own natural resources.

How many lives might have been saved, how much history would have been changed, if the United States had continued to work with Ho against Japan? The West might have made a Tito out of him, after all.

# CHAPTER 23

# Odd Friends and Confessions

APRIL 1955 IS WHEN I AM TOLD "HO CHI MINH OR ZHOU ENLAI CAN still follow Tito's example," by Malcolm MacDonald. The dragons of notional proximity leap across the calendar and remind me that this is when China lacks transport planes for long flights and Nehru makes available the Kashmir Princess, pride of India's commercial aircraft, so that Zhou and his staff can fly directly to that first Afro-Asian conference. I am invited to join the Chinese delegation for the journey to Bandung on the island of Java in Indonesia. At the last moment, I am warned not to board the plane in Hong Kong by a phone call from the New China News Agency. The British embassy in Beijing is also told the Kashmir Princess is a target but brushes this aside as another case of Maoist neurosis. There are no US diplomats in China and US newsmen are still forbidden by the US State Department to enter the country. Washington still treats "the Gimo," Generalissimo Chiang Kai-shek and his Nationalists, as the rightful government of China although Chiang has retreated to Taiwan, also known as Formosa.

Zhou takes an alternative route, using short-range Chinese planes to cross to the northern tip of the Burma Road, refuel in Kunming, and slip across Burma and Thailand to Singapore. I fly by a Western airline from Hong Kong and meet MacDonald in his role as High Commissioner for South Asia. He invites Zhou Enlai to "arrange to have some engine trouble" on the last leg of his journey to Bandung. If the secret rendezvous in Singapore leaks out, it will inflame British expatriates in Singapore and Malaya who think MacDonald is so far to the left that he might as

140

well wave his Party membership card. While he confers with Zhou in a discreet corner of Singapore airport, news breaks of an explosion on board the Kashmir Princess in mid-flight. All Zhou's support staff are lost. MacDonald later provides Zhou with physical proof that a bomb was planted by the CIA proprietary in Taiwan, Western Enterprises, after the Royal Navy finally recovers the telltale fragments.

MacDonald describes his stealthy meeting with Zhou Enlai as "the start of one of the most fascinating friendships of my life." He says Zhou really does want good relations with Britain and cites Tito's cooperation after breaking with Moscow, saying, "Yugoslavia stays communist but outside Moscow's control."

In Bandung, Zhou speaks as China's foreign minister, telling some thirty Afro-Asian delegations that most of their countries "suffer from neocolonialism. If we seek common ground to remove the misery imposed upon us, we can respect and help each other."

Mao, in an official Chinese version broadcast from Beijing, reverses Zhou's appeal to "let us all live together in peace." This follows the disclosure that a bomb was set to explode when the Bandung-bound Indian airliner reached cruising altitude. Although in Hong Kong this is never disclosed, everyone in that colony seems to know that one of the airport ground staff slipped back to Taiwan the second he was identified as the saboteur.

MacDonald continues to believe that a form of Asian Titoism can emerge in opposition to policies dictated from Moscow. He hoped I would find a ready ear in Ho Chi Minh. Neither Ho nor Zhou is willing to ignore US displays of military might along the periphery of communist Asia. Someone along the Beijing-Hanoi axis made the decision to stop me from boarding the doomed Kashmir Princess. The tantalizing question is why and who?

I ask Intrepid. In our swift INTER-STEVERITE exchanges, Sir William Stephenson and I mask details. Cables are composed with care. References to people and locations are oblique, sometimes made comprehensible with follow-up air letters that read to the uninitiated like harmless gossip. This is safer than sending telegrams in code, easily intercepted by hostile cryptographers who have the talent to solve such riddles.

"Rena tells me she hates Jacson as much as she does yellow flower." Up comes this example of one such air letter, more detailed than most, understandable to Stephenson as referring to past notes on Rena in Mexico, to the false name used by Trotsky's assassin, and to Mao's closest aide, Yellow Flower.

I had bumped into Rena at Moscow airport after flying there from Kiev, where I interviewed the president of the Academy of Sciences. With me was Welles Hangen of the *New York Times* and Niels Bohr, the physicist who helped the United States build the first atomic bomb. We are told about Sputnik, the first man-made object soon to be launched into space. Hangen is later killed in the secret US war in Cambodia.

An old photograph reminds me of how I got into Russia in 1956–57. It is an informal and, yet in retrospect, a very revealing, picture of Nikita Khrushchev after his condemnation of Stalin's excesses. His "de-Stalinisation speech" emboldened him and Nikolai Bulganin to break out of the closed Russian world and plunge into the West's old colonies with enticing promises of Soviet support for local pro-communist uprisings.

I am in India, standing in front of Khrushchev. Brilliant sunshine shines through the back of the tropical straw hat that he waves to the crowd. I take the shot with my old Rolleiflex, and Cyrillic characters are clearly etched inside the crown of Khrushchev's quaintly imperialist hat. It is unique. The unified communist world is still run out of Moscow and it has a face. That face—deceptively jolly, visibly topped in this moment of exposure by a shiny gray-fringed dome—belongs to Nikita Khrushchev, general secretary of the Soviet communist Party, grandson of a serf, son of a miner, fizzing with ruthless energy and unschooled native intelligence. I have read that he is a chronically optimistic opportunist. On a hunch, I mail a color print by way of the *Toronto Star* "To Mr. Khrushchev c/o The Kremlin." Then I apply for entry into the Soviet Union. It seems like mere days before I am directed to the Russian fisheries liaison office in Tokyo. But in Japan, the Soviet fisheries team tells me sternly: "Russia has no diplomatic relations with Japan. Try Istanbul."

In Turkey, at some sort of disguised Russian diplomatic outpost, I am told my only way to reach Moscow is by way of Latvia. The only

Soviet-approved Latvian flights to Moscow, it turns out, originate in Sweden. I am still based in Hong Kong but I have my handy air-travel credit card by which to fly from pillar to post. Later dragon notes explain this odd dance of the visas.

In Moscow, I find little to inspire news reporting that will escape Soviet oversight. I never see Khrushchev again. Doubtless my visa was deemed reward enough for my photographic initiative. But I can at least see a lot of Russia if I fly from Moscow to Beijing. I explain this is the most convenient way to rejoin my family in Hong Kong. At Moscow airport, a Polish girl asks me how to get to China. It's Rena! I am astonished when she greets me as an old friend from odd encounters in strange places. I recall she is still Poland's representative on the three-nation ICC Control Commission in North Vietnam, known as The Dragon Lady by other ICC peacekeepers because she sabotages the purpose of the mission. Rena is flying back to Hanoi by way of Beijing. "Moscow airport never puts up departure boards!" she explodes. "Citizens are treated worse than animals."

We find the same puddle jumper to China. She sits with me for the longest flight of my life. All along the way, she savages the Kremlin's invocation to its satellites: "Build socialism first in the Soviet Union." She says it's a confidence trick. "Russia sucks up Poland's resources while we sink deeper into poverty."

Fellow passengers are privileged members of the Party or they would never be on a flight to anywhere. They could spend the rest of their lives in jail, trying to convince the KGB they did not agree with the Polish girl's tirades. Luckily, on this bulky Antonov biplane, the single piston engine and four wooden propeller blades make enough noise to drown conversation beyond each pair of its twelve seats, and the pilot is isolated inside a closed cockpit. The An-2 is a rare sanctuary. Rena takes full advantage.

We hop between little fields. The An-2's range is limited. It can plonk down into small farm plots. Its top speed is 130 miles an hour. In 35 mph headwinds, of which there are many, it flies briefly backward. If the speed drops below 40 mph, slats on the leading edge of its wings extend on elastic rubber bands and it descends in stately fashion like an enormous parachute. It is impossible to stall. Rena knows all this because Poland builds this model, nicknamed "kukuruznik" in honor of workers in the fields of maize. Best of all, she knows she has an eternity to blow off steam. She is interrupted when we stop at a real airport, because I am the only passenger allowed ashore, a foreigner who warrants the facilities of a regular airline.

"Eat! Drink!" booms the bosomy boss of a restaurant barred to my fellow passengers. It looks like a hangover from Tsarist days: food displayed behind finely woven curtains, lace doilies, hefty steaks, and lots of vodka. Terrified by this giantess, I gorge under her gaze. She can tell I'm a wicked capitalist. She intends to convert me. All other passengers meekly wait in the Antonov. My matronly hostess wants to load me with so much booze and protein that I shall never nurse a single solitary misconception about the benefits of life behind the Iron Curtain. I wobble back to the plane and stagger down the narrow aisle, aware of covert glances of envy or hate. I sink beside Rena, who is drinking vodka the Polish way, slicing salted radishes with a pocket knife smeared in butter. I suppose she smuggles vodka and radishes the way she smuggles Kalashnikovs into North Vietnam. But I have never seen her touch alcohol in Hanoi. Now she ceases to be the Kremlin's obedient servant. All her personal rage and frustration has been bottled up, waiting for this chance to explode.

"Reserved for the Party aristocracy," she says, nodding in the direction of the restaurant, dissolving in a cloud of snow as our biplane swivels for takeoff. "And for rotten capitalists, so you report Russia is paradise." Rena picks up the thread of her complaints and confessions. "This very morning, in my hotel, I go for breakfast at the first-floor restaurant and order bacon and one fried egg. The waitress says, 'Comrade, here you get two eggs. One egg is on second floor.' I tell her, 'Then slice off one egg. I don't want to go upstairs.' She insists: 'One egg is on second floor. Here is two eggs.' I am a bad egg for wasting good Russian eggs."

I really cannot believe she is here to entrap me, even if, in Hanoi, she does betray other ICC truce commissioners trying to keep the peace. In Beijing, she continues to blast the Russians when I invite her to dinner at The Three Tables, where everything remains the same as when I was last

144

there. Comradely Chinese waiters treat her with respect, unlike the Moscow bumpkins. Rena announces that "even Chinese mao-tai is better than Russian vodka." She adds hastily, "Although Polish vodka is best of all."

She tells me that her comrades at the Polish embassy are furious.

"Goodness! Why?" I ask innocently.

"They wait for months to get a reservation at The Three Tables. Not even the ambassador can jump the queue. But you just walk in. You! The wicked capitalist."

"Perhaps Mao needs foreign friends to counter your ill-mannered Russian allies," I suggest half-jokingly.

"Russians have contempt for Chinese." Her laughter is bitter. "Mao thinks the Russians are primitive but he always needed their arsenals. Now he's close to breaking off relations." She confides the astonishing details, gleaned from her Polish embassy colleagues.

I file from Beijing that Nikita Khrushchev, having denounced Stalin, now launches fierce criticisms of Mao. My report enrages foreign leftists who suck up to Beijing's rulers for scraps of news. How can an outsider get such an exclusive? My source is Chairman Mao's translator-turned-diplomat, Yellow Flower, Huang Hua, angered by Khrushchev's mockery of Mao's campaign to "Let all flowers bloom." Yellow Flower's pseudonym seems like a sour comment on Mao's invitation to dissidents to voice criticisms. Millions who think that letting all flowers bloom is an invitation to speak freely expose their dissidence and die or go to Reform-Through-Labor camps. Even the most revered cultural figures are sent to toil as anonymous peasants in remote regions.

Rena speaks frankly because I show up in Moscow just when she needs a safety valve. She is angry with Khrushchev for bullying Poland's Peoples United Workers Party. Wladyslaw Gomulka was First Secretary in November 1956 when the Party defied Moscow. Stalinists in Warsaw lived like aristocrats. The workers became bold in their protests. Khrushchev tried to win time with promises of fair trade and cancellation of Poland's "debt" of more than two billion rubles. My earlier talks with Poland's leaders had been thinly disguised disclosures of dismay at Kremlin domination. Now those camouflaged criticisms jump across timelines.

Rena senses I understand her own inner rebellion while she still serves old doctrinal ideals.

In Hanoi later, she will do what she sees as her duty. Here in Beijing, she talks frankly. It's always the same. I roam through regulated societies and trigger frank disclosures: I guard against agents-provocateurs who might try to provoke me into self-incrimination. Rena's outbursts are genuine. She gets nothing out of them except The Three Tables' Peking Duck, roasted crispy brown, served in three courses: skin dipped in thick soya bean paste: raw green onion wrapped in tortillas: meat and bones boiled in a grand finale of cabbage and mushroom soup. And a continuous flow of mao-tai. "Makes Russian vodka taste like horse piss," she confides.

My first exploration of Poland had followed Rena's studies at the London School of Economics. When I revisit Warsaw, Rena's colleague Jana asks me never to identify her, for her own safety. My long relationship with the widely known author Han Suyin never requires such precautions. Her friendship with me becomes fractious after I write my first nonfiction book, *The Yellow Wind*. She misconstrues the title. The jacket on the US edition calls it "An excursion in and around Red China with a traveler in the Yellow Wind." This refers to the yellowish wind shrieking out of the Gobi desert, shrouding Beijing in much the same way Mao obscures political realities. The London edition has a cover showing masses of yellow-faced Chinese. Han Suyin mistakes the title, the blurb, and the UK cover as demeaning "the yellow races."

HCH ignores the book. It was written on *Toronto Star* time without his approval. I'm a dunce in the burgeoning business of plugging books. I never draw attention to a *New York Times* review by Edgar Snow, an authority on China, but I draw consolation from his comment: "More than any political or specialists' study, it gives the American reader some understanding, in human terms, of a new people and the secret of their power." I let this float on a private reflection that my mother would have deemed it worth reading to us children long ago.

# CHAPTER 24

# Double-think and Double Lives

HAN SUYIN, RENA, AND OTHERS ARE TRAPPED INSIDE TWO WORLDS. SO
I comment in old notes resurrected by the dragons: notes which quote
Han Suyin's lament at being torn between her bisexual and biracial per-
sonas. "In China I was a half-Belgian Eurasian. In the West I don't
belong to either."

She writes about Mao's benevolent reforms during the late 1950s.
I report that salaries, if any, remain the equivalent of US $4.00 a week
on which a Chinese family with two working parents might afford an
occasional movie. "Foreign films are more interesting," I quote a street-
car driver. "He has a family of ten crowded into a tiny brick house near
the Thieves Market. Soon, Mao's Cultural Revolution sniffs them out as
'enemies of the state.'"

Mao brainwashes the masses with double-talk, foreshadowed when I
studied psychological warfare. Zhou Enlai tells me, "When Mao achieved
power, we truly planned an agricultural and industrial infrastructure suited
to the China of 1949. Then US forces in Korea crossed the thirty-eighth
parallel. We could not remain passive."

On November 24, 1950, Zhou appealed for caution at the UN General Assembly but failed to stop 100,000 US troops from advancing to
the China border. "I had to send in 'Peoples Volunteers.' We forced US
forces into full retreat by the end of December. The UN branded us the
aggressor. I ran our Military Affairs Commission and had to take Russian
aid, which I had wanted to avoid. We paid heavily for Stalin's 'unselfish
fraternal help.'"

Han Suyin says I distort such realities. Yet I had happily reported an earlier Beijing, when the old city wall encompassed ancient traditions. "Sword dancers pose for photographs and tumblers ham it up. A fat little eunuch tells stories while juggling from the top of a swaying pole, and throws me a stepladder to follow his movements above a ring of onlookers. Behind cotton screens, jazz bands pound out a discordant "Tiger Rag" on rickety instruments. Workers roar with friendly laughter when they hear me speak 'Chinglish.'" I later describe "an old man with a bucket of crabs. If one crawls to the top, he knocks it down with a big stick. He reminds me of Mao."

This infuriates Han Suyin, who says she has exercised her influence to stop me returning to China. Then she says she is sorry. This double-think reminds me of Zhou Enlai, split between China and his sophisticated studies in Europe. On one of the several journeys I make along the Burma Road, he speaks about the need to protect China's southern borders against United States–backed Nationalist armies, pretending to guard against Maoist invaders while creating in Thailand the so-called Golden Triangle, center of a global trade in drugs. He quotes Mao's speech on New Democracy during the Long March when victory seemed a distant mirage. "Mao told us the only yardstick of truth is the revolutionary practice of millions, which seemed to mean the revolution could be whatever the masses wanted. But Mao also warned: Either you cooperate with the communist Party or you oppose it . . . The moment you oppose, you become a traitor (and) must be prepared to be ground into the dust."

Zhou had repeated these words during the Long March, and warned young Chinese not to turn Mao into a god. Mao took this to confirm Zhou's ambition to lead the Party. Mao's distrust degenerated into a deadly suspicion of Zhou's skill in handling China's relations with noncommunist governments.

Later, it was Zhou who was ground into the dust, and left to die by Mao.

Han Suyin, in another of her self-revealing books published in 1994, describes her own relations with Zhou. Her harshest critic, David Pryce-Jones, reviews her latest book in the London *Times* and describes Zhou

The author's first encounter with Red China's Mao Tse-tung was here at the Temple of Political Diligence (formerly Temple of Heaven). Mao's authority was still uncertain in 1950 when this picture was taken of survivors of his Long March to bring communism to China. All these traditional officials were executed by Mao by 1960, when his power was firmly established. This photo was presented to the author by Premier Zhou Enlai on one of his last visits to China.

"as one of the most cold-blooded and sinister characters in the entire historical phenomenon of communism." Ross Terrill, in a more kindly *New York Times* review, predicts that "some day, when all Zhou's contradictions are sorted out, we shall witness the myriad dramas of an exploding Chinese society."

Zhou always seems caught in contradictions like those plaguing Han Suyin. Her lover, Ian Morrison, understood her inner confusions. "Her contradictions were understandable," Morrison had told me before he was killed in Korea. "She was the daughter of a Chinese father and a Belgian mother. She was a fourteen-year-old typist at Beijing Hospital

149

in 1931, discriminated against for being Eurasian. She became wife of an anti-communist, National Chinese army general killed in the civil war. She graduated from London Free Hospital and became a doctor in Hong Kong, where she felt like an outsider among English colonizers."

*A Many-Splendored Thing* describes her affair with Morrison. She offers to share royalties with his widow, who does not respond. This baffles Han Suyin, living in two worlds, each with different rules. Her autobiographical novel of 1944 had disclosed her bisexual and biracial persona and this is echoed in her 1980 autobiography, *My House Has Two Doors*. And having said she will have me banned from China, she attends the baptism of my Sally, born in Hong Kong. Her Singapore husband is seen leaving the home of a murdered prostitute. She asks me to join her at the trial. "I must save him," she says. She ridiculed him in her novel, *The Mountain Is Young*. He is found innocent. He dies later and his police colleagues say his male pride was destroyed by her fictional version of his sexual incompetence.

She asks me to help buy a car in Singapore because, she says, "I know nothing about cars." I drive her home to Johor Bahru, where she already has a car. She asks me to look at a new book she is writing. She changes into nightwear. I read into the wee hours, then phone for a taxi back to my hotel, the Cockpit.

In Hong Kong, she visits my home. From our beach, she swims, slender as some exotic fish. Here she meets other correspondents. Phil Potter of the *Baltimore Sun* laps up her observations on Mao's China, where she is no longer despised as Eurasian, but is sent from Beijing on what she later calls "missions in America." But Madame Kung Peng tells me that Han Suyin bounces between opposite ends like a ball in table tennis.

If I dance with her at dinner dances anywhere between Hong Kong's Marco Polo Club and the Cockpit Hotel in Singapore, the band strikes up the theme of the movie about her love affair with Ian. She writes about the Cockpit as "the breeding ground" for gossip. It is, in fact, the only unregulated meeting place for interesting people. When Canada's prime minister John Diefenbaker comes here, I introduce his brother Elmer to a rich Chinese girl who whisks Elmer away in her sports car, delaying an official Canadian delegation's departure to Djakarta. The enchanting chanteuse at the Cockpit marries the editor of the *Straits Times,* Ron Baxter, who joins the British Foreign Service, which sends him to India, where he becomes my close friend and adviser. The Cockpit is more than a gossip's whispering gallery. Here Alex Josey writes pamphlets on Marxism to win friends in Red China. He is finally admitted into Beijing, and is thunderstruck when I turn up there from Moscow.

It is while lunching at the Cockpit that Han Suyin speaks of her abandoned husband's trial and repeats: "I must do what I can to save him."

I reply, "But you landed him in this mess in the first place."

"That's why I have to do what I can for him now."

Self-contradiction marks the lives of those dwelling on both sides of mutually hostile societies. Han Suyin befriends Glenys, who travels with me through India while I produce and host a TV documentary. Glenys leaves early to get back to our children in Hong Kong. Han Suyin meets her at Calcutta airport with offers of help. Yet Suyin also continues to maintain that she will stop my re-entry into China. A Xinhua news agency correspondent tells me that his cousin Zhou Enlai, who for now has the title of Premier, prefers visiting writers who are critical but not anti-Chinese. By contrast, Mao does not want foreign observers who like the Chinese people but expose his brutal reforms. Each admiring book that Han Suyin now writes on China is outdated before publication because of maverick changes in Mao's policies.

Nehru approves of Han Suyin's marriage to an Indian army officer in Nepal. This might help the Indian prime minister counter Chinese intrusions along the Himalayan frontier. But Nehru also lives in two worlds. He tells me, "I was jailed by British imperialists, yet adopted things they left behind, like rule of law." He pursues a love affair with Edwina, wife of Lord Louis Mountbatten, who divided the old Indian empire between Muslim-dominated Pakistan and the rest of the subcontinent. Lady Mountbatten dies suddenly in Borneo. I am with Nehru at a public event when her death is announced. Everyone looks for his reaction. He betrays nothing. Something transformed her from a pre-1939 rich socialite to a woman who served tirelessly the causes of the poor and wretched in

South Asia. She had questioned me in Nehru's presence about things I had seen and heard. One name sticks in memory: Auschwitz.

I write the book *After Nehru What?* He juggles conflicting influences. He reminds me of Han Suyin and others like Rena who confessed her hatred of the Soviet Union. Han Suyin finds ultimate security in Switzerland. Rena goes back to Hanoi to continue smuggling Soviet arms into North Vietnam, using her role as one of the ICC peacekeepers. A kind of civil war tears at the insides of such intelligent observers.

HCH had based me in Hong Kong for six months in 1954, and then he left me there for six years of nerve-wracking uncertainty. It is difficult to plan ahead. I keep up a rapid flow of reports from around the globe to confirm HCH's belief that the colony is the least costly base from which to dart in and out of developing conflicts. Glenys accepts my abrupt departures and swift returns. Sometimes she travels with me. She is still the girl who survived Coventry and, as a nurse, twice fished me out of smashed warplanes. She, too, recalls with nostalgia the lines, "I have slipped the surly bonds of earth" from High Flight. Now I find the alternative to high flight is under water.

The proprietor of "Jimmy's Kitchen" in Hong Kong does more than run a famous restaurant. He fought an underground war against the Japanese occupiers here. Now he owns underwater gear, an advance on aqualungs used to plant limpet mines on enemy warships. Jimmy asks me to join a fisheries research vessel heading for the Pratas Reef, source of legends about monsters of the deep and undiscovered submarine wildlife. I recall fragments of Charles Kingsley's "perfect naturalist . . . able to swim . . . if he go far abroad."

I am as far abroad as ever I dreamed, though far from a perfect naturalist. Now I have an opportunity to go far abroad into another region. The Pratas Reef is the graveyard for ships passing through a narrow strait bounded westward by Maoist China and eastward by the Nationalist Chinese strongold of Formosa.

# CHAPTER 25

# An Underwater Escape to Boyhood Dreams

JIMMY OFFERS ME A SUBOCEAN CAMERA TO FILM HIS SEARCH FOR SPEC-
imens in the coral lying some fifty to sixty feet deep. Our shipmates are
marine biologists looking for rare forms of underwater life and are based
in Hong Kong in the late 1950s. They are limited to masks and snorkels.
Jimmy has underwater gear for the two of us, complete with cylinders of
air. Pratas Reef is roughly the shape of a horseshoe. A stiff Force Six wind
recently drove the 1,200-ton Filipino freighter Don Rene onto its rocks.
Commander John Melton, later of the Britannia Royal Naval College,
rescued the Don Rene's crew, after walking across a dangerously slippery
coral shelf, dragging two inflatable Gemini craft behind him. Remembering this close call, our skipper anchors near a sand spit.

Jimmy leads me down to the deep calm of coral and flashing colors
of strange sea life. We have nets and sacks to scoop up fish and deep-sea
growths not found in current textbooks. Weightlessness makes it easy to
maneuver. We rise regularly to the surface, pausing at intervals on the way
up to avoid "the bends." Soon the deck is full of flopping fish and huge
shells with weird horns and razor-sharp gaping "mouths." We dive back
into a world I never imagined as a schoolboy. Sand sharks lie still, dark
shadows dreaming, bellies flattened on golden grains of sand. A giant bar-
racuda hangs motionless above a flat-topped chunk of sandstone, lit by
beams of sunshine shredded into narrow shafts of greenish light. Sting-
rays glide past like V-shaped warplanes in close formation. Out of a pillar
of rock emerge tiny spider crabs that perch like friendly gnomes on my
open palm.

Each time I follow Jimmy back to the surface, it's like returning to a world of ugly realities. Alarms and despondencies await us. The ship is buffeted by rising winds. Scientists and crew frantically cram our specimens into huge steel canisters lashed to stanchions. In the belief that we have collected as many unidentified objects as we can, we head back to Hong Kong through heavy seas that sweep across the open decks and tear away at least half our hard-gotten gains. In later reports, I do not identify Jimmy to save him from retribution by those who protected Masanobu Tsuji, the sadistic Japanese torturer of Allied POWs. Tsuji was called God of Evil by Lord Mountbatten, who wanted to hang him. Americans hired Tsuji when he claimed to be an expert on Red China. He is now a prominent parliamentarian in Tokyo. Much later, I write about Mountbatten's evidence that Tsuji, disguised as a Buddhist monk, killed a young king of Siam, the Eighth Rama.

Now Jimmy watches the boiling seas swallow much of our catch. The adventure is in the spirit of my boyhood stories. "Back to reality," I yell between struggling to save valuable tokens of the unexplored and unexpected world below. Jimmy roars with laughter and shouts back, "That's life!"

The next time we meet, he is checking the *Official Guidebook of the Hong Kong Hotels Association*. At the top of a list titled ATMOSPHERE is "Jimmy's Kitchen, founded 1936. Hours 9:00 a.m. till 1:00 a.m. daily . . . Dress informal except on mezzanine after 7:00 p.m. Australian Oysters HK $12.00 . . . Satellite Deep Fried Ice Cream HK $4.50 . . . "The HK dollar is worth US $0.17, or less than two dimes. Jimmy has adjusted to the real world.

I edit and produce the first-ever documentary film of this unseen life under the waves, and contemplate an offer to become correspondent for a TV-newspaper combination. It might help with my re-awakened schoolboy yearnings. It eventually leads to the prolonged exploration of Africa with my family. I manage to get assigned to Arabia, too, and then comes a time when I join the first undersea search for the *Titanic*. Later I learn the wisdom of the whales from my eldest son, Andrew, but that is long after I escape from the murky depths of politics.

Right now, I must justify to HCH my absence beneath the waves. I report: "Mao's China and Generalissimo Chiang Kai-shek's Nationalists on Formosa lob artillery shells at each other on alternate days. Chiang shoots from the Pratas islands of Quemoy and Matsu on even days of the week: Red Chinese artillery responds on odd days. Beijing broadcasts each 'provocative action' and Formosa responds with bulletins of communist 'adventurism.' It's in the spirit of Sun Tzu's *Art of War,* written some two thousand five hundred years ago to show warlords how to win a war without wiping out the enemy camp."

At other times, when I report from inside both Mao's and Chiang's camps, no Chinese official on one side is ill-mannered enough to ask what I glean from the other side. In moments of schoolboy naiveté, I even wonder if my miracle undersea world might evolve, like Jimmy, into an amiable live-and-let-live tolerance.

Then I stumble upon an ugly reality. High-society patrons of Jimmy's Kitchen whisper ugly bits of gossip. "He works night and day to get rich . . . He plans to leave Hong Kong to go back to his own people."

Jimmy is Jewish. I hadn't noticed. I had forgotten the anti-Semitism I glimpsed during that first assignment to Poland. In a hurried trip to Cairo, I discover Goebbels's chief aide skulking under an Arab name, and broadcasting anti-Israel propaganda from Egypt's Ministry of Political Enlightenment.

Cairo is where I see Ambassador Herb Norman again. He talks of a suppressed diary by Mackenzie King, the Canadian prime minister who wrote volumes of personal reflections. But this one diary was always kept hidden from public scrutiny. "Because," Herb tells me, "it records how much King detested Jews and admired Hitler."

I am reminded again of past, seemingly disconnected, encounters. First there was Rena in Poland. At Auschwitz, she spoke of Holocaust survivors who tried to enter Canada after World War II and were rejected by Prime Minister Mackenzie King. Then Ambassador Norman tells me of King's diary, hidden from public view because it recorded his pre-World War II adulation of the Fuehrer when King met Hitler and wrote, "I could not but think of Joan of Arc." The facts deeply affect Herb Norman's view of politics. He knows about King's anti-Semitism and his ruling that "None is too many" when asked if Jews from Hitler's camps might enter Canada. Herb speaks to me of the steamship *St. Louis,* loaded with Jewish survivors, forced to sail back to Europe. By the time another prime minister, Brian Mulroney, publishes details "to ensure Canadians never forget a voyage of the damned," Herb has suffered in Cairo his own personal tragedy after being smeared as a communist.

I return to Tokyo with the owner of another North American daily newspaper and his editor. They want a quick introduction to Japan. I cable ahead to a friend in the British embassy who feels he owes his life to the Canadian who discovered penicillin, Sir Frederick Banting, and so meets us at the airport in an embassy limo flying UK flags. This offends my two potential employers, sensitive to any suggestion they owe allegiance to a queen-empress. They have business to conduct with Sony, the first major challenge to the zaibatsu industrial consortium that always domi-nated the Japanese economy. While General Douglas MacArthur reigned supreme, the zaibatsu was allowed to revive its age-old monopoly. Now Sony is on the brink of fame as Japan's first independent giant. Our time spent at Sony's research center follows our promise to keep secret all its surprising technical innovations that will beat the powerful competition.

I escape briefly from foggy explorations of Japan with the press barons and join Mikimoto pearl divers. Girls free-dive to pick through the oyster beds. They work on lungsful of air, beyond my ability to linger on the sea-bed. I free-dive to the bottom and stay for a fraction of the time they spend before surfacing. All are freezing after an afternoon extracting pearls. The cure is an enormous wooden tub of hot water. An old photograph shows my shaggy head surrounded by Japanese girls laughing through the steam. Dragons bring up my dizzy poetic notes I wrote about "straightforward challenges presented by Mother Nature in contrast to what humans call the real world." It looks a trifle immature today, and reminds me of Jim Bell, a *Time* correspondent in Hong Kong, taunting me with "feminine sentimentality" he detected in my news reports. I retort that the femininity of the pearl divers showed more guts than his kowtowing to his boss, Henry Luce who, in this time period, fires paper darts at communist China with a spinsterish certainty that everything there is irreparably wicked.

A later *Time* column accuses me of romanticizing British military preparations to confront an Arab threat to the Suez Canal, the age-old

With Japanese pearl divers who prove that they can stay underwater far longer than the unskilled author.

seaway to major Eastern sources of raw materials vital to the survival of the UK's modest living standards. In the last war, thousands of our men had been slaughtered or disabled in the effort to stop the Nazis from cutting this lifeline. I am in Egypt and threatened by the Muslim Brotherhood. I would much rather write sentimental stories about the more easily perceived challenges of Nature. Jimmy had re-awakened my schoolboy yearning for a simpler life, away from political strife. I'm not alone. My news editor, Borden Spears, would rather return to his prewar Greek studies, and Herb Norman longs to continue studying Japanese cultural history. But Herb, as Canadian ambassador in Cairo, is again attacked by McCarthy's witch hunters. They bring up old accusations leveled against him when he was ambassador in Tokyo. These are denied by the current Canadian Prime Minister, Mike Pearson, who tells me: "Herb always had his head in academic clouds as a student who, like so many, flirted with socialism and eventually rejected communism."

## CHAPTER 26

# Goebbels's Old Puppet Finds
# a New Trumpet

I AM IN CAIRO TO REPORT BRITISH, FRENCH, AND ISRAELI PREPARATIONS in 1956 to prevent Gamal Abdel Nasser from seizing the Suez Canal. A senior Egyptian official, frank about his Muslim Brotherhood links, warns that if I continue to write critically of Nasser's policies, "You will find yourself rolled up in a rug and dumped on your embassy's steps." Borden Spears cables me: "Mike says get out now."

"It's all Greek to me!" I jokingly tell Herb. "Spears is a Greek scholar who could never afford to continue his studies after wartime service in the air force."

"If he's a former fighter pilot, he won't be in a panic now," Herb replies. "He must have good reason. Don't you know 'Mike' is Mike Pearson? He expects trouble."

Herb insists that Nasser is a patriot who wants to shake off what remains of Western control. We argue about the Muslim Brotherhood. They have reformed, he claims. They are no longer religious extremists. I point out that they burned or trashed some three hundred buildings in Cairo on January 26, 1952, and one of its leaders had threatened me for a report estimating that 30 percent of the Brotherhood holds clandestine power. Herb's wife follows me outside their high-rise apartment and says hurriedly, "Herb's not himself. Don't be offended."

Herb Norman the idealist despairs of ever clearing his name after renewed attacks launched against him by McCarthyite zealots. He jumps to his death soon after our last meeting.

The tragedy goes back to the defection of the Soviet agent CORBY. Section two of the British Official Secrets Acts stopped me from disclosing what Herb knew about CORBY's escape from the Russian embassy in Ottawa, clearinghouse for Stalin's atomic-bomb spies in North America. CORBY named Soviet sympathizers in the Canadian capital, but he never implicated Herb, whose home in Ottawa was close to where Allied scientists continued atomic research. This had started *before* the Nazi invasion of the Soviet Union, under the code-name Tube Alloys. In 1941, British intelligence moles were reporting this to Moscow, and mischievously named Herb Norman as a collaborator. When Churchill sent William Stephenson to North America, free from Whitehall's oversight, the man called Intrepid had not signed the Official Secrets Acts. As Sir William Stephenson, he told me: "Whitehall is the most dangerously secretive bureaucracy. It controls the Secret Intelligence Services, SIS, MI5, and the officially nonexistent MI6, which harbors Soviet-run moles." In March 1946, a royal commission heard behind closed doors the full testimony from CORBY. Two days later, Winston Churchill delivered the famous speech in Fulton, Missouri: "It would be wrong and imprudent to entrust the secret knowledge or experience of the atomic bomb while it is still in its infancy . . . From Stettin in the Baltic to Trieste in the Adriatic, an iron curtain has descended."

The so-called Corby Case triggers the Cold War. A published version of his testimony mistakenly includes the name of Herbert Norman. This is not made public for almost thirty years. Details were known to Ian Fleming when he wrote his first James Bond thriller, *Casino Royale*. Intrepid read the original draft and told Ian: "It will never sell. Stick to nonfiction." I know now that the Corby Case *is* nonfiction. I have seen the true story, in a thick volume titled Top Secret, of which only a few copies were distributed to former US and UK leaders.

CHAPTER 27

# I Find a New Life in a
# New World of My Own

I FLY TO EGYPT AFTER LEAVING MY HONG KONG BASE TO REPORT AGAIN
from Pakistan. There I receive an INTER-STEVERITE message fore-
telling hostile action against the West's control of the Suez Canal. I tone
this down in a brief pigeon-post proposal to HCH, who agrees it might
be worth a quick look at Cairo. This, the Suez crisis, leads to my reunion
with Mrdjn Lenka, my former minder in Yugoslavia. Her husband now
works with former top Nazis, recruited by Egypt's Nasser. At the bar of
Cairo's Metropole Hotel, she scribbles for me the Arab name adopted
by a notorious German Jew-baiter, now broadcasting anti-Israeli propaganda. Dragons jump me back to 1950 in Berlin when an Egyptian doctor asks me: "Why do ex-Nazis want health certificates for Cairo?"

Now I learn the answer. They planned to continue their war on Jews
from Cairo. The Germans include the former Waffen SS General Wil-
helm Farnbacher and Otto Skorzeny of Nazi special operations, freed
by US captors after he claimed that he was really fighting communists
during the Hitler years. Other known Nazis now work on new versions
of German flying bombs and V1-rockets to be aimed at Israel. At the old
Gezira Sporting Club, an Argentine diplomat who is one of the post-
Peron radicals gives me a list of 240 Germans who fled from Allied justice
to continue their Nazi vendetta against the Jews.

Mrdjn Lenka cannot be seen talking openly to me because her husband is a chemist now working for the Egyptian regime. I discreetly share

Mrdjn's disclosures with Anne Sharpley of London's *Evening Standard*. It's always wise to team up with a correspondent who is not in direct competition. It's hard to discredit an exclusive story from two independent reporters. Anne is dubbed "Shapely Sharpley" by Randolph Churchill, in Cairo for the first time since he left in World War II to join Tito's partisans. Randolph is now back to report for the London press on the growing Suez crisis. He relishes his unplanned reunion with Mrdjn, his former translator, and he praises Anne for humiliating Egyptian army popinjays who tried to put down an Englishwoman by challenging her to perform on a shooting range. Anne gets a bull's-eye, and then another and another. Randolph Churchill asks where she learned to shoot. "Never fired a gun in my life 'til now," she says cheerfully. "But Dad was an army major. He used to misquote Doctor Johnson, 'Imminence of hanging wonderfully concentrates the mind.'"

Randolph recalls the Hitler-Stalin pact on the eve of Nazi Germany's war on Britain. He has a lot of faith in Mrdjn, who quietly warns him that the Nazi-Soviet pact of 1939 is in effect being revived by Russian military and intelligence experts now infiltrating Egypt to work with former Nazis. A few years later, when I spend time with the Israeli Air Force, I see evidence of Soviet pilots flying Egyptian jets, and Soviet SAM-2 missiles lining the Suez Canal, more proof of the revival of the old Soviet-Nazi joint actions against Jews.

Anne comes with me to search through the Ministry of Political Enlightenment for the former Nazi now masquerading as an Arab. A real Arab in the building, loyal to former British employers, is happy to help. He points upwards and whispers: "Fifth floor. Room 502."

I shove open the door and bark, "Johannes von Lehrs!"

"Ja!" He jumps to attention. He has been repeatedly held in POW camps, questioned by American captors, and then released. His response is automatic.

"It's him!" Anne says softly before snapping at the little man, "Why are you here?"

He's fooled so many American tribunals since Hitler's day. "I am innocent of all offenses. I fight communists. Never I kill Jews." But he hates them and returns to the old rhetoric. Then he suddenly comes out of this trancelike state and reaches for a phone to call the guards.

Anne and I quickly leave. We mingle with noisy crowds in crooked side streets. Mrdjn Lenka intercepts us on the way to our hotel. "Be careful," she says. "They're waiting for you." Then she's gone.

We climb the hotel's rickety back stairs, grab a few essentials, and quickly quit our rooms. We squat on the curb behind a noisesome market, bang away on our portable typewriters, and file our stories through Cable & Wireless, the British telegraphic service that covers the globe. We buy air tickets. These are the days when you do this without going online. Rome is immediately available as a safe destination. Randolph Churchill and other correspondents hear of our impending arrest and arrive at Cairo airport to see that we get away.

From Rome, Anne must fly home to London. I head for Istanbul. I had been earlier told to go to the Russian embassy there to get my first visa for reasons obscure. Anne and I part on the tarmac, never quite holding each other. These encounters are always unplanned, always intense, always doomed. *Time* magazine runs a photograph of me hiking across London Bridge alongside a waspish column claiming that if I cannot find a story, I make one up. The *Time* correspondent who filed this from Hong Kong thinks I'm a leftist because I can enter China, whereas he cannot. And he obeys his boss, Henry Luce, who opposes any battle for the Suez Canal.

Anne reports later that the English Cable & Wireless manager in Cairo who handled our telegrams, Tom Little, is arrested. She's also heard that I found a way to re-enter China from Moscow. She loves dangerous faraway places, and writes, "But it's still a man's world. I got the Cairo assignment only because the Beaver likes me." The Beaver is Lord Beaverbrook, who owns her paper. Envious editors tie Anne down to London. It is full of secrets I never uncovered as a boy and she later shows me historic hideaways, dens of vice dating back to Henry the Eighth, goldsmiths in the maze of alleyways around the Rothschild banking complex, and places still hoarding the secret slips identifying the Scarlet Pimpernels who saved French prisoners from the guillotine in a time of revolution. Anne says I remind her of the original Scarlet Pimpernel, but my pen is more powerful than his sword. She is a romantic soul. Because of this, I lose her to a medical mishap she never foresaw.

After we part in Cairo, I see that the Anglo-French-Israel war to seize Suez, although a failure, gives Moscow the opportunity to suppress Hungarian resistance. Suez is also a distraction in Southeast Asia. Notes recovered by my dragons once again cross conventional timelines. With press attention focused on the Mideast, Cambodia's Prince Sihanouk cuddles up to Mao, and communist leaders blaze new jungle trails into Vietnam for future combat. Groupthink portrays Sihanouk as "innocuous" until there comes a time when the Khmer Rouge slaughter untold millions of fellow Cambodians. My datelines range from Japan to Pakistan, London to New Delhi and Zanzibar. My airline credit card, now outdated like my portable typewriter, in those days let me fly when and where I wanted. I stumble into a bunch of Indonesian revolutionaries in a Borneo shop selling birds' nests and write another nonfiction book, *Birds' Nests In Their Beards*. A *New York Times* book review calls it: "A colourful recital of his adventures with pirates in Indonesian waters with insights into problems of race, economics and politics." I had not seen it in quite this way. I remember telling Mama, when I was a boy, "That is how I want to live." I am still influenced by her reading aloud Charles Kingsley's definition of "the perfect naturalist" who can climb, walk all day, sail a boat. . . . " Airline credit cards do not seem the equal of such romantic visions. I find my bearded piratical revolutionaries by sailing across the Makassar Strait. Today's dragons remind me that the voyage to Indonesia is made aboard a low-lying "kumpit" blockade runner whose wheezing engine luckily breaks down so that my Bugi sailors turn back: President Sukarno's warplanes bomb our destination on the day they have been forewarned will mark our arrival. I'm lucky the engine broke down. The warplanes are MiG-17 jets and Ilyushin bombers that foreshadow Indonesia's drift into either the orbit of Russia or China. The Kremlin and The Forbidden City are rivals for control of the former Dutch colony.

## CHAPTER 28

# The Emperor Loses His Clothes

IT's 1950 AGAIN. DRAGONS BRING UP THIS PERIOD WHEN I AM NOT YET banned in China. Airline credit cards are unknown, and air transport is still only domestic, passengers restricted to those approved by the Party. I ride a train, refreshed hourly by hot tea poured from huge watering cans by attendants who roam past at hourly intervals. In Beijing, I fill out a new form labeled: "Person you wish to interview." I remember my children asking, "Does China still have an emperor?" and amuse myself by scribbling across the form, "Emperor of China."

I am astonished to be taken by truck and train to Manchuria to meet the last emperor, now Comrade Henry Pu-yi. He receives me in a peasant's blue jacket and baggy trousers. "He is being reformed through labor," I am told by Zhou Enlai's interpreter, Huang Hua. He monitors the ex-emperor. Pu-yi tells his story in the old Imperial form of Mandarin used in 1900 by his mother, the last Empress. She was formidable until the British crashed through doors closed against Western traders. Now here is Pu-yi telling me what it was like to be a boy clothed in the trappings of the old imperial court. He describes being enticed by the Japanese to become Emperor of Manchukuo, which Japan claims until the atomic bomb ends all their imperial pretentions in China. Pu-yi tells me about his life as a puppet emperor whose strings were pulled from Tokyo. He seems relieved to be saved from the elaborate nonsense of being the emperor with no clothes. He plans to write his own story under the title From Emperor to Citizen, a sad tale by someone born into an elaborate web of imperial intrigue, then used as a cat's-paw by political rivals in a modern world. Nobody, until I meet him, revealed the Soviet Union's attempt to control him in Moscow where, for a while, he lived in mock-imperial style. He gives the impression of someone relieved to enjoy the simplicities of farm work. He is still haunted by memories of how he had to imitate the intricacies of life in the court of China's last imperial ruler, and later dress up as the Emperor of Manchukuo before Mao taught him "reform through labor." The stories he tells me are finally published by China's Foreign Language Press in 1965 and serve as a background to my first novel, *Emperor Red*.

The origins of the book begin in 1956. My dragons take me back there, traveling to Hanoi by truck on the Burma Road, and pausing to walk along old trade routes. My schoolboy dream of following the recommendation by Charles Kingsley to be strong enough to "climb a rock, turn a boulder, walk all day" is tested. It is so much easier to flourish a credit card. By this other and most strenuous route, I find Rena again, with the International Commission for Supervision and Control. The ICC monitors the armistice in Vietnam. The ICC's Indian chairman calls Rena "the Polish version of Machiavelli" and the Canadian member, Sherwood Lett, says he doubts if the Soviet Bloc could have a more effective representative than Rena. She is helping the Viet Minh smuggle Russian arms through China. Yet in Beijing, Rena was fiercely critical of Nikita Khrushchev's arrogance, although she had agreed with his denunciation of Stalin's "cult of personality" at the 1956 XX Congress of the Communist Party of the USSR. Now she fears Khrushchev is growing dangerously arrogant. In Beijing, he denounces Mao's same overbearing cult. I note with a twinge of envy that Khrushchev travels to China by air.

Rena has seen my published reports from India, foreshadowing Khrushchev's takeover from Nikolai Bulganin as Chairman of USSR Ministers. "B&K" the new Soviet leaders were called. But "K" eclipsed "B" and Prime Minister Nehru at the dramatic durbar in Old Delhi to coincide with Russia's launch of the first man-made vehicle in space. The word "durbar" is from an ancient Hindi word for a big reception held for an Indian prince. This durbar is populated by huge crowds. Many have trudged on foot from miles around. Still, they represent a long and impressive history, whatever Russian technology is used to dazzle them. This is the date of Sputnik's launch, precisely disclosed to Welles Hangen and myself at that meeting with Niels Bohr and the Kiev university president. Now that Hangen has been killed in the United States' "secret" war in Cambodia, I am the only journalist who has heard, from the horse's mouth, the prediction of the first unmanned satellite into space, Sputnik. Now I wait to see if it comes true.

## CHAPTER 29

# Sputnik and the Death of
# a Great Indian Aviator

Eventide 1957. India. The sky is splashed with fading blue and pale pink colors. Crowds squat in the open space near the Red Fort. Curiosity about the stranger from Moscow swells the mass of onlookers. Khrushchev advances in front of Nehru to the front of an improvised wooden platform. "Russia sends you . . ." The VIP's heavily accented growl comes over the loudspeakers as he lifts his arms: "Sputnik!"

A tiny twinkling dot rises over the horizon. No star ever moved across the sky at such speed, nor descended so quickly into the obscurity of advancing night. The whole thing seems inexplicable, although foretold in Kiev. Now, in Delhi, Khrushchev's interpreter takes over. He translates in an Anglo-Indian English accent, left over from a British empire long gone. "See how Russia now leads in science and industry."

My original Sputnik report had been cut to a brisk paragraph in the *Star's* back pages. HCH's readers would say Russians cannot make a wrist watch, let alone a rocket. So, as STEVERITE, I wrote to INTER a full account of the Kiev disclosure to Niels Bohr. In Nazi-occupied Denmark, he had once aroused fears that German physicists would learn his nuclear secrets. British intelligence smuggled him out to help develop the first atom bomb. I had told Intrepid what Bohr learned in Kiev about the date Sputnik would go into orbit. Which is today.

The showmanship in Delhi is synchronized by Soviet scientists with this first venture of Soviet leaders into non-communist territory. When they later leave India from Calcutta, an Indian Army band strikes up the cheeky soldiers' version of a British military march: "Bollocks! And the same to you!" Mistaking this farewell for a fanfare, B&K innocently wave good-bye from the plane taking them deeper into South Asia. Some good comes out of my own encounter with B&K: My first visa to enter Russia. But before that comes tragedy.

Earlier in Bangalore, Khrushchev boasted of Russia's superior manufacturing methods. India's top test pilot, Captain Namjoshi, later takes me through the nearby Hindustan aircraft factory. He watches my reaction to the spectacle of workers in dhotis and sandals, welding air frames of aircraft uncannily similar to the Canadian de Havilland Chipmunk. I have flown Chipmunks. The difference is that here, these copies are assembled by men dressed in traditional Hindu style. Namjoshi asks what I think of their work. I politely express appreciation of their speed and skill. He calls my bluff. "Then take a test flight with me."

We climb into one of the neat little monoplanes, straight off the assembly line. He takes control, performs loops and spins and all the usual initial tests. By the time we land, it's time for lunch. He needs to make further test flights and so I return to my hotel and enjoy my favorite Indian lunch of curry and beer, with a follow-up siesta. My bedroom telephone rings. Would I write a few words about Captain Namjoshi for the company magazine?

"Why?" I ask. "Is he okay?"

"I fear not," says the caller. "He is, sad to say, dead." Captain Namjoshi had put the same machine through its paces again. "He is making his final approach behind a Vampire jet landing just ahead of him, la? He got caught in the Vampire's slipstream. Unhappily, violent movements cause his tail to fall off."

That night I sleep with my pajama collar turned up again, not against vampires so much as a silent vow to make Namjoshi's death mean something: a better world, a better life for his own people, things he wanted above all. I write about his dedication to honest values in my article for his company's magazine, with a warm account of his outstanding flying skills. Captain Namjoshi was already a national hero. Prime Minister Nehru pays tribute to him and quotes from my valedictory. I had been deeply impressed by Namjoshi's faith in the future of the Indian aircraft industry. The tragedy could not have come at a worse time. When B&K visited the factory, Khrushchev gratuitously advised his polite hosts to visit Magnitogorsk to see how Russians build multi-storied factories, pointing at the same time to the flat roof of the two-storied Indian aircraft works.

"Excuse me," Namjoshi interrupted the Russian leader. "This factory is still in the process of expansion. We do not need instruction in adding five more levels we have already planned."

A great Indian aviator felt challenged by Sputnik-sparked Russian arrogance and thereby met his death. I may well think this, but I do not say so. What never emerges in 1967 is that B&K and Sputnik's designers took a big risk of failure. A decade later, I learn what terrifying chances were taken to make the Soviet Union's totalitarian methods seem far in advance of capitalist profit-seeking inefficiency. The first space vehicle is Russian, and shoddily constructed. The cosmonaut, Vladimir Komarov, is about to crash full speed into Earth, his body turning molten on impact. United States listening posts in Turkey hear him "cursing the people who had put him inside a botched spaceship." KGB officer Venymin Ivanovich Russayevth knew the space capsule was not safe to fly and that Komarov knew he would probably die. But he wouldn't back out because he didn't want Yuri Gagarin to die. Gagarin would have been his replacement. The plan was to launch a capsule, the Soyuz 1, with Komarov inside. The next day, a second vehicle was scheduled to leave with two additional cosmonauts. The two vehicles were to meet and dock. Komarov would crawl from one vehicle to the other, exchanging places with a colleague, and come home in the second ship. It would be, Brezhnev hoped, a Soviet triumph on the fiftieth anniversary of the communist revolution. Brezhnev made it very clear he wanted this to happen. Gagarin, the first man ever in space, had inspected the Soyuz 1 and found 203 structural problems that would make it dangerous to navigate in space. The mission, Gagarin suggested, should be postponed. Who would tell Brezhnev? Gagarin gave a ten-page memo to his friend in the KGB, Venyamin Russayev, but nobody dared send it up the chain of command. With less than a month to go before the launch, Komarov realized postponement was not an option. He met with Russayev, the now-demoted KGB agent, and said, "I'm not going to make it back from this flight. If I don't go, they'll send the backup pilot instead—Yuri Gagarin." Vladimir Komarov couldn't do that to his friend. Komarov then burst into tears. On launch day, April 23, 1967, Soyuz left Earth with Komarov on board. Once it began to orbit the Earth, the failures began. Antennas didn't open properly. Power was compromised. Navigation proved difficult. All the while, US intelligence was listening in. The National Security Agency (NSA) had a facility at an Air Force base near Istanbul. Perry Fellwock, an NSA analyst, described overhearing Komarov tell ground control officials he knew he was about to die. Fellwock described how Soviet premier Alexei Kosygin called on a videophone to tell him he was a hero. Komarov's wife was also on the call to talk about what to say to their children. Kosygin was crying. When the capsule began its descent and the parachutes failed to open, American intelligence "picked up Komarov's cries of rage as he plunged to his death." The Gagarin of 1967 was very different from the carefree young man of 1961. Komarov's death had placed an enormous burden of guilt on his shoulders. At one point Gagarin said, "I must go to see the main man [Brezhnev] personally." He was profoundly depressed that he hadn't been able to persuade Brezhnev to cancel Komarov's launch. The intensity of Gagarin's rage became obvious. "I'll get through to him [Brezhnev] somehow, and if I ever find out he knew about the situation and still let everything happen, then I know exactly what I'm going to do." Russayev, after his demotion as a KGB agent, reports: "I don't know exactly what Yuri had in mind. Maybe a good punch in the face. I warned Gagarin to be cautious as far as Brezhnev was concerned and said, 'Talk to me first before you do anything. I warn you, be very careful.'" Those words resonate when my dragons leap me forward several years to when I am free to write some of British Security Coordination's work in my book *A Man Called Intrepid.*

# CHAPTER 30

# Return of the Trotsky Case

I FINALLY LEARN WHY INTREPID SUGGESTED I TELL THE STORY OF Trotsky's assassination. It has ties to the Soviet defector Igor Gouzenko, who escaped with masses of secret Russian files. Details of the so-called Corby Case could not be disclosed. The Gouzenkos were warned for decades that they could still pay the extreme penalty for escaping from the Russian embassy on the eve of the re-opening of the Canadian Parliament for the first time since the start of the Second World War. This resumption of Parliament in 1946 signaled a return, they supposed, to free speech and no further risk of being returned to SMERSH. But their testimonies before hush-hush government committees were heavily censored. Why such secrecy? Full disclosure would reveal MI5's incompetence, and expose the internecine warfare among the UK's Establishment secret agencies. This threatened Britain's survival between 1939–45 when anti-Nazi European governments had their own secret services in London. Some of these exiled intelligence agencies, it is now disclosed, feared the existence of links between their UK patrons and the Soviets.

In April 1987, William H. Webster testifies at a Senate Intelligence Committee hearing on his nomination as Director of Central Intelligence. The *New York Times* publishes a front-page photograph of Webster reading from my biography of Intrepid his cautionary preface that two immensely powerful weapons were forged during World War II. One was the atom bomb; the other was secret intelligence of such hidden powers that it must be entrusted to leaders of the utmost integrity. "That," says Webster, "is what I believe."

By then, Igor Gouzenko has died. His widow, Svetlana, steps out of anonymity. She breaks her thirty-eight-year-long silence at a press conference to declare that every word is true in a book I write about the Gouzenkos. Her late husband came under critical fire from historians who denounced his early public testimony as "unconvincing." But the French government wanted all the testimony to be declassified in what they called *L'Affaire Gouzenko*. It cast a new light on the intelligence services of the Free French, and how they were betrayed by moles. An authorized history of MI5 appears in 2009 and seems to end the hiding of inconvenient truths by the imposition of secrecy oaths. But in 2010, the UK government promises a full inquiry into "the distortions of intelligence leading to the invasion of Iraq." This dashes any hope of genuine reform because the investigation will be held in secret, before a "Truth Commission." It is appointed by the same government that rushed into the Iraq war on doctored intelligence.

This "Truth Commission" sounds Orwellian, never answerable to democracy's questions. There are enough subsequent protests to make the commission open its doors to the Press, but questions and answers are orchestrated in ways that remind me of "psychological warfare" preached to us young pilots. CORBY is finally confirmed as Igor Gouzenko: his wife, Svetlana, is declared a former Red Air Force pilot. Both were always in fear of betrayal as a consequence of the public's disbelief in moles. Reports on the Trotsky assassination in the journal of the Royal Canadian Mounted Police reflect a change of opinion about Gouzenko. The best RCMP officers are vindicated for having protected the Gouzenkos after they left the safety of Camp X. Reports about Trotsky as victim of Soviet Special Tasks, and about the Gouzenkos as victims of Soviet disinformation, swings attention to Kim Philby, who worked for what was still unknown to the public as MI6, the foreign intelligence service. Philby was in Beirut as Mideast correspondent for the *Observer*. The public finally learns how Philby fooled the UK intelligence services into letting him escape. My dragons draw me back to the mid-1950s when Zhou Enlai and his supporters in communist China saw through the Soviet Union's black propaganda. So many of Mao's henchmen conveniently forgot that their present arch-enemy, Chiang Kai-shek, was in Moscow as a student of communism before siding with the Americans, who treated him as President of China until he was forced to retreat to Taiwan. Beijing shows signs of waking up to the Kremlin's double-dealing, its use of informers and moles within Mao's own foreign intelligence agencies, and the hollow claim that the Soviet Union leads the world in industrial and inventive power.

# CHAPTER 31

# Moscow's Spyglass on China's Atom Bombs

ZHOU ENLAI, AFTER HIS OWN EARLY DAYS IN THE SOVIET UNION, BECAME uneasy about Russian claims to superior manufacturing methods. He does not want China to rely on Russian power. He is at cross-purposes with Chairman Mao and recognizes the same Stalinist duplicities. Mao urges the people to speak their minds, a trick to draw out enemies lurking "like lice" in China. Madame Kung Peng tells me of a schism between Mao and Nikita Khrushchev. Foreign observers in Beijing who fancy they get an inside track on events by professing pro-Maoist sympathies are kept in the dark about what happens in China after the time from July to August 1958, when Nikita Khrushchev denounces Mao and brags that Russian-style communism will overhaul capitalism throughout the world.

I arrive from a puzzling journey to one of Russia's frontiers with China, and report from Beijing a widening division between Kremlin and Forbidden City. The East German finance minister, my unwelcome companion with Zhou on one of my Burma Road explorations, asks why a wicked capitalist gets this exclusive information. Other foreigners who suck up to Mao's regime are furious that I scooped them on this sensational development.

My source, Yellow Flower, Huang Hua, is not only Mao's interpreter. He also oversees the China Travel Service, which spies on its foreign clients. Yellow Flower tells me, for his own devious reasons, the details. HCH treats this as a minor sidebar interview. I write more fully, STEVERITE-to-INTER, about the rift between Moscow and Beijing. Khrushchev also fails to get a summit meeting with India, the UK, the United States, and France to cap the eruption of Arab power. He wants

174

the UN Security Council to curb Muslim troublemakers but this requires recognition of Chiang Kai-shek's Nationalists who occupy China's seat on the UN Security Council. Then Khrushchev attacks Mao's Great Leap Forward as a Great Step Backward. Zhou Enlai secretly agrees, but to present a united front against the Kremlin, refuses to let Soviet scientists install nuclear plants in China. Khrushchev jeers, "Even your peasants don't make trousers to wear." Zhou responds, "Even if we have to go trouserless, we shall keep nuclear power in our own hands."

This is the backstory to a journey I make across Russia to a region normally barred to Western observers but where I am shown China's testing grounds for its own atomic bombs.

It all begins in Moscow. I go to a party given by a satirical magazine tolerated by Khrushchev as a safety valve for "cultural critics" where I meet The *London Evening News* correspondent who writes under the name of Victor Louis. In truth, he is a Russian agent, a survivor of Stalin's slave labor camps. Khrushchev atoned by assigning to him all visible royalties for the Russian version of *My Fair Lady*. Victor Louis invites me to spend Sunday at his dacha outside Moscow.

Back at my hotel later, I review hours of drunken chatter at the dacha. I recall escaping to get some fresh air among snow-laden fir trees. A man in heavy furs and on crude wooden skis asks for directions to the nearest railroad station. I haven't a clue. Anxious to seem helpful, I point him in an easterly direction. I wonder if I sent the poor chap to ski into the unknown forever. Of course that's nonsense. Then I recall Victor Louis saying, "Why don't you go to Alma-Ata?" I dismissed this as a bit of propaganda to make all Russia seem wide open for foreign tourists. Nonetheless, next morning, I ask at the Intourist desk. "Can I fly to Alma-Ata?"

"Yes," the Intourist girl says with suspicious promptness. "Midnight tonight."

This is not a period when outsiders casually fly anywhere in the USSR. Clearly, someone decided I should be prompted to visit Alma-Ata, today known as Almaty, back then the capital of Kazakhstan. It is so far away that I wonder if, by some miscalculation, I might end up back in China. A "guide" drives me into the Altai Mountains.

175

He speaks excellent English and it is quickly evident that he enjoys silly jokes. I ask him where he learned his English. "Foreign Language School," he replies. "Best in world."

"In my world, linguists get sent to places where the stuff they are taught is not spoken. You seem luckier."

"No! No!" he bubbles. "I have friend learns difficult Uzbek Chinese and is sent to Iceland."

"Iceland?"

"No, no! You not understanding. Icelam. Lunatic icelam."

"You mean he went mad with frustration and got sent to a lunatic asylum?"

"Is correct. Same like everywhere."

From a mountaintop, he points. "Down there is where China tests atomic bombs."

He glances at my cameras. "Take pictures."

I peer into the wide-open spaces far below, and faintly recall a precipice called Lord of the Sky above a Chinese desert. I had earlier obtained a film of Peoples Liberation Army horsemen galloping into the fallout from a nuclear bomb test, to prove that radiation is Western propaganda. Now I shoot footage of the plains below, using the 16 mm Bolex-Paillard camera I carry without the tiresome formalities of getting permission. Soviet internal security will report on what I film. Back in Moscow, I change my plans and fly to London. The gatekeepers at Moscow airport studiously ignore my cameras. In London, the rolls of 16 mm film are developed. The former head of the Hong Kong government broadcasting service asks me, "How in hell did you get this?"

Puzzled British intelligence specialists finally conclude that the Soviets are alarmed by China's bomb tests but fear that if they voice official concern, the CIA and the UK's officially nonexistent MI6 will suspect Moscow's motives. Better to have a foreign correspondent convey the message. I later produce a TV documentary titled *The Dragon and the Bear*, with a cautious commentary on the desert. Today, it is known as Taklimakan, the test site near what is now called Baicheng from where traders, or perhaps Chinese nuclear scientists, can enter

Afghanistan by way of a short and narrow passage now named the Baroghil Pass.

I fly from London to Hong Kong. It's holiday time for local schools, and the family is away on vacation, so I stay at the Foreign Correspondents Club. A girl from East Germany seeks me out. "The Soviet security services thought you were taking the train to Beijing. They put me on board to seduce you." She is intoxicated by the free air of the colony. She tells me about bitter squabbles between East German leaders, including her Australian parents, who moved to the Soviet world and now quarrel over opposing views on Russian communism. The more she lets off steam, the more she talks of flying to Australia, never to return to be stifled again within a Russian satellite.

I introduce her to a friend at the Security Liaison Office, Rider Latham. At the end of World War II, he parachuted on his own into Norway. He was fluent in German after pre-war studies at Heidelberg University, but he was not sure the Norwegian garrison would surrender. Armed only with a pistol, he faced the German commander, whose troops stood stoically alert behind him. There was a painfully long pause before the commander raised his arms. Rider only told me this when he was dying in later years. In Hong Kong, he was master of "the artful mumble." One of his SLO colleagues, Eric Kitchen, used it to make others talk. Glenys and Helen, the wife of Rawle Knox, agreed to match Eric's artful mumble when he invited them to a small lunch. "It got smaller and smaller," Glenys said later, "because nobody let slip a word, other than 'please' and 'thank you.'"

There was a different kind of MI6 interrogator in Hong Kong: Tim Milne, related to A. A. Milne, who created Christopher Robin, the boy celebrated in English literature. Tim was tired of being teased as Christopher Robin, but he could use the nickname to disarm those he cross-examined from behind a mask of amiable chatter. He devoted several all-night drinking sessions to chatting up the girl comrade sent to seduce me. When it became blindingly obvious that she was addicted to freedom, "Christopher Robin" arranged her passage to Australia, from which she never returned to the Democratic Republic of East Germany.

# CHAPTER 32

# Afghans Erase All Who Get in the Way

AFTER THE DISCLOSURE OF SOVIET PLANS EAST OF SUEZ, I PROPOSE IN the usual way, by pigeon-post express: "HCH: Afghans worth watching for return of Russians? WS"

"OK: HCH" comes the terse reply. Then follows an advance on expenses. These help inflate the children's pocket money, so long as my Hong Kong money changer values the Canadian dollar at 10 percent more than the US dollar. I fly to Pakistan to begin a long overland journey through Afghanistan, with memories of my *Boy Scout* magazine stories about the Great Game played to stop Russia breaking south from frontiers stretching from the Caucasus Mountains to Kazakhstan. I drive through Peshawar, and find the road winding north through stark mountain moonscapes. If I blink, I can imagine I'm back in the Kazakh mountains. Imagination gives way to reality. I glimpse in a Kabul alley the new Soviet Special Tasks chief: Ivan Serov of the KGB. "Christopher Robin" had told me Serov reported to Khrushchev on internal East German squabbles. So what is Serov doing here?

I ask the British ambassador if this means the Russians are coming.

"Let them come!" He rubs his old-soldier hands. "It took us three hundred years at a terrible cost to learn that no foreign army can ever control Afghans. They clobber themselves. Go watch 'em in a game of buzkashi. It's the origin of our polo, except these players kill each other."

I film *Buzkashi,* a documentary I later produce. Gigantic horsemen lean far over the side of their fierce steeds and swing hooked sticks into a dead goat whose stomach is stuffed with some ghastly goo to produce a substitute for the ball. Spectators and players are killed when the riders, obsessed with winning, charge into the crowds. Applause comes from anyone still left standing. My later commentary notes that China has bitter memories of trying to stop "Mongol invaders" piercing the Great Wall on just such massive horses. Decades later, the Russian chief of army education during the Soviet occupation of Afghanistan tells me about this tribal taste for mayhem. "That kind of fury forced us to pull out in 1989. We tried to warn the Americans but . . ." He tells me this after becoming a big businessman in Canada. His father-in-law is the Soviet general who turned back the Nazis in the epic Battle of Stalingrad and hammered a very big nail in Hitler's coffin.

I buy karakul lambskins for Glenys and drive back from Kabul in a British embassy Land Rover with George Evans of the *London Daily Telegraph*. Tribal boundaries are mere lines in the sand. Local fort commanders question us. In southern Kandahar province, Evans speaks politely in the local dialect to tell the ethnic Pashtun community chief that his fort's flag is "accidentally" hoisted upside down. The commander orders a warrior to shin up the flagpole to fix it, and waves us on with a warm and toothless grin.

Evans explains this jolly interlude. "Kandahar is the traditional fulcrum of insular Afghan wars. Pashtun subtribes are forever in conflict with one another. But any non-Afghan intruder unites them. Their proximity to Pakistan encourages a mafia-style network of oligarchs and elders." We drive the relatively short distance remaining to reach Pakistan. In Peshawar awaits a cable from Evans' editor, reminding him that his name is in the news-desk diary to cover the annual Pancake Races at Olney in Bedfordshire next Tuesday. Today is Sunday. He has time to make it, if he takes the next flight to London. I ask him, "Where'd you learn to speak Pashtun?"

"It wasn't at the Pancake Races," he jokes. He is a reporter of the old school. If your name is in the newsroom diary for some annual event, you cover it. Evans had done his military service in Afghanistan and learned local tribal tongues. His tutor was Charles "Dick" Ellis, who frustrated Russian efforts to control the region between two world wars. I know

Ellis as Intrepid's former deputy. He authored *Transcaspian Episode,* a classic textbook on how to thwart Russian intrigues. Ellis outwitted Soviet enemies after his battlefield service in 1914-18. He studied Lawrence of Arabia, Mao, Tito, and the causes of France's sixteen years of defeat in Indochina and Algeria. "Nothing rivaled The Great Game for control of the Muslim belt from Siberia to the Mideast," he wrote. "Nothing is more impossible to win than Afghanistan . . . Our frontier officers all read Kipling's Kim and observed Uzbek traders who came to Peshawar through the Khyber Pass with their rugs, silks and lambskins."

My own karakul furs are so badly cured that a tailor in Hong Kong rips the lambskins apart in front of Glenys. She sees her dreams of a Persian lambskin coat torn apart, and swallows her disappointment after hearing how I wrapped myself in the skins for warmth driving through the high Afghan passes. I confess I was warned not to buy such furs, originating in Urumchi, the Chinese Muslim province from where terrorists enter Afghanistan and raise funds by the sale of furs and drugs. The warning came from an Indonesian friend, Jana Warawantu, working for some unspecified secret service. She gives me shelter later in Djakarta, capital of Indonesia during its war of *konfrontasi,* the confrontation attack on Malaysia that is portrayed by the communist world as not truly liberated from the British yoke, although Malay by then is an independent member of the British Commonwealth.

Indonesia's armed forces are supplied with the latest Russian warplanes and weapons, a modern extension of the centuries-old Great Game.

# CHAPTER 33

# A Boyhood Dream Dies

A NEATLY HANDWRITTEN LETTER FROM GEORGE EVANS IS CALLED UP from the past. I had asked him to take a pair of shoes, purchased in Kabul, to my mother in London. In his neat handwriting, he reports that he delivered these unusual shoes with upturned toes. I had expected they would amuse Mama. But Evans writes, "I'm sorry to report your mother has medical problems and unfortunately she cannot wear those wonderful Afghan clogs."

Glenys urges me to fly at once to see Mama. I worry about the cost, about the kids, about my job. We live month to month but I suspect I can get HCH's agreement to cover a story in London. In 1955 I had flown there to inquire into Khrushchev's protest against a bungled attempt by a frogman of MI5, "Buster" Crabbe, to inspect the hull of the new Soviet cruiser *Ordzhonikidze* on a goodwill visit to Portsmouth. Crabbe disappeared in waters I know well from days when I began training as a naval airman. Now I hear from Mrdjn Lenka that she is in London with Tito. I send HCH a cable: "Perhaps useful to report Tito talks with new UK government. WS."

"OK HCH" comes the prompt reply. Now I can see Mama. She had been out of reach in Turkey with my father at his post in the UK embassy. I remember my schoolboy vow to take her to Hong Kong. Did foresight prompt me? Why Hong Kong? I no more believe in foresight than in my parents' religious beliefs. These days I try to understand Buddhism and how monks passively resist dictatorship. Mama teaches me about resistance. She still will not admit illness. She is home again in the same

181

The author's mother, Alida Deleporte.

dispiriting London house but still seems young as ever in her devotion to English literature, and she is now happy to watch reels of film I project proudly on one wall: scenes of the children in Hong Kong and shots of junks and the family sailing, swimming, and riding horses. But it's not the same as taking her there. I say good-bye to Mama. It's a cheerful parting, neither of us expecting it to be the last.

182

The affairs of the world have drawn a curtain across the years since Mama was a small boy's guide to the future. I still sleep with pajama collar turned up, not because I crept under a cinema seat to watch an Adults Only movie about vampires, but because of a promise to Spud Murphy to justify his sacrifice and my survival by helping to make the world a better place. I leave the old London home with a timeworn version of Dad's advice ringing in my ears: Leave my body in the cockpit and my mind outside to watch how events unroll. Did he foresee so much, without fear? Without favor?

Before I can examine such questions, raised by my return, I hear from Mrdjn Lenka. An attempt has been made in London on Tito's life by his oldest enemies. German Nazis? Or aging survivors of Stalin's Special Tasks? I resist the urge to dig deeper and book the next flight back to Hong Kong, saddened by my failure to fulfill my silent childhood promise to Mama. I console myself with the memory of her conviction, shared with Dad, that a new world of strong ideas is destined to emerge from what they called the Far East.

# CHAPTER 34

# Tender Traps

FROM THE 1950S TO 1962, MY PARENTS' FORESIGHT IS SHARED BY DENIS Corley-Smith. The Reuters news agency correspondent divides his time between Hong Kong, Hanoi, and surrounding regions. He explores a patchwork of mystifying neighborhoods, especially Cambodia. He takes me there for a more cheerful picture of the region because Cambodia "is absolute paradise." Even this astute reporter, with a brother who is a British ambassador and also a specialist on Asia, does not expect this paradise to become a hell as the result of Mao's Great Famine. It kills fifty-five million Chinese between 1958 and 1962 while Mao's allies in Cambodia sink into a nightmare of shifting alliances. Mao's cat's-paws bring out Cambodian evildoers whose wickedness is rooted in a different history. It will take fifty years before a professor in Hong Kong digs out the buried Chinese archives on the Great Famine.

Today I get old notes about an early inkling of the nightmares to come. I relish the old Beijing. Embracing the capital, there is an ancient wall guarding a sense of age-old continuity: creak of farmers' carts, clatter of tinsmiths, chipping of hammer and chisel, cries of hawkers, and Gobi Desert sandstorms that invade every crevice of human bodies and *hotung* lanes. Then Mao issues an ominous decree to Zhou Enlai: "We inherited a blanket full of holes and you must be the housekeeper who patches up the blanket."

Zhou is in trouble for having once warned against "making Mao a deity" at a closed meeting with Party cadres. This is never made public until long after Beijing's first ugly attempts to patch up its blanket. Zhou has foretold sinister changes, such as the directive from the Bureau for Religious Affairs that "Freedom to worship is a State license to perform rituals in places called churches." The famous Lama Temple is rebuilt to pacify several million Buddhists, but the golden idol "seventy elbows high" only survives for as long as Mao allows. Towers rise with red tiles stuck on top like a tipping of hats to the dismissal of China's grand old architecture. The country is swept by campaigns disguised as "Reform Through Labor." The modern guardians of a past culture, opera singers and writers, philosophers and teachers, once lauded as guardians of past greatness, now die in jail or are driven into labor camps. Those who confided in me are now destroyed, even if they implicate me.

Zhou Enlai's man in Hong Kong, Liu Pengju of the New China Xinhua news agency, asks to visit my home. Beijing representatives are never known to visit Westerners at home. Liu wants to talk in my garden, away from hidden microphones. Later, a wildly inaccurate CIA account is shown me by MI6, for the British Security Liaison Office spies on the CIA and the CIA spies on the SLO. The SLO is disguise for MI6, collectors of foreign intelligence, but with no official presence in Hong Kong and not yet known to exist by UK taxpayers. MI5 guards colonial possessions like Malaya and Singapore. MI6, camouflaged as the SLO, operates here in the colony and keeps watch on neighboring China. These serpentine differences between security services cause fierce rivalry. Hong Kong does a huge amount of business with China. This frustrates the CIA. It angers MI5, whose operatives are physically waging war against Chinese communist guerrillas in Singapore and the Malay peninsula.

Liu Pengju confirms what has been disclosed before. "My comrades in Beijing are discussing you. Some want to ban you and only want to let in writers like Simone de Beauvoir and Han Suyin who never criticize us. I must ask: 'Are you critical because we are communists or because you are a friend of China?'"

I tell him I would not devote so much time to China if I did not respect its people.

"That is what I say," he responds. As the local Xinhua correspondent, he normally calls me by telephone. But during the Suez crisis of 1956, he warned Glenys that I am being thrown out of Egypt: "I did not want you to read it first in tomorrow's newspapers." My wife appreciates his concern. She likes the glamour that lets me roam far afield, of coming with me to Japan, India, and the high Himalayas, while amahs and friends watch over the children whose lives are full of activity: swimming, boating, horsemanship. Son Kevin helps Ah Wong in the kitchen, and what that boy learns about cooking is surprisingly useful later when I take him trout fishing with Andrew in Kashmir. Jackie learns seamanship and is a champion swimmer. Baby Sally is not too small to reinforce my dreams of taking the children on those worldwide adventures I imagined as a boy.

Other foreign correspondents use Hong Kong as a base from which to freely cover vast regions. The Foreign Correspondents Club is evicted from mainland China and now overlooks Hong Kong's shipping lanes. Its members include veterans of the Korean War: Keyes Beech of the *Chicago Daily News;* Bud Merrick of UPI; *Time* magazine's chief of Asian affairs; a future editor of the *New York Times;* Russell Spurr of the *London Daily Express;* Jim Robinson of NBC; Rawle Knox of the *Observer,* who comes from a family whose intellectual talents range from revising the Bible to editing *Punch,* then the most successful of satirical magazines; Gordon Walker of the *Christian Science Monitor;* Dick Hughes of the *Sunday Times* of London; Bob Elegant of *Newsweek;* Hank Lieberman of the *New York Times.* Some feature in strange events. Glenys and I go to dinner with Hank and I stupidly leave in the back of our car my original 16 mm movie footage shot in China: all the film has vanished when we return to the car: nobody knows how or why. Gordon Walker dies from injuries after we cover the American evacuation of a coastal village in mainland China; Jim Burke of *Time-Life* is killed in Nepal; and Dick Hughes is stunned by what he is told about his dead wife by a blind monk in Laos who never before met him, nor myself. Bob Elegant is ridiculed in a novel by Han Suyin: this only confirms his distrust of her.

Han Suyin repeats that she will stop me from ever again re-entering China. She is described in the London *Times* as "a leading apologist in the west for communist China." In her earlier volume of memoirs, *My House Has Two Doors,* she admits "lying through my teeth" to diplomats

186

and newsmen about famine in China. The *Times'* reviewer damns her for "pure Stalinist kitsch. . . . Only a psychiatrist can probe the whys and wherefores of her willful denials of reality." Her attempts to inform the outside world of Mao's policies are not always applauded within China's hierarchy. Zhou is uncomfortably aware that her enthusiastic endorsements are overtaken by events, even before her latest plaudits are printed. "Chairman Mao's actions change completely by the time the West reads her accounts of his latest reform plans," confides my stealthy visitor from the official New China news agency. "Any Western inclination to build bridges with Beijing is discouraged by her unintended disclosure of Mao's erratic behavior."

Some CIA residents in Hong Kong dismiss correspondents as "police reporters." Many intelligence agencies are based here. Their reports, being secret, cannot be checked. Our mistakes are there for all to see. A farcical CIA account of my meeting with the New China news correspondent comes from my CIA neighbor, annoyed because I reported to Hong Kong police that his guard dog tore open the face of my son Andrew. Rabies is common in the colony, and antidotes often cause severe reactions and even death. When I ask the police to "put down that blasted dog," I am told by the Security Liaison Office that "it's against British policy" to interfere in CIA activities.

This nest of newsmen shelters families while some correspondents are away on assignment. Glenys has an amah and cook-boy to handle the basics for our three children. They came to Hong Kong when they were younger than five years old. A fourth child, Sally, is born here, but still HCH never raises my salary. Cheapness of life in Hong Kong applies to penniless refugees from mainland China. Western residents live full lives on modest incomes. I share the cost of a sampan with John Horton, a wartime submariner. He is CIA but understands the mutual benefits enjoyed by the colony and China, in contrast to our CIA neighbor, whose job is to sabotage Western-Chinese commerce. A time comes when I see Horton again in Washington, D.C., following his well-publicized resignation in protest against having his reports altered to suit White House policies.

Mao needs the commerce with Hong Kong. He keeps Premier Zhou Enlai busy with foreign affairs. While I was a mere child, Zhou's aide, Madame Kung Peng, was enduring hardships of the Long March. She seldom speaks of the past. Instead, she tells me where to find culinary delights in places I visit with my minder, Chan, who has never forgotten that Glenys helped him in London. Beneath his cautious solemnity, he retains a sense of humor that is useful when he comes with me on yet another trek along the Burma Road.

I fly more and more frequently between Hong Kong and Delhi where Nehru monitors Mao's military ventures along the borders. Nehru talks to me of India as China's economic rival. He foresees clashes. It helps India if foreign correspondents observe his efforts to come to terms with China. I can move freely in both countries, and I keep a house in the colony and rent an apartment in New Delhi that belongs to Khushwant Singh. This brilliant Sikh writer is a regular on BBC-TV's Brains' Trust debates. My latest Hong Kong residence, "Normandie," looks like a castle aloft on The Peak, and rents for a laughable one thousand US dollars a month. From home, we peer down on airliners landing at Kai-tak on the far side of deep-water shipping lanes.

Dragon-mail includes *Toronto Star* expenses for December 1960, totaling the equivalent of US $1,800, including staff salaries and running a car. Properties in Hong Kong are cheap, for its future is so uncertain. Leaving the colony is going to be painful but is inevitable. It is not in any boastful spirit that I wrote *The Yellow Wind* and called it, "A solitary attempt to examine the tender trap fashioned out of Marx, Lenin and Confucius." I explore places that once paid tribute to the Dragon Throne: Vietnam, Laos, Cambodia, Thailand, and Burma; the Malay Peninsula; the three thousand islands of Indonesia; Korea and the islands of Japan; the borderlands of Inner Asia; the Himalayan kingdoms; Turkestan and the Russian Far East. "Everywhere the tender trap of Chinese communism closed slowly and irresistibly," I write. "Visualize the author as a lonely wanderer groping through unfamiliar darkness, hoping Oscar Wilde could have been wrong when he wrote: 'I can stand brute force but brute reason hits below the intellect.' For the secret of all tender traps is that they strike below the intellect."

The tender trap snaps down on the Minister of Communications, Chang Po-chun. Fooled by Mao's call to "Let All Flowers Bloom," Chang proclaims, "China is a country of five hundred million slaves ruled by a Single God and nine million Puritans." Chang vanishes, leaving no trace.

Mao's free-speech movement catches Chang and all such dissenting "flowers." Mao's Cultural Revolution and the Great Famine follow. There is still no public record of the devastation. Many years later, in 2008, I ask a young professor, "Why the silence?" He looks down and whispers, "Because we are ashamed."

My dragons now remind me that, while I had to anticipate my departure from Hong Kong with my family, I drafted a book in which I would lay out the long history of Chinese civilization as well as Mao's ill-judged efforts to wipe out the past and use modern political and military power to command foreign respect. I reconstruct Marco Polo's journeys through China, his establishment of the neighboring colony of Macau in 1557, the arrival of the English East India Company, whose agents were called Western Barbarians and had to obey the Middle Kingdom. I research the Opium War that followed the Chinese Imperial Commissioner's efforts to suppress trade in opium, denounced as "foreign mud" undermining Chinese civilization and spreading corruption. By the 1840s, British forces had held Shanghai, Amoy, and Ningpo. They were ready to occupy Nanking when China agreed to the establishment of Hong Kong as a free port in 1842. Chairman Mao Zedung denounced the "unequal treaties" of that time, but he also now tolerates Hong Kong as the largest source of Chinese commerce.

I look at things from India's viewpoint. Both countries are still treated in the West as backward. China is poorly understood but regarded as a massive threat. India is seen by the UK as emerging from under the benign guidance of the British Raj, still guided by incorruptible local officials trained by the British civil service and advancing through a muddle of uncertainties. My family's transit from one to the other is more poignant because we sail on the maiden voyage of a new cargo vessel that makes speed trials around the colony before heading for Calcutta. All the old familiar places pass us by: islands, ocean-going junks, and the "Nine Dragons" that gave Kowloon its name eight hundred years ago when the Boy Emperor Pang counted eight mountains and saw in each a dragon. Because ships could take on fresh spring water, China's name for this deep-sea retreat for the world's largest vessels was Heung Kong: Fragrant Harbour. The name holds for us strange memories.

We are the young who pack eternity into little satchels of time, linked by my dragons in defiance of mulish calendars. We see things differently, act more swiftly. Time is foreshortened, as if Glenys is still observing me in a Hellcat, looking no further than the end of an ADDLES runway. Fragrant Harbour is just another example of the opposing pull of two cultures. A third pull is our shared longing to follow in the footsteps of naturalists who "sought to capture and catalogue the natural world and build a great and permanent body of knowledge."*

Tiring of HCH's lack of commitment to a long-term post in Hong Kong and the nerve-wracking domestic anxiety about family needs, I join the staff of the press barons I took to Japan. I write for Toronto's *Globe & Mail* and report on radio and TV after drafting a final message to HCH that breaks our pigeon-post brevity: "Either balance of your mind is disturbed in making no promises or mine is unbalanced by lack certainty about my future." But before it is sent, HCH dies. He would have had the last laugh. The *Globe & Mail* publishes a long article by Premier Zhou Enlai that contradicts my repeated criticisms of the Cultural Revolution as a form of Newspeak in George Orwell's prediction of a new world where individualism is crushed. Han Suyin, in her 1994 book about herself and Zhou, *Eldest Son,* boasts of persuading *Globe & Mail* executives to print her enthusiastic endorsement of Mao's acts of repression. She forgets to mention the Great Famine.

She also fails to report significant misunderstandings between Zhou and the West. During the pioneering visit of US President Richard Nixon in the early 1970s, Zhou responds to a question about the impact of the

---

* The words are echoed later by Richard Conniff in his book, published in 2010: *The Species Seekers: Heroes, Fools and the Mad Pursuit of Life on Earth,* pub. WW Norton. Reviewed in the *Financial Times of London,* Nov. 21, 2010, by Manjit Kumar, author of *Quantum: Einstein, Bohr and The Great Debate about the Nature of Reality.*

French Revolution. "Too early to say," says Zhou. This is interpreted as a reference to the French Revolution and the Paris Commune nearly two centuries earlier, and taken as evidence of China's ability to think long-term, unlike the impatient Western powers that react to each twist and turn in world events. Many years later, an enormous misunderstanding is disclosed by the US Foreign Service officer who was present, Charles Freeman. He discloses that Zhou Enlai had been referring to student riots in Paris three years earlier, in 1968, and wished to avoid a more open reference to radical French Maoist protests in riots of that year. Zhou's cryptic caution had been influenced as well by a murderous political climate festering in Beijing at the time. Zhou's response, though, had been quoted as an example of China's far-thinking ability to soar above events, and his supposed reference to the French Revolution proof of the Chinese wisdom in viewing events in the context of the distant past and far into the foreseeable future.

Such mystifications become wearisome for an observer trying to muddle through the supposedly ancient wisdoms of the East. I can untangle the undeniably tangled threads of politics at home, but these seem relatively easy to discern, and susceptible to critical examination. I am missing the challenge of visible lies, and I miss threading a path through political chicanery that can be exposed in the course of democratic processes.

I am missing straightforward and visible truths. I miss sitting solitary in an aircraft cockpit, away from all the muddle of meddlesome players in squalid games of political mischief. Then I read in the *South China Morning Post* that a flight engineer in the back seat of the prototype Avro Canada CF-100 is killed after firing its seat ejector system to bail out above Toronto. I sat in that same back seat and was meant to bail out from that same prototype. And the very same seat ejection system was in use when Jan Zurakowski demonstrated for me his new aerobatic.

# CHAPTER 35

# End of an Ace and an Honest Man

SUMMER OF 1959. MY DRAGONS HOP ME BACK ACROSS TIME, FROM HONG Kong to 1950 and a flight in the same CF-100. The hydraulics fail. Zura cannot fire the Martin-Baker seat that should shoot me out of our crippled craft in Canadian skies.

I met Zura's future wife during my first assignment in Poland, after meeting Zura while I was at Elementary Flying School. She was a young girl in love with the fighter pilot when he flew old biplanes against formidable German warplanes during the Nazi attack on Warsaw in 1939. They had sworn, somehow, somewhere, to meet again. After the war, she posed as the very model of a fervent young communist. She played the role so well, the Polish Communist Party sent her to Paris for further studies. She skipped Paris, made her way to England, and found Zura. He was, by then, Britain's hottest test pilot.

"I must get as far from communism as I can," she told him. Zura married her and moved to Canada, where he became Avro Canada's chief test pilot. His part in the Battle of Britain is the stuff of legend. Before the war, he had qualified as an aeronautical engineer. That discipline helps him coldly analyze every move he makes as an aviator. He takes me up in the CF-100 to demonstrate its unsurpassed qualities. I am reporting on a black cloud that hangs over the new and independent Canadian aircraft industry. My dragons pull up old reports from days of dashed hopes when the CF-100 and its creators of Avro Canada are all endangered by a Canadian government under pressure to buy US warplanes. Zura was committed to proving that

Canada could design and make unprecedented fighters to deal with its own special challenges.

There is one flyable prototype of the new CF-100 fighter with enough range to cover Canada, which has to protect the broadest skies in the world. Zura demonstrates for me the first new aerobatic since the First World War. This is his own "Zurabatic." We climb straight up with the two jet engines at full blast until the CF-100 seems to stand stationary on its tail, balancing force of gravity against pull of jets. Zura cuts back the port engine. This throws us into a vertical spin. "Gor' blimey! Arse over tit!" I might have thought, but would never say to Zura. One never indulged in such crudities, even if they were used by other pilots in that air war fought for Britain by my Polish comrade. He was a man who shrank from any kind of bad language.

I hear him say over the intercom: "Beel, we have a problem." Soft and calm, as always. I hear no more. He has blown the canopy enclosing us. The slipstream tears off my helmet. Will he fire my ejection seat to make a parachute descent? A blast of air floods my eyes. I cannot see his hand signals. Perhaps the violent maneuver locked the landing gear in the up position. In this prototype, fuel tanks are not yet fireproofed. If we make a belly landing, friction can make the fuel explode.

I clear my goggles and two jet fighters appear. My friends Michael Cooper-Slipper and Don Rogers fly on either side and tap their helmets, as if urging me to jump. But I know Zura. He won't abandon the sole working model of a long-range aircraft needed for defense of Arctic air space bordering Russia. Our escorts peel away. Zura bleeds off altitude and circles the control tower. Our wheels remain retracted. Commercial flights come to a standstill. Fire trucks creep along the main runway and spill foam to cushion a wheels-up landing.

Zura tries to shake down the landing gear in sick-making bunny hops. Rogers and Cooper-Slipper give us a thumbs-up. The wheels are down. But our instruments do not show if the wheels are locked in position. Zura gently approaches the moment of truth, flying the heavy fighter just above stalling speed, feeling his way down, ready to open up if the landing gear begins to buckle. Blood-wagons roll on either side, keeping pace.

The CF-100 rides high on its storklike legs. The landing gear holds! Zura shuts down both engines. We scramble out. Our two escorts scream low over the airport and then climb straight up into victory rolls.

Zura drives me back into town along the Queen Elizabeth Highway. He stays in the slow lane. "I do not wish to die in a car crash," he squeaks, as he always does when driving me home. I never report the incident for publication. Avro Canada is in enough trouble. Later, the flight engineer in my same seat succeeded in firing it and was killed when he struck the CF-100's tail. The seat's guidance rods were installed at the wrong angle. The error was never discovered until ejection explosives were fired electronically for the first time.

"There, but for the grace of God . . . " I tell Glenys. She remembers Bill Dryly, war veteran, an editor at the *Toronto Star,* telling her, "If your husband fell into a bucket of shit, he'd come up smelling of roses."

Zura continues his test flights and the CF-100 goes into service. Then the first delta-winged military aircraft, the Avro Arrow, takes shape in a secret hangar. Nearby, the world's first jetliner is ready to go. But John Diefenbaker, a prairie boy-cum-prime-minister, brutally cuts all further government funding. The Avro Canada Jetliner is sold to Howard Hughes. Test-pilot Don Rogers goes with the deal. Cooper-Slipper and Canada's brilliant team of specialists are snapped up by NASA. Zura's whole adult life has been spent in defeating identifiable enemies in the sky, not wading through the muck of politics. He is beaten for the first time and retreats to run a hunting lodge in the backwoods. There is no official history to trace the real political causes of this abandonment of an enterprise too big for small minds. Politicians yield to Canada's big neighbor. Another prime minister, Pierre Trudeau, repeats in public, "You can't challenge an elephant when you're a mouse in its shadow."

## CHAPTER 36

# The Mole Who Gagged Soviet Defectors

"DRAGONS IN EUROPEAN MYTHOLOGY HAVE WINGS TO SOAR FREELY AND view a vast panorama of events below," I am told by Ian Fleming. He knows my early exchanges with The Boxing Parson. My dragons give me a fresh view of Fleming when we meet before I move my family to India from Hong Kong. He is "roving foreign editor" for the *Sunday Times* of London, paid to travel abroad and research his James Bond thrillers. It makes him unpopular with Ian Lang, the official foreign editor who resents Fleming's rival role. "He never recovered from the shutdown of *Mercury News* as a source of intelligence," Ian Lang tells me in Formosa while I am there to discuss a series of *Sunday Times* reports on this off-shore island occupied by Chiang Kai-shek.

When I return to the colony, Fleming says, "You're finally a man of the world. Show me what you see." I take him to the vice dens of Macau and learn how diligently he researches his thrillers. His James Bond is a deadpan secret-service agent with high tastes and low instincts, esti-mated to command 1,250,000 readers. His sixth James Bond novel, *Dr. No*, published in 1958, emerges from our Macau explorations. I see now the foundation of Fleming's Bond-style secrecy. He suggests that I tell for the first time the story of a real-life version of Bond, Bill Stephenson, and his Intrepid secret intelligence agency, BSC, that readers would find more fantastic than fiction. Ian Lang is unaware of my STEVERITE-INTER exchanges and that Stephenson has asked me to delay writing his memoirs until a time when disclosure may be essential to remind democracies that the new advances in secret intelligence, hidden from public scrutiny, demand leaders of utmost integrity. Fleming recommends me to Nick Elliott of MI6. The old-boy network still operates. Elliott later tells me what really happened when he was asked in January 1973 to collect Kim Philby without any publicity. Nothing must undermine public faith in the inscrutable secret bureaucracies. Elliott used a well-honed technique for drinking a suspect far enough under the table to loosen his tongue. But Philby is even more experienced in such methods. The mole drinks far into the night until he moans, "I let the school down, Nick, old chap." He was a schoolboy at Eton when Nick's dad was headmaster. "I'll come quietly," says Philby. "Let's meet for breakfast." By breakfast, he is on a Russian trawler to become the first Englishman dubbed a Red Army lieutenant-general.

Nick Elliott is retired when I finally get him to explain how Philby escaped. I had interviewed General Reinhard Gehlen, Hitler's chief spymaster on the Russian front and postwar chief of West German intelligence. His disclosures led me to write *The Bormann Brotherhood*, a 1973 biography of Martin Bormann, who was the least visible but most powerful of Nazi warlords. This intrigues a Welsh physician, responsible for the health in Spandau prison of ex-Deputy Fuehrer Rudolf Hess. The doctor gives me X-rays to prove the prisoner of Spandau is not Hess. Such encounters excite the interest of former intelligence chiefs like Nick Elliott, who invites me to his country house. On the ground floor, it resembles a rambling old vicarage. Monika, my present wife, now a *60 Minutes* TV producer, is with me. She slips upstairs to use the loo and tells me later, "Up there, it's like a James Bond movie set." Nick's elegant wife serves a brunch of foie-gras freshly flown from France. Her husband was also suspected of being a mole after Philby escaped, but that ghost no longer haunts him. In Nick's old garden shed, which leans a trifle drunkenly on the other side of the village lane, we mumble artfully. My mind wanders to when I was a *Toronto Star* reporter. HCH liked old truisms coined by great men, from C.P. Scott of the *Manchester Guardian* to Shakespeare. One day HCH reminded me of Doctor Watson's surprise that Sherlock

Holmes never knew the earth and moon orbited the sun. "Sherlock said he kept in his memory only what he needed to know for his work."

I disagree. After schooldays when I delivered newspapers, I wanted to keep alive all memories, however widely separated in time and place. The memories are milestones. Too many are forgotten because keeping them in notebooks seemed enough. Now I recover an old note from Anne Sharpley: "The further back you look, the further forward you can see." I look back to 1964–65, shortly after my family lived in Kenya while I roamed across the African continent. I'm a producer and presenter in London of Independent TV's *Dateline News* and the further back I look, the further forward I see myself forever confined to a TV studio. My Kenyan friend, Nick Carter, expelled by African nationalism from protecting rhinos, survives in London for a few weeks. "I'm suffocating," he groans and heads for South Africa and a game warden's job. I can only return to Africa in my head. I write a novel based on my eldest daughter, Jackie, and her Kenyan animal pet, a bushbaby. Anne finds me a publisher and the book becomes an MGM movie, *The Bushbabies,* with Hollywood stars playing Jackie and her black African guardian. In Japan, in the 1990s, it becomes an animated forty-week TV series when another bushbaby is the pet of my youngest daughter at the Thai palace school in Bangkok. Memories of wildlife are more vivid than notebooks.

In London, stifled by city life and office politics, Anne Sharpley tells me later that Tom Little died in the Cairo jail to which he was sent after handling our Cable & Wireless telegrams about Nasser's hired Nazis. My curiosity about such distant mysteries is fired up again. Within a year, I am back in Malaysia. My children attend the British Army School in Singapore. Anne dies after telling me the horror story of a faulty medical diagnosis by a group of doctors who missed the subtle evidence of a rare cancer. She would have laughed at the claim by a disgruntled CIA defector who publishes a book identifying me as MI6's man in Egypt. There's no way to disprove this; no way to prove a negative. How my dragons do foreshorten time. Too often, they spout fire and brimstone.

CHAPTER 37

# The Burma Road Leads to China's Future

THIS LATEST ASSIGNMENT IN THE MALAY PENINSULA PUTS A NEW FACE on one of the strangest of journeys I made along the Burma Road, in the mid-1950s. Others follow. By 2009, I am back on the road yet again, and see it as a strategic highway into regions once disputed by US arms. By 2011, it is a symbol of China's growth into the world's second largest economy, causing a global demand for copper, aluminum, steel, tin, and coal. For some commodities, China is reported in a *London Financial Times* survey to be responsible for more than 100 percent in the rise in demand for natural resources overseas. All this is within the half-century since New China was deeply suspicious of the outside world. I am astonished to be invited to travel again on the road that was a tortuous, daunting ribbon of red dust when it was used by Western democracies to bring massive support for China's Nationalists in the 1941–45 war with Japan.

My dragons go back to my first drive along this unique road. Beforehand, I tell Madame Kung Peng that my then wife Glenys would like to visit Beijing. This is 1956 and Kung Peng is pleased by this gesture of trust when North American newspapers report atrocities in China, and US correspondents are forbidden to see China for themselves. Glenys leaves the children in Hong Kong, care of the *Observer*'s Rawle Knox and his wife, Helen. Rawle comes from a long line of distinguished English literary and religious personalities. His favorite occupation is composing poetry while soaking in his bath.

Malaya and its neighbors are populated by Chinese migrants who launch small businesses, work long hours, and send all the money they can spare to their families in China, even during Chairman Mao's tightening of the screws. In Hong Kong, my children are always under the eyes of our amah, Ah Mei, and her husband, Ah Wong. He confides that he will return to China when things get better. He is disillusioned by Western expatriates who quit Hong Kong and abandon servants who develop strong emotional ties with the expats' children. Ah Wong listens to Red Army marching songs on Beijing radio, and Mao's version of the 2,500-year-old Confucian promise that, "The truly great General serves best by mastering the art of conquering hostile territory without bloodshed . . . and of vanquishing the enemy without giving battle."Ah Wong hopes China will win equality without fighting the great powers that reduced to servitude the Chinese in this Chinese place run by foreigners. It is many years later that I fly from Malay to Hong Kong and get an unexpected invitation to visit Americans I have never met. I go to the address specified. A smiling Ah Wong opens the door. Ah Mei giggles in the background. I have no idea how they know I am back, yet they had asked their latest employer to wine and dine me. All evening they carry out their duties until I nip into the kitchen to answer a barrage of questions about my children, my wife, and the state of my health. Loyalty shines out of their faces. They will eventually go back to their home in northern China, but only after the riots in Tiananmen Square challenge Maoist tyranny.

Now up comes an old STEVERITE communication to INTER, dated 1956: "We shelter amahs and cook-boys in Hong Kong, but we shall pay a far higher price than the few dollars we give them now. Zhou wants to counterbalance the Soviet Union. Ho Chi-minh is driven into the arms of our enemies. The debacle at Dien Bien Phu shows we squander 'advanced weapons' on Asians who beat us with the old traditional weapons hand-built out of wily unorthodoxy. The Chinese drive a strategic military road through East Ladakh in Nepal to reinforce their expanding highway, the Burma Road. . . . " And I repeat Mao's quotation about "mastering the art of conquering hostile territory without bloodshed."

On Burma Road author travels with China's Premier Chou Enlai on his way to meet Burmese leaders for talks on China-Burmese cooperation. 1960.

Old photographs and notes come up from that 1956 journey to the border, foreshadowing China's claim that territories to the south owe allegiance to Beijing. Trails are unpaved and resemble East Africa's red earthen roads: none so serpentine as this old Burma Road, looping around steep hills and doubling back upon itself for what feels like hundreds of miles. The actual distance, I am told by Madame Kung Peng, is a state secret. It's an ancient trail, opened up by African-American soldiers to provide a strategic link with Chinese opponents of Japanese invaders in World War II. Flying supplies was in those days both dangerous and wasteful. "The Burma Hump" was a barrier consisting of the worst of unpredictable thunderstorms. Cargo planes vanished without trace. Now Red Army trucks rumble along the road from Kunming to Burma. This is December and it is difficult to imagine the cumulonimbus barriers between Calcutta,

200

the old wartime source of supplies, and The Hump. Here the skies are a cloudless blue, and the winter rice is said to be just as abundant as that of spring and summer. Visible are the snowy peaks of Tibet. My guide, "Chairman" Chang, says his government will restore all the ancient trading routes that wind into Tibet, and cross the high plateau to the Silk Road and Russia. "We have more manpower to restore traditional paths to the South China Sea and Tibet than any other country in the world," he says, his chubby face expressionless.

At the Burma border, I find Rawle Knox. He arrives with Burmese leaders because he cannot get a visa into China. I ask Kung Peng to bend the rules and let Rawle enter to report this meeting between Zhou and Burma's premier, U Ba Swe. She agrees but wonders who is caring for my children. Rawle says my wife is back in Hong Kong after "a most illuminating sojourn in New China." Then he joins me and several thousand locals who spend all night singing the praises of the joint friendship between national minorities and Beijing. They parade local costumes, sing tribal songs, and bang drums as different in design as their vivid clothing. The underlying message is that China will show Tibetan and other South Asian minorities the same goodwill—under Chinese law. Rawle winces. But he remembers George Orwell's sour vision of British imperial bullying when Orwell served in Burma's Imperial Police, before Aung San Sun Kyi's father fought for freedom and was murdered.

Rawle brings bottles of whiskey to sustain us during the long comradely speeches. A couple of Red Army officers stand in front of us to yell support for Sino-Burmese development of the Mekong and other mighty rivers fed by the melting snows of Tibet. Rawle and I apologize to two officers blocking our view. We explain that unfortunately we have to grab them by the tail of their army tunics and yank them back down into their seats so that we may properly show our respect and admiration for such rousing promises of joint prosperity. The officers share a stone bottle of mao-tai with us. In return, they take a few slugs from our Johnnie Walker scotch. They must reason that if Rawle and I are here, we are honored guests from some primitive corner of the Soviet Union and our uncouth manners should be tolerated.

Next morning at breakfast in one of the community huts swiftly improvised out of the surrounding jungle growth, Rawle watches me and turns deathly white. "What's that you're eating?"

"Goats' lungs," I reply, chewing away.

Rawle claps a hand over his mouth and rushes outside. He returns some while later and murmurs apologetically, "I drank too much scotch last night. Sorry, old boy." Really it was the realization that he, too, must have eaten goats' lungs that he mistook for some awful local sausage. I had consumed them as part of the PLA's cuisine on the road, and acquired a taste for them. "You've been brainwashed," Rawle tells me, and perhaps I had. I certainly learned to see Malaysia and the surrounding countries through Beijing's ambitious and yet traditional viewpoint. The "national minorities" were going through a kind of brainwashing to play a future part in China's domination of South Asia. Not that it always succeeded. Ironically, after US armed forces left Vietnam, war broke out between America's communist enemies in Hanoi and China's Red Army.

⸺

Decades later, in the twenty-first century, in China's Year of the Dragon, I travel again down the Burma Road, now a modern multilane highway. My present wife, Monika Jensen, and our young daughter, Alexandra, are with me. Monika recognizes US Marine Corps decals on our battered old jeep "liberated" during the short, sharp, and deadly frontier war between China and Vietnam that followed the US withdrawal. That later conflict is almost ignored in the Western media. "It cost many more lives than those lost in the French-Indochina and Vietnam wars," claims an INTER message to STEVERITE. Burma is now part of China's economy and thumbs its nose at Western accusations that tyrants oppress this scenically gorgeous country. Sucked into playing a role in China's development of their resources, Burma's military dictators ignore Western sermons about personal liberty.

Our driver in 2009 calls himself John. He was a PLA major who fought in the brief and nasty Sino-Vietnam war. I ask if we can drive to the Burma border. He apologizes: Foreigners are not allowed there. I say I've been there before, with Zhou Enlai. John looks embarrassed. He remembers how Zhou died. What I remember is that Madame Kung Peng was also allowed to die from cancer. It's a creepy feeling I get now, because John wants to be helpful, in much the same way as Zhou and Kung Peng. I try another tack and confide that my wife and our daughter lived in Thailand between 1989 and 1995, and often entered northern Burma with the mother of the king. We saw Burmese kneel in affection for the Princess Mother, who is Chinese.

John digests this and talks of big projects to be jointly developed with Thailand. "The lower Mekong is to be broadened in partnership with other Asian countries. It will be like before. China will deliver valuable cargoes everywhere. Tibetan products will again be shipped around the globe. This new Burma highway is the main stem of many great projects to bring prosperity to south-western regions whose development was stunted by Western colonizers." Because Alexandra speaks fluent Mandarin Chinese, he adds, "You are friends of China."

"In that case, surely there can be no objection to driving us to the border," I suggest hopefully.

Before responding, he takes us to a splendid little teahouse. Nearby is a village that looks as if it has not changed in a thousand years, except that on the thatched roofs there is now the glitter of government-supplied solar panels for converting the year-round sunshine to electric power. And in place of little pigs rushed to market by farmers in need of a fast turnover, there are the biggest of hogs. John tells us "the Party pays the farmers to wait until the hogs are so large, they sell for much higher prices at market. Everyone benefits."

He says foreigners can no longer go all the way to the border without a special dispensation. "But I am free to come and go whenever I please." He murmurs something about being also an officer in the Burmese army. He wears civilian clothes, scrubbed many times. He could be an offshoot of Ah Wong and Ah Wei or any number of house servants in Hong Kong when it was still a colony. Now thousands of Chinese are working in Burma for Chinese corporations. No wonder the military dictators of Burma defy Western pleas to free Aung San Suu Kyi, the jailed leader of the pro-democracy movement, and daughter of Aung San, paramount leader of the six Burmese ministers who were cut down by assassins in 1947. I remember Aung San's successor meeting with Zhou Enlai on the frontier that year. It is out of bounds. Dragons bring up notes on questions I submitted on this first journey to the Burma border when I asked about the investigation by Major-General Tun Hla Oung, former chief of Burma's Imperial Police, into the killing of Aung San. "He was disliked by the British for successfully challenging their colonial grip," I was told. "Much is still hidden under British laws on secrecy."

King Bhumibol, the Ninth Rama of Thailand, in 1991, tells me, "The secrecy hides an inquiry into reports that a group of British military officers shot him." The king trusts his people, and astonishes me by his rejection of the elaborate security precautions surrounding other leaders. Twenty years later, though, I see that he has few trustworthy advisers to help him save the kingdom from being sucked into dangerous waters.

—◦—

I learn something about dangerous waters of the more obvious kind after I shuttle between Hong Kong and India, renting an apartment in New Delhi to cover China-India fire fights. Finally I move the family by cargo ship to India at the end of 1960. We have to navigate around Typhoon Alice, off the Vietnam coast. Glenys, the children, and I occupy all the extra accommodation. This is a time when such vessels have space for passengers who enjoy long voyages by sea and good food and wines at the captain's table. Sally is just old enough to walk when we tuck her up in a cot. We return from fine dining to find Sally gone and a porthole open. Huge waves rock our vessel. We must be closer to the typhoon than our Norwegian captain expected. He navigates in wide circles to create a smooth patch of water in the forlorn hope of finding her. And we do find her—safe with the ship's Chinese cook in the galley. "Baby cry!" he explains, rocking her gently. "So I sing baby bye-bye."

Once in Delhi, my boys attend an Indian school, trout fish in Kashmir, exercise the president's horses, and fly in Tiger Moths. Jackie teaches Sally to swim in the pool of a luxury hotel and Glenys agrees that she should take a ship from Bombay to England with the girls because many dangers surround the Delhi apartment. We dodge swift attacks from wasps nesting under the balcony of our neighbor, an Afghan diplomat, who lives above. I am with Glenys and our girls in Bombay when a horse-drawn wagon rumbles along the street and we recognize our goods and chattels, sent ahead from Delhi, now strapped on board the cart. We have learned to laugh at the unexpected, swinging between astonishing revelations to bad moments handled with help from loyal Indian friends.

"Am I reckless as a father?" I ask myself that night as I turn up the collar of my pajamas. Our family would never have such experiences if I were a banker, I try to convince myself. Take Kashmir, for instance. I fly my two sons there from Delhi for adventures I could only dream about as a child in the London slums.

## CHAPTER 38

# A Splendid Secret Love

I AM IN KASHMIR WITH MY TWO SONS, ANDREW AND KEVIN, IN 1961. Aboard our wooden houseboat on Dal Lake, I keep notes on the strife between Muslims and Hindus. This has grown steadily worse in Kashmir since the British Raj ended in the partition of Pakistan and India at the urging of Lord Mountbatten. Lady Mountbatten's close affection for Nehru is discreet but the lovers cannot hide it. I see them holding hands in Chandigarh, the new capital of the Punjab, which Nehru tries to keep united despite the discord sewn by Muslim fanatics. She is now titled Countess Mountbatten of Burma, which seems to me ironic in light of Mao's conviction that Burma is historically Chinese until colonized by Britain. This freshly minted Countess of Burma is often present when I talk with Nehru. She shows particular interest in my ventures into Bhutan, the Himalayan kingdom where I first saw a small girl, later famous as Aung San Sun Kyi, who fights against Burma's dictators. Lady Edwina is well informed about my journeys elsewhere, and one aspect sticks in my mind: her interest in my reactions to Auschwitz, and my understanding of Poland's entry into Moscow's orbit after the West's indifference to wartime appeals for help from the Polish anti-Nazi underground armies.

Nehru is familiar with my work. India's foreign-affairs department reprints my news reports, a procedure inherited from the UK government, which copied and filed all telegrams sent through its postal service and Cable & Wireless. The Foreign Office IRD (Intelligence Research) now condenses suitable material for the Near & Far East News Agency (NAFEN). Its manager, based in New Delhi, is Ted Howe, who fought with Tito's guerrillas against the Nazis. He arranges for me to write for NAFEN. It's another outlet for reports on events that get little or no attention from regular news services.

Nehru talks about infiltrating and outflanking Chinese border posts in Ladakh. He values my STEVERITE-INTER telegrams because Stephenson is in regular touch with the Mountbattens. At the end of February 1960, I recall again, I was at the Indian Council for International Affairs in Delhi. All 563 seats were occupied when Lady Mountbatten's sudden death in Borneo was announced. Everyone turned to watch Nehru's reaction. He adores the Countess Mountbatten of Burma, for her beauty and for her work throughout South Asia, locating prisoners of war and other victims of Japanese atrocities. It is a startling transformation from her pre-World War II reputation as a social butterfly. Now she represents the American Red Cross, the St. John Ambulance Brigade, and the Save The Children Fund, among other welfare agencies. Her white tropical uniform, when she wears it, displays five rows of medal ribbons, including the Brilliant Star of China. Her grandfather was a German Jew whose family moved to London, where her father became the richest man in England. She is sensitive to hostile comments about the German origins of her husband, Admiral Lord Mountbatten, who served in the Royal Navy and then became Supreme Commander, South East Asia Command, SEAC. "Dickie" Mountbatten was portrayed as "a jumped-up playboy" and Edwina as "a spoilt Jewish playgirl of doubtful morals" in newspapers owned by the press baron Lord Beaverbrook, who detested them both.

Edwina's transformation is recorded in published diaries kept by Mountbatten. An entry dated August 22–28, 1945, refers to her "great experience in Europe." She arrives at the Normandy beaches after D-Day and plunges into saving survivors of German prison camps after hearing the first public accounts of Auschwitz. She is in Burma on the heels of the retreating Japanese, in a role code-named "Operation Edwina." She helps save the hundreds of thousands of American and British battle-shocked prisoners in camps stripped by the Japanese of everything.

Word of surrender had not reached some Japanese commanders who were also battling packs of armed "bandits." Nehru, as first leader of an independent India, had to tour a region that would be of immense importance to the new republic. Lord Mountbatten had written in a diary shared with Nehru: "Few people realize the immense scale of the enlarged South East Asia Command. A million and a half square miles of territory ... half a million Japs and over 200,000 prisoners of war and internees to be repatriated. .... SEAC starts a few hundred miles west of Karachi, down to easternmost limits halfway through New Guinea, a distance of 6,050 statute miles. This is 150 miles more than the distance from the northwest corner of SEAC to St. John's, Newfoundland!"

Nehru told the UK journalist Ray Murphy, "I first met Lady Mountbatten when I found her sleeping on the floor of a hut in Singapore after the Japanese had gone. Emaciated ex-prisoners occupied the hut's few bunks and she was afraid to disturb them." This began his fourteen-year romance with Edwina.

Mounbatten is not with Edwina only days before her death when Nehru stands with her on January 26, 1960, at the Republic Day Parade in Dehli. Soviet President Voroshilov is the guest of Nehru, who needs Moscow's goodwill to counterbalance Red China's intrusions into Ladakh, challenging the Indian army along the northern Nepalese borders. Nehru turns to the woman whose uncle by marriage was the last tsar of all the Russias: "Edwina, I would like you to meet the Russian President ..." Soon Voroshilov is deep in conversation with Lady Mountbatten, related by marriage to most of the crowned heads of Europe. They are joined by Nehru's daughter, Indira Gandhi, who will assume Nehru's mantle. Later, after she takes over, I ask Indira: "Did your father wish he could marry Edwina?" Indira's eyes water and she shakes her head, as if avoiding the issue. When she is later assassinated, I remember that silent, enigmatic gesture.

On this Republic Day in 1960, Lady Mountbatten is fifty-eight years old and looks gorgeous: sparkling blue eyes, long graceful neck, beautiful bone structure. Stiffness in one cheek betrays her angina. Nehru is now seventy, bronzed and handsome. Their affair dated back to when they worked closely together during the 1947 transfer of power from Britain to this vast subcontinent.

Edwina joins Indira in the Moghul Garden at the close of these latest festivities. "The Bright Young Thing of the twenties has made something of herself—nothing to do with status—a great deal to do with vitality," reports Charles Wheeler, the BBC correspondent who shares his Delhi office with me. "When Edwina leaves Nehru's house for the last time, the lovers display sheer joy on Nehru's lawn. He wears garlands to join Punjabi Bangra dancers, and Edwina shines in pink sandals and a vivid red suit."

Before a grueling journey to Sarawak in her few last days of life, she questions me about Indonesia. She knows I had sailed there from Borneo with rebels against the Djakarta regime. She flies to Borneo on Thursday, February 8, 1960. Her duties and social exchanges fill all her waking hours, and are orchestrated by the Acting Governor, Bob Turner, locked up by the Japanese when they invaded, freed by Nepalese Gurkhas after he suffered almost four years of cruel internment. He shows her Mount Kinabalu, 13,500 feet high. . . . Today's dragons bring e-mails from my youngest daughter Alexandra, aged twenty when she climbed this same mountain decades later. By then, few remember Edwina's final hours. On the morning of the twenty-first of February, Edwina is found dead in the spare bedroom of Bob Turner's house. Nehru knew she had concealed how seriously ill she was during their last reunion. He had accepted with a terrible, private sadness that she would never return from serving causes to which this "Jewish playgirl" devoted the second half of her life.

# CHAPTER 39

# Dalai Lama Is No More "On Top"

BEFORE THE DEATH OF LADY MOUNTBATTEN, I AM AGAIN TALKING WITH Nehru. We sit on the usual wickerwork chairs on the lawn outside his modest residence. He has never forgotten our encounter in the Forbidden City with the Dalai Lama. Since then, the Indian leader has tried to thwart Chinese excursions across the Northwest frontier. One afternoon, while Edwina hovers, a messenger brings a telegram from Tibet reporting that the Dalai Lama has fled. Nehru tells me, "He's not running away. He's coming here to fight in his own nonviolent Buddhist way."

I leave for Nepal and intercept the Dalai Lama. He recalls our meeting in Beijing, when he pointed to his autograph above that of the Panchen Lama. Now he tells me, "I had to warn you that Mao wanted the Panchen Lama on top. I was careful. Mao sent his last emperor to Manchuria as a puppet."

To persuade Nehru to make peace on another front, I am asked by David Astor, proprietor of the *London Observer,* to advise "Dingle, one of The Three Left Feet." Dingle Foot is the youngest of three British left-wing brothers. Eldest is Michael Foot, the Labour Party's most strident socialist, who came to Nehru's rescue when he was detained as a leftist troublemaker by British authorities during the war. Michael is remembered for his battle cry: "We are here to provide for all who are weaker and hungrier, more battered and crippled than we. . . . If you ask me about those insoluble economic problems that arise if the top is deprived of their perks, I reply, 'To Hell with them!' The top is greedy and mean and always finds a way to take care of themselves." His views, considered

Author demonstrates photographic equipment to Dalai Lama's court merchants in Nepal, where they had just arrived from Tibet looking for supplies to take back to the Dalai Lama. 1958.

outlandish then, seem prophetic today. The London *Financial Times* in 2010 comments that after major international banking upheavals, "perhaps the time has come for his socialist solutions."

Dingle Foot's assignment is to dampen conflict between India and Pakistani Muslims in Kashmir. He tries to persuade Nehru to forget the murderous consequences of Mountbatten's swift partitioning of India. Nehru foresaw the aftermath: the worst Islamic atrocities against Hindu Indians ever recorded. Now he refuses to give up Indian protection of a sultan who rules part of Kashmir claimed by Pakistan. Nehru has hardened since he lost Edwina. He dies four years later, a troubled prime minister, impatient to build a nation united across religious and political divides. He never budges on Kashmir, where conflicts attract little attention in the foreign press until the twenty-first century when Pakistan turns Kashmir into a battlefield with the aim of driving out all Hindus. Edwina Mountbatten had hoped Nehru might prevent the religious and racial hatreds that she foresaw would spread into Afghanistan.

# CHAPTER 40

# The King and I Share Dragons

THE DALAI LAMA'S JOCULAR WISH NOT TO BE BANISHED TO MANCHURIA like China's last emperor had been woven into my novel *Emperor Red*. Now I want more than ever to write about the world of nature. I work with the only king ever born in the United States. He teaches his people that understanding wildlife will counter the human drive to self-destruct. He is King Bhumibol, the Ninth Rama of Thailand. Siam is the old title to which royalty clings. Today, I recover a handwritten letter signed simply "Bhumibol." It foreshadows more Far East adventures. His letter praises Sir William Stephenson's unconventional approach to warfare and asks for permission to translate into the Thai language my biography *A Man Called Intrepid*.

We meet at Narathiwat, the king's "working palace" on the Malay border, in company with my second wife, Monika. From here, the king reasons with Muslims at odds with the smaller Buddhist population in his four southern provinces. I had earlier discussed with Bhumibol the confusions of Muslim militancy during the "confrontation" war Indonesia launched against the moderate Muslims of Malaysia. In September 1987, I explore Bhumibol's need to use homemade weaponry instead of the expensive hi-tech US weapons employed against the communist Vietminh. He flies us to see his improvisations, such as a jungle factory making artificial limbs from local materials instead of paying through the nose for US supplies. With us is Queen Sirikit. Both studied in Europe when she was a striking girl of seventeen who appeared on covers of fashion magazines all over the world. I say his land-reform programs revive my schoolboy dreams about

Author walking along jungle trail with King Bhumibol, Ninth Rama of Thailand. The author's wife follows with Queen Sirikit and Princess Sirindhorn (in gray safari suit).

wilderness places. The king says his mother was born in the slums of Bangkok. She is Chinese. His daughter, Crown Princess Sirindhorn, looks for Siam's origins in China along the Burma Road. It symbolizes, for her, historic ties between China and its southern neighbors.

Bhumibol, Queen Sirikit, and the crown princess escort Monika and me along jungle footpaths. We discuss how we can live as a family in the kingdom. He asks Monika not to chronicle this period. He knows Monika first worked with me on documentaries in Israel when I fell head over heels in love with her, and that she is now working on a book and documentary for New York media. Our daughter, Alexandra, now age four, attends Chitrlada, the palace school, where she becomes part of court activities. My own strictly private, one-on-one discussions with the king often continue for hours. I discover a king wise about world affairs. He followed Zhou Enlai's efforts to avoid war when Chiang Kaishek's Nationalist armies claimed to be fighting communists after Mao

The author's wife in close discussion with Queen Sirikit.

had assumed power. "The Nationalists' real aim was to develop the drug trade, sanctioned by their US patrons," he says. He asks about Auschwitz, voices horror that for years after 1945, most of the outside world forgot about it. He talks of Israel's rise out of the ashes and what he learned about national self-reliance from the Israelis. He knows I publish as much as can be told about Intrepid, skirting UK secrecy laws that prevent the inclusion of findings about a Japanese war criminal who, disguised as a Buddhist monk, in 1949 shot dead Bhumibol's elder brother Ananda, the Eighth Rama. This king's enemies spread stories that he killed Ananda. Later I get a document detailing prolonged investigations into the murder, including the findings of British experts. There is no clear explanation of why Ananda, aged twenty-one, had been shot through the head early one morning in the Grand Palace, but all the circumstances demonstrate that he could not have been killed by his young brother, who was twenty at the time.

The Ninth Rama admires Edwina Mountbatten's work in Burma, but is less impressed by her husband, who swept into Bangkok on the heels of the vanquished Japanese. The published Mountbatten diaries "paint a

214

grotesque portrait," says this king. He was born in modest circumstances in Boston, Massachusetts, in the same year as myself. His father, who never felt high on the royalty ladder, was studying medicine in Boston when he met a nurse, the former slum girl, and married her. Bhumibol's older brother was born in Germany, and was shot dead soon after SEAC's Supreme Commander, Mountbatten, met him in Bangkok on Friday, January 18, 1946. Bhumibol has not forgiven Lord Mountbatten's portrayal of his older brother as a "Boy King . . . a frightened short-sighted . . . sloping shoulders and thin chest behung with gorgeous diamond-studded decorations, altogether pathetic. . . . " The king deplores an entry in Mountbatten's published diary: "Some 40 years ago, a small baby was found in a basket and taken to the Queen (the present Queen grand-mother) where she was bought up to become an additional maid . . . The foundling girl chose to become a registered nurse and went to America to be trained. The then-Queen's youngest son, a doctor attached to an American hospital, met what was probably the only Siamese woman in American medical circles. They fell in love, were married, and produced three children, a daughter (who is unfortunately married to the son of the leading war criminal of Siam) and two sons. They settled at Lausanne in Switzerland and then the Doctor Prince died . . . His eldest brother had abdicated as King Prajadibok some 12 years ago."

Siam, as it was called during the Japanese occupation, wanted to re-establish the monarchy through the ex-nurse's small family in Lausanne. "They paid a brief visit to Siam but were so horrified by Siamese Court life that they hastily returned to Lausanne. . . . " noted Mountbatten's diary. "The 1942 leaders of Siam were violently pro-Axis and declared war on the British and Americans." He neglected to record that Siamese resisters fought a savage underground war against the Japanese occupiers, nor that one young Siamese prince was killed piloting a Hurricane RAF fighter. When the war ended, Bhumibol and his brother Ananda left their studies in Switzerland and went to Bangkok with their mother. After Ananda was shot dead, Bhumibol took over as the Ninth Rama, instinctively aware that a swift restoration of the monarchy was the only way to save the country from chaos.

The Ninth Rama has a detailed memory of Anglo-American operations in the Second World War. In his first handwritten letter, dated April 22, 1978, he writes that Intrepid is "an inspiration for our people, especially young officers in the armed forces, to follow the example of a man who has dedicated his life to combat injustice and uphold world peace by conventional and 'unconventional' means. With the latter, the spirit of dedication and honour is always present. Our country is subject to tremendous pressures from every quarter. Perhaps we are in the most critical period of our history; though we have always been able to weather all crises using the very strong spirit of unity which emerges in difficult times. But our people are thus that when they don't see the physical dangers we are facing, they tend to be lax. And the new kind of danger before us does not show its face, because it is even more than total war: it is what I would call 'mental war.'" The modest address on the king's letters is "Chitrlada Villa," where he lives, rather than the Grand Palace, for reasons I discover in ensuing years.

He startles me with anecdotes about the old Swordfish. "Your 'Stringbags' proved that what counts in war is the dedication of fighting men, not reliance on advanced weaponry." He wants to work with me on unconventional "booby-trap" warfare. His intelligence adviser "Woodie" is descended from Prince Damrong, who explored prewar Burma. Woodie later discloses that his king is not amused by Mountbatten's assumption of a Burmese title on the eve of Burma's release from fiefdom within the British Empire.

Woodie is our companion during exhausting journeys with Bhumibol throughout the kingdom. Woodie, sophisticated and widely traveled, is delighted that in Africa, I knew the famous J.A. Hunter, who claims to have bagged the most elephants in the history of white hunters. But when Monika finds a starfish on a beach and proposes to bleach it, Woodie protests against killing any living thing. "What about killing in combat?" we ask. Woodie says, "If a living thing runs into my bullet, it's not me who kills." He travels in Burma and hostile neighborhoods. I learn how worldly-wise Woodie and the royals are when I reconstruct the complicated history of their family tree. My dragons again link past and present. Monika had already flown to Lausanne to be scrutinized by Bhumibol's older sister Galyani, now Princess Galyani, having re-married into royalty. She had divorced the son of another pro-Japanese war criminal. Exercising her new authority, she discloses more about how much is known about us by the time Bhumibol invites us to live in the kingdom.

At the Narathiwat meetings, we are joined at dinner on September 29, 1987, by Crown Princess Sirindhorn, adored by Thais who hope she will succeed the king. The problem is her older brother's claim to the crown. He is disliked for his closeness to drug barons, brothel-keepers, and the CIA. Big brother is absent from this family dinner. The menu lists items from the king's farms, run by folk taught in his rural schools to modernize farming. Bhumibol is a land reformer, influenced by China's initial Maoist revolution. He goes into the jungle to persuade young Thai communist guerrillas to join his campaign to transform the country. The menu at our first family dinner lists, in French, consommé au sherry, followed by krapong, a nontraditional fish introduced by the king as best suited for village ponds, and ends with Fruits de Passion.

The king also has dragons in the basement of his mind. The murder of brother Ananda haunts him. Born in Germany in 1923, Ananda later became very much aware of Jews sent to death camps. The Ninth Rama confesses his unease at reports of King Rama the Seventh visiting Hitler in Nazi Germany. "The Fuehrer told him that stern measures were required to solve economic woes caused by 'international Jewry,' thinking this pleases a monarch whose predecessor wrote, 'The Chinese are the Jews of the East.'"

But the Seventh Rama rejected anti-Semitism and neo-fascist Siamese leaders. He abdicated in January 1934, moved into a thatched-roof cottage at Virginia Water in Surrey, and took to bicycling along English country lanes. The abdication left Siam without a king until Ananda was murdered and Bhumibol revived the monarchy. He reads my books about Jewish survival and draws a parallel between his kingdom and Israel: "Like us, a tiny country surrounded by immense populations under hostile dictators." His father, at university in Heidelberg, was shaken by the discovery of Auschwitz and other death camps. Bhumibol wonders why so much hatred is directed at Jews and all who resist dictators. "There is much to be learned from the balance of nature," he says, and quotes from memory a speech by Hubert H. Humphrey, US Democratic vice president, on January 14, 1966: "There is in every American, I think, something of the old Daniel Boone who, when he could see the smoke from another chimney, felt himself too crowded and moved further out into the wilderness."

Bhumibol lives close to Nature. He says that if we ignore Nature, everything will unravel. Nature builds resistance to hostile neighbors and bad politicians. He cultivates new sources of food, supervises farms on land around his home, shows me fresh village ponds where he introduces new kinds of fish. He takes me to mangrove swamps that now provide an abundance of shrimps. I hear echoes of the Boxing Parson, Prince Charles, and biodiversity on the farms of the Duchy of Cornwall. I tell this king about Prince Charles challenging "bastions of conventional thinking" and Charles' lament: "I am dismissed as a dreamer in a modern world that clearly thinks itself too sophisticated for 'obsolete' ideas, but if we ignore Nature, everything starts to unravel."

I seem to have soared all this way across space and time to meet an oriental monarch who practices lessons that the chaplain to an English queen offered me. I tell the Ninth Rama about the Boxing Parson's definition of "dragons in the basement of the mind." Bhumibol speaks of his own dragons, going back to when the likelihood of becoming king was inconceivable. This is why he is forever driven by that moment when his brother said "I walk behind you" though dead from a bullet in the head, his body already encased in the Golden Urn. Everything Bhumibol has done since then is driven by the reformist plans of two idealistic young brothers, then both alive. He agrees with Prince Charles: "China, once seen as dirt-poor, will run rough-shod over our old imperialist snobbery . . . Former colonies always understood biological diversity . . . None of us will survive if the underlying well-being of the planet is destroyed."

Bhumibol translates for his armed forces an English biography of Tito, whose Yugoslav guerrillas used unconventional ways to defeat the Nazis. This king talks freely during our private sessions about the growing difficulty in curbing the greed of palace courtiers whose numbers multiply. He recalls a simpler time when I came through Bangkok to Djakarta to enter Indonesia during its war to destroy Malaysia. He is uneasy about one US ambassador, "Wild" Bill Donovan, creator of the Office of Strategic Studies (OSS), who tried to involve the kingdom in wars against Asian communism. The king knows that Donovan once paid public tribute to Sir William Stephenson as having "taught us all we know about gathering foreign intelligence." But Bhumibol feels threatened by more recent US "adventurism like the secret bombing of Cambodia. He fears this led to the growing nightmare of the Khmer Rouge. He says Zhou Enlai began with youthful dreams of social reform, and could have restrained Chairman Mao in the early days. Now it seems inevitable that China, playing so big a part in Thai business, will bring into its fold all of Southeast Asia. He says of Crown Princess Sirindhorn, "It is wise that she speaks Mandarin and writes for Chinese journals." This, plus his reformist agricultural programs, fuel the view of his CIA opponents that he encourages "a form of communism." He reminds me that Siam is unique in resisting foreign domination. "This is why the royal standard is a *garuda,* like an eagle with a beaked but human head. It holds apart the forces of good and evil."

He paraphrases the question raised in the *King and I,* banned by his parliamentarians but which he greatly enjoyed in New York: "If allies are weak, isn't the king better off alone?" He argues that Buddhists have never fought a holy war. He has become a godlike figure among Thais, although he went to Catholic schools and sends me to the local Catholic cardinal who runs a web of intelligence informers in communist neighborhoods. He quotes Sirindhorn's gentle spirit, reflected in a poem she wrote about him, in Thai and French as if to bridge two worlds: "Through the dark jungle, very dense / Which stretches out interminably, somber and immense / I follow without stopping the footsteps of my Father as a strong right arm. / Oh Father, I am dying of hunger and I am tired. / Look! The blood is running from my two wounded feet. / Father, will we arrive at our destination? / Child! On earth there exists no place / Full of pleasure or comfort for you. / Our road is not covered with pretty flowers.

/ Go! even if it breaks your heart. / I see the thorns prick your tender skin. / Your tears are rubies on the grass / For all the human race does not lose its courage in the face of pain. / Be tenacious and wise and be happy to have an ideal so dear. / Go! If you want to walk in the Footsteps of your Father."

She walks in his footsteps by appearing, on his behalf, at the 2011 royal wedding of Kate the commoner, and William, son of Princess Diana. Royals from around the world parade in all their finery. Sirindhorn appears in the unassuming style she has always adopted, her black hair pinned back by a couple of simple clips. Her presence fuels speculation that Bhumibol still wants her to take over when he dies, despite the resolve of her older brother, the Crown Prince, to occupy the throne. Sirindhorn is the very opposite of her mother, Queen Sirikit, who was once feted everywhere. Crown Princess Sirindhorn is most at home amid wildlife, and feels no need to be anything but herself, loyal to her father's ideals. She mentored our daughter Alexandra when, as a child, she was suddenly obliged to speak Thai as the only non-Siamese attending the palace school. Sirindhorn knows a special language, otherwise jealously guarded in the one village where it is used to communicate with elephants. When a baby elephant is brought in from the jungle because it shows markings of royalty, the Crown Princess writes traditional Siamese "lullabies" for the new addition to a palace stable of white elephants. She is horrified that I knew J.A. Hunter, killer of elephants. After she and the king ask when it became possible to write about Intrepid, I had to stutter that Ian Fleming pushed for it after I met, of all people, "Mister Hunter in Africa."

Sirindhorn wants to know how this happened. My dragons dredge up a picture of J. A. Hunter, standing still as an elephant on the dirt road from Nairobi to Mombasa. He wore black safari gear, dark and bulky like the elephants he shot. "He loved them but some destroyed native crops," I explain. "So he saw hunting as a way to cull an excess of destructive elephants. He lived where my friend Nick Carter saved wildlife from poachers until he was expelled from Kenya after the British colony became an independent republic."

The king asks if this was also when Sir William went ahead with giving me details of unconventional Intrepid-style operations. "Yes," I say.

Author's daughter Alexandra with a young elephant preparing to enter the sea near the palace of Jua Hin. The small Thai palace is known as "Far from Worry."

"It followed an earlier time in Kenya when Independence Day marked freedom from British colonial rule." Woodie's intelligence reports are For His Majesty's Eyes only. His dragons pour out tales of past resistance to would-be colonizers. After much earlier research, I blame the Eighth Rama's murder on Tsuji, the Japanese war criminal. General MacArthur's successors in Tokyo had saved Tsuji when he pretended his only crime was to fight Asian communism. In Tokyo, evidence was never admitted into US courts of inquiry that Tsuji killed Bhumibol's brother. The regicide is never discussed at the Grand Palace. Sirindhorn is more concerned about the slaughter of elephants in Africa.

She question me at a private dinner, and makes my own dragons leap back across time again, back to a distant past in what was known as the Dark Continent, to the day of independence for a former British colony in Africa. Prince Philip stands with Jomo Kenyatta. Searchlights focus on the Union Jack, which will be lowered at midnight when the lights go out. This follows tradition. Each newly liberated colony unfurls its new flag before the lights go on again. Free Kenya is born. It is the mid-1960s. Arafat becomes leader of Al Fatah and directs Arab guerrilla warfare against Israel. Later will come terrorist bombings in Nairobi. But here, tonight, I only hear the joyful beat of drums heralding self-rule. The new Kenyan banner is run up the flagpole in the darkness of the midnight handover from colonial rule. Queen Elizabeth's husband nudges the new leader of this freshly born republic and asks jovially, "Are you sure you won't change your mind?"

I remind Jomo Kenyatta of this "schoolboy joke" when Jomo is in London for a Commonwealth conference. I am presenter-producer for a British ITN TV news show and interview Jomo. He laughs, as he did back then, and taps me playfully on the head with his fly-whisk for "being naughty." With this we open the evening news. Yet Kenyatta was tagged "Leader to Death and Darkness" by a British governor during the Mau-Mau uprisings prior to 1960 when I first moved with my family to Nairobi. Our housekeeper is reported by the governor to have been a Mau-Mau oath taker. We keep her. She's a dear thirty-three-year-old woman and reminds me of the misleading tag, "Lack of Moral Fiber," pinned on US soldiers in Korea.

# CHAPTER 41

# A Difference between Elephants

MY CHILDREN, IN OUR EARLIER DAYS IN AFRICA, LOVED WILD ELEPHANTS. In Thailand, as Crown Princess Sirindhorn knows, elephants work hard at building wooden forts with their *mahout* drivers. In Africa, where elephants are visibly different from those of Asia, we can walk among huge African elephants if we tread quietly. Some have to be moved from the region of villages where they smash fences and strip the cultivated land, gulping the crops in enormous quantities. Nick Carter darts rhinos with tranquilizing drugs to move them to safety. He is joined, during school breaks, by my eldest son, Andrew. Jackie has the bushbaby she later takes to school in England and smuggles into Malaysia. Kevin and Sally wander freely through our garden's lush avocado trees, down to a river of crocodiles. Andrew befriends a baby rhino dubbed "Little Owl," and finds a bat hitherto unknown, and now displayed in Nairobi's natural history museum, with his name incorporated in a Latin title for this rare specimen.

Sirindhorn eventually meets these children from my African past. She understands the need to break free from sorting out incomprehensible human conflicts. The king, her father, later wants to know more, being proud of Siam's history of escaping colonial domination but also uneasy about the new form of US exploitation.

I describe taking the family into the tranquility of Africa's open spaces under brilliant skies. Nature is in balance here: every species except man is tidily organized. I hear from Ian Fleming. He spends winters in his Jamaican home, where World Commerce secretes one of its major

Author in Kenya with son Andrew and his baby rhino, nicknamed "Little Owl."

projects behind the innocent title of Caribbean Cement. Sir William Stephenson moves from there to Bermuda. Fleming telegraphs me, via INTER: "Western world needs to boost morale as Cold War intensifies. The Soviets push our backs against the wall."

I see an example when I cross the Kenyan border in 1962 and enter Somalia, infiltrated by the Soviet Union. In the capital of Mogadishu, a crowd of agitators in threadbare rags, but endowed with shiny metal badges stamped with the hammer-and-sickle, surround me, claw at my US-made cameras that I lift high above my head, hoping nobody spots the cameras' decadent origins. I yell "Russkie! Me Russkie!" I pray nobody speaks Russian or I'm a goner. Word spreads that I'm a comrade. The attackers back off.

I learn from this attempt to take the measure of human self-destruction in the ex-Italian colony: respect for English District Commissioners who will soon disappear along with Union Jacks. District Commissioners are underpaid but stoically organize meetings of African headmen to settle

224

feuds on both sides of the Kenya-Somali frontier. These durbars, these gatherings, are surprisingly joyful and deflate anger built up over misunderstandings between tribes. The District Commissioner has no other powers than their respect, and his mastery of several tribal languages to settle disputes. Hateful memories of the long-departed Italian colonizers also encourage Russian intervention. In Ethiopia the Soviets bring in weapons but do nothing to improve public welfare. I discover this firsthand in an Addis Ababa hospital when I suffer from the inevitable dose of diarrhea, lying on a wooden floor until my health improves with the help of an amiable "witch doctor" who simply employs natural remedies of ancient origin.

Back in Kenya, I'm thrown by a horse and break my back. A Nairobi neighbor let me ride his horses on Sunday mornings but this time lent me a new one with the caution that "gears are in reverse and when you pull back on the reins, it goes faster." The horse takes me downhill toward the local cathedral just as worshippers are pouring out. I have a vision of flattening the congregation. I do exactly the wrong thing. I pull back on the reins. The horse gallops. I yank its head to one side, and we go over a fence. I fall flat. My back seems broken. In the hospital, my surgeon is a well-known Harley Street specialist who left the UK because he conducted abortions in a time when these were illegal. He stretches me out, my legs and arms locked forward and back, so that I cannot move. In the adjacent cot is a friend whose Land Rover rolled over. At night, when the hospital virtually closes down, the doctor's gorgeous blonde daughter sneaks in to where my friend is also anchored, and whispers to him, "My fingers are going on safari." When she turns her attentions to me, I grind out loud protests. She desists. My spine mends, up to a point. I don't deserve the long-term consequences of chronic back pain, since I am innocent of permitting her fingers to wander on safari over me.

My house in Nairobi is rented from an Italian who would have been Governor of Kenya if only Mussolini had won the war. I meet a former Security Liaison friend from Hong Kong. As usual, his funds are limited. We split the cost of flying a small monoplane to Urundi-Burundi, renamed Ruanda after French colonial rule evaporates. Tribal tensions will later lead to genocide in the ex-colony. The UK ambassador, in this earlier period, shows me his dispatches. We sit in the Coconut Bar beside Lake Tanganyika. It is the season of heavy rains. Rising waters make us balance in the lotus position on bar stools. I say I'm astonished by so many acronyms in his files: TTUC and ARKO and other odd initials suggesting lots of organizations in this primitive setting. He says, "I make 'em up. Only way to get London to read my dispatches. Locals couldn't organize a tea party but the Huntus know how to kill the Watutsis and vice versa." He adds, "Don't look now but there's the Tutsi Minister of Justice."

On my other side squats the minister, picking his nose.

This same ambassador turns up again in Indonesia when it is exhausted by its "konfrontasi" war against Malaysia. I covered this Soviet-backed war as bureau chief of Near & Far East News (NAFEN). Its reports go to the Intelligence Research Department at the Foreign Office. In Indonesia, many were silenced by Maoist Chinese. Survivors now flock to the UK embassy's revived celebration of Queen Elizabeth's birthday. In a long waiting line, I finally reach the ambassador. "What-ho! Not quite so wet as the Coconut Bar!" he cries. In this vast crowd, after all these years, he remembers, and sheds his former cover as a kind of P.G. Wodehouse silly-arse Jeeves.

I go to see Sir William Stephenson in Bermuda to begin assembling some of the Intrepid story. I have to sort out recollections, make connections, prepare to discuss with him the same kind of untidy leaps across the calendar that, during overt and covert wars, were needed to link events separated by calendar dates. He has his own dragons, and shares my reliance on "notional proximity, for what happened in past months, or days, or years," he says in one of our recorded interviews, "become significant when tied together outside the march of conventional time."

## CHAPTER 42

# Adventures of the Imagination

MY PRESENT CROP OF CHILDREN PREPARE FOR UNIVERSITY. GLENYS herds them to Canada in yet another cargo ship, loafing through Asian waters, loitering in Japan's inner seas, and progressing calmly across the Pacific to North America. She comes to terms with "normal" motherhood. No more sharing in exciting sideshows to my foreign assignments. I settle down to making TV documentaries. In spare hours, I write the kind of fantasies I lapped up as a boy. The future now holds out a prospect of assignments abroad minus marvelous benefits we all shared while I challenged the children's imaginations, defying the conventional view of what constitutes a "proper schooling in a stable environment." Those last words come from my old friend Arthur Hailey. I find a less impermanent home in Toronto, and walk to work at the Canadian Broadcasting Corporation.

The wicked spirit of the inquisitive wanderer is revived when a New York publisher invites me to investigate legends that Hitler's shadow, Martin Bormann, escaped Berlin with other Nazi criminals to Latin America. This follows Intrepid's belief after World War II that leading Nazis slipped into the bailiwicks of other dictators. All these years later, I can again combine the normalcy of a regular job with excursions abroad. My CBC salary barely covers domestic expenses, but again I choose to accept a modest income in exchange for freedom to roam. Often, I can travel as a producer of TV documentaries because of experience in foreseeing a news story worthy of lengthy treatment, if only in some STEVERITE-INTER chronicle.

After such a long end to Hitler, it should be easier to track the fate of surviving Nazis. I return to Israel to meet a former chief of the Israeli secret service, Issar Harel. He tells me how he felt after he caught Eichmann, and flew with him from Argentina to Israel. "I was not prepared to be in the company of a meek little old clerk," he says, "instead of a monster in jackboots."

To learn more, I fly to England to meet Dr. Otto John, the German who came out of East Berlin. He had worked for a commercial airline in pre-Nazi Germany and for a time thought communism offered alternatives to Hitler. After the war he was disenchanted by what he knew as "the Gehlen Org." This anti-communist intelligence agency was headed by General Reinhard Gehlen. I had interviewed him as an expert on the Soviet Union. Otto John recalls that Gehlen won US support after claiming he was never a Nazi but merely Hitler's intelligence expert on the Soviet Union. Gehlen took over Reichsleiter, Martin Bormann's old mansion, six miles south of Munich, where wartime Nazis in charge of Dachau took breaks when the sights and sounds in that concentration camp became too sickening, even for them. Known as "the settlement" after its use as a Hitler Youth training center, it later flew the Stars and Stripes, replacing the Nazi swastikas in 1945. On a brass plate appeared the disarming sign: SOUTH GERMAN INDUSTRIES UTILIZATION. The mansion had become a training school for spies. When the so-called Gehlen Org became part of the federal German government, it continued to get US financial support and, in 1971, General Gehlen published a claim that Martin Bormann was alive, inside Russia.

Otto John seemed likely, after the 1939–45 war, to become chief of the Gehlen Org. He was smeared by Gehlen, who declared him a traitor. Before and during the war, Otto John was a German liberal who hated Nazism. His brother was killed after the British-backed bomb plot failed to kill Hitler in July 1944. In talks with Otto John, I conclude that he was among many good Germans torn between loyalty to their country and hatred of Nazism. Some chose communism. Otto John worked with British intelligence after he left East Germany. In London, we meet on park benches near the Serpentine. He tells me how he was disenchanted by the pro-Nazi actions of ex-King Edward VIII and his former paramour who became Duchess of Windsor. He makes me think of Rena, and all those others I had known, who felt betrayed by the West and turned to the East, only to be trapped within the Soviet tyranny. Otto John was fortunate. He made his way back. He describes this as "moving twice between the lines." He speaks of his youthful ideals and how those who feared Nazism turned to communism after Hitler was courted by the Windsors, who had been seen as part of English royalty. Otto John lost confidence in Western democracy. Did he win the full trust of British intelligence? The full basis for his misgivings about the Windsors was not openly substantiated until the twenty-first century.

CHAPTER 43

# The BBC and "The Nazi King"

THE MISGIVINGS OF OTTO JOHN AND OTHER GOOD GERMANS ARE validated much later, in a BBC-TV documentary, dated 2009, entitled "The Nazi King." This exposes the ex-king who abdicated, became Duke of Windsor, and married the former Baltimore belle who insisted upon the title Duchess of Windsor. The BBC is funded by the UK government. The documentary had official approval and discloses the ex-king's links with the Nazis and Hitler, before and during the 1939–45 war. The facts can no longer be suppressed by the application of Oaths of Secrecy or their draconian clauses. The UK's Freedom of Information Act opened secret files in the year 2000 and prompted protests from historians that some secrets remained hidden. It was some years before they won access to information still deemed to be potentially harmful. But harmful to whom?

Damning proof of the ex-king's Nazi sympathies almost fell into the hands of Americans in 1945. After Nazi Germany collapsed, Hugh Trevor-Roper and Anthony Blunt stole, from a castle in the postwar US sector of Germany, old letters from ex-King Edward VIII to prominent Nazis who might restore him to the throne. These letters had to be kept secret. They could seriously embarrass Buckingham Palace. Blunt's silence was guaranteed as Keeper of the Queen's Pictures. Only later was he exposed as another Soviet mole within the UK Establishment.

On their secret mission, Blunt and Trevor-Roper, recovered correspondence from the Duke of Windsor to Hitler. The letters had been lodged by the Prince of Hesse at the family home near Frankfurt, along with a full record of one conversation in which Hitler spoke of restoring the ex-king of England to the throne. Other papers reflected the closeness between the Duke and Duchess of Windsor and the Fuehrer before and during World War II. If questioned while trying to recover this damning evidence, Blunt and Trevor-Roper were told to say, by King George VI, that they were retrieving letters from Queen Victoria to her eldest daughter, Empress Frederick of Prussia. The Prince of Hesse family home, Schloss Kornberg, had been commandeered in 1945 to serve as an army club and dormitories, with an American WAC captain in charge. The Princess of Hesse authorized handing over the evidence, but the WAC woman officer was under instruction to stop Blunt and Trevor-Roper from taking anything. The two agents had to smuggle out the incriminating papers and hide them in a pickup truck. It was only in 1979 that UK prime minister Margaret Thatcher confirmed that Blunt was a Moscow-run mole. Blunt was stripped of his knighthood. Trevor-Roper was elevated to the House of Lords.

Intrepid was in trouble for gathering such damning details when Whitehall was instructed to cover them up. His fiercest postwar critic was Hugh Trevor-Roper, treated as the UK's ultimate authority on Nazis until he lost credibility by authenticating fake Hitler diaries sold to the *Sunday Times* of London. Whitehall had long since buried Intrepid's wartime reports of the ex-king's flouting of wartime financial controls while, as Duke of Windsor, he served as Governor of the Bahamas. The appointment followed the proposal in 1940 by the UK's foreign secretary, Sir Samuel Hoare, an admirer of the ex-king, that a deal should be made with Hitler.

"The quicker we get the Hoares out of the country, the better," Sir Alexander Cadogan, permanent undersecretary to the UK foreign office, wrote on May 20, 1940, in his diary, published after the war. "But I'd rather send them to a penal settlement. He'll be the Quisling of England when Germany conquers us and I am dead."

The greatest threat is posed by ex-king Edward and his pro-Nazi wife, the Duchess of Windsor, after they flee from exile in Paris, ahead of Germany's occupation of France. While the bulk of British armies in Europe are evacuated from Dunkirk, the UK foreign secretary, Lord Halifax, echoes the wish of the Windsors to negotiate peace with Hitler.

Winston Churchill calls for their return to England. Instead, they flee to Spain and arrive in Madrid on June 23, 1945. There the US ambassador, A. W. Weddall, reports to Washington: "The Duchess of Windsor declared France lost the war because it was internally diseased. . . . This doubtless reflects the views of an element in England, possibly a growing one, who find in Windsor hope to come into their own."

While the Blitz hits British cities, the ex-king and his wife shelter in neutral Lisbon. Churchill wants them out of there and they sail to Bermuda. There the ex-king golfs with Canadian troops, and insists that everyone address his wife as "Her Royal Highness." He wires Nazi contacts in Portugal that he will return to negotiate peace. Churchill hastens the Windsors' elevation to the Bahamas, and he sends Bill Stephenson to New York to create BSC, British Security Coordination. Stephenson reports that the ex-king wants to go to Canada "to visit his ranch in Alberta." Intrepid fears the ex-king will then rally American isolationists with pro-Nazi sympathies.

The Windsors are told not to enter North America. Their communications with pro-Nazis are scrutinized by censors sent to Bermuda and the Bahamas. The Windsors' evasions of wartime currency restrictions are investigated by one of Intrepid's staff, H. Montgomery Hyde, sent from Bermuda to the Bahamas. "The role of the Duchess is paramount," he reports, "She was born in Baltimore, out of wedlock in June 1895, and was christened Bessie Wallis Warfield. 'Wallis' the divorcee who caused Edward VIII to abdicate as symbol of Britain's imperial power, continues to encourage Edward's links with Nazi Germany in time of war."

A pro-Nazi Swedish businessman, Axel Wenner-Gren, establishes the Bank of the Bahamas, linked to the institution financing Hitler's Gestapo, the Stein Bank of Cologne, and also to the Banco Continental in Mexico City. By April 7, 1941, Intrepid has proof of the Windsors' financial dealings through these intermediaries, subverting the UK's effort to conserve dwindling foreign currency reserves. Sumner Welles at the US State Department confides to BSC banking experts that the Windsors are siphoning currency to the Banco Continental. The FBI reports the ex-king is promised that Hermann Goering will overthrow

Hitler and restore the duke as king of England "when Germany wins the war." The Duchess emerges from the conflict as a millionaire in her own right. Goering ensures his own silence by committing suicide during the Nuremberg war-criminal trials.

The Windsors' conduct takes me back to Mama's work for the anti-Nazi resistance and Dad's undertaking of poorly paid secret work. All their sacrifices were threatened by betrayal. BSC knew too much. I first see the BSC reports while working on Intrepid's biography. I can only skim fragmented documents. I feel the old urge to escape into a wilderness where conflicts are readily visible. Have I roamed with the open mind of a child in an adult world? Did I fool myself into believing I can always tell right from wrong? I recall the integrity of fellow pilots: the risks taken by honest journalists like St. Exupery, who wrote magical books before he crashed his warplane in Nazi skies. I count those who died for what seemed good and true. Were they betrayed by this English ex-king and his American wife? If Spud Murphy had known, would his ghost still lay upon me the need to justify his death? Was the truth of ex-king Edward's support for Hitler known to the Jewish underground fighters who fought the British during and after the war against the Nazis? Were the efforts of Jews to settle in British Palestine distorted by anti-Semitic prejudice bolstered by this ex-monarch of the British Empire? Did this incite Jewish agencies like the *Irgun Tsevai Leumi* to bomb British officials and kill British soldiers in Palestine? The violence aroused concern among mainstream Zionists. The Jewish Agency was asked to help suppress terrorists who earlier struck at British leaders in Cairo with oversight of Palestine. Is this where it all started, when the tiny new state of Israel found itself surrounded by oceans of Arab hatred?

I hear my mother reading aloud: "A rock pile ceases to be a rock pile the moment a single man contemplates it, bearing within him the image of a cathedral." I need to see the good that lies within the piles of lies. I consult Rider Latham's relative by marriage, a British army general who attended a school to which I might eventually send my children. I ask the general if the school is any good. "I'll tell you how good," the general says wryly. "I promoted Idi Amin while I commanded troops in Uganda."

# CHAPTER 44

# A Piece of Cake

My dragons return to Uganda when I reported from Africa in the sixties. Then I am thrust forward to July 1976 when a cable from INTER reports to STEVERITE that "Big Daddy is in for a big surprise." I tell Oscar Dystel, my Bantam publisher. Big Daddy is Idi Amin, cannibalistic dictator of Uganda. Oscar says I should fly to Israel to write a book for Bantam. We avoid paperwork and save time by shaking hands at Grand Union Station. From New York, I catch a flight to Tel Aviv. Oscar begins the costly business of marshalling paper mills and typesetters and copy editors. He and I stake everything on mutual trust, not written contracts.

Betrayal and hostile propaganda dogs Israel. Now its air force must rescue Jewish hostages on a hijacked Air France flight, grounded and under Idi Amin's control at Entebbe. His Uganda air force was once trained by Israeli pilots when their tiny country's technology might serve Africa despite anti-Semitic pressure. Now when Israel pilots protect their narrow borders, their warplanes are accused of intruding into the air space of hostile nations. The rescue flight to Entebbe must skirt the east coast of Africa, head south to Zanzibar, then turn north, the only friendly air space arranged by a Brit who stayed after Kenya's independence. As Minister of Agriculture, he helped black farmers. For helping Israel, his own private plane is sabotaged and he is killed. I do not identify him, for the sake of his family. In *Ninety Minutes at Entebbe,* a book I later write, photographs of Israeli airmen are smudged to disguise their identity. Also for security reasons, I do not link Jonathan, killed leading the rescue, with

Entebbe commandoes preparing in Israel for rescue of hostages held in Uganda. Faces in this operational photo were blacked out to conceal identity of the Entebbe raiders.

his brother Benjamin Netanyahu, a future prime minister whose tough leadership is driven by a memory of Ben's special-forces dedication, and the bravery and sacrifice of the Entebbe action.

During sojourns in Bermuda, I assemble Intrepid's publishable records. For us both, Bermuda's attraction is its closeness to nature. I can slip underwater to revive my curiosity about sea life. He can handle Whitehall's disapproval by taking comfort from wildlife. "At least creatures of the wild," he says, "fight clean." His Big Daddy forewarning coincides with concern for my fast-growing children, who need a more conventional education after far more adventurous lives than I had ever imagined as a child.

Sir William Stephenson, the name by which Intrepid is known in Bermuda, wants to hear more about these other lives. I recall explorations of wildlife in Malaysia, where three of our children attend the British

Army school. Sally, our fourth and youngest, attends a local kindergarten, and at home studies the construction techniques of highly organized weaver ants. These march head to tail along a forest canopy on the open side of our dining space and build a kind of metropolis with suburbs linked by commuter routes. The ants seem insensitive to gravity and form air bridges. They are endlessly fascinating and closest to us among many other mysteries. We drive into the Cameron Highlands and giant Atlas moths float beside us above dense jungle. We listen to the haunting cry of gibbons. We puzzle over the mystery of Sarawak turtles surfacing at full moon to lay eggs, always on the same beaches after incredibly long undersea journeys. Their precise navigation, we don't understand. I remember that as a boy, I imagined superworlds where space bends. This mystery, and its possible association with the Sarawak turtles, is the foundation of a story I write for *Harper's Magazine*. I know a bit about sea turtles since diving at the Pratas Reef off Taiwan. Up come old cans of 16 mm film for a documentary I shot on Taiwan, produced with the title *The End of the Beginning*. It refers to the end of the initial phase of Taiwan's defiance of China's communists. Jimmy Wei, intimate aide to Taiwan's Nationalist Chinese chief, Chiang Kai-shek, had told me why he spent long nights copying the calligraphy of past emperors "to enter the mind of whatever emperor I choose." This is something Intrepid understands as completely as my reports on a classical Chinese "war" when Maoist guns on the mainland opened fire on even days in the calendar, and Taiwan's guns shot back on uneven dates. He thinks it a mature arrangement which left warlords with their armies intact. It often seems to me that some such spirit prevailed when I slipped from one side to the other in the Malay-Indonesian conflict. After it ended, President Sukarno, in disgrace but still in charge, sees me in Djakarta. "I always knew when you were here," he says as he pokes me with a swagger stick. "Never pass an open door, eh?"

Sir William keeps our STEVERITE-INTER correspondence about Jana Warawantu. Her presence in Pakistan once aroused my curiosity. Now she is said to have been an agent for Sukarno. Again I stay at her Djakarta home. In the war against Malaysia, she paid lip service to anti-colonial feeling. Her garden is designed to resemble a jungle. A large

The "Queen of West Irian," mother of Jana Warawantu. She was still known as Queen of West Irian after moving to the mainland. She became a famous artist under the regal title.

woman appears. "My mother," says Jana. "Still calls herself Queen of West New Guinea." The unexpected queen takes me to a neighboring house, and says, "I'm primitive. But he's more primitive. Straight down from the trees." She indicates a small man wearing what looks like a crown fashioned from vines and slender branches. He joins her side. Their artless smiles are contradicted by large canvases propped against an impenetrable tangle of jungle. These are impressionistic paintings of such a high order that I look to Jana for enlightenment. "My mother is an artist and my father sells them, since neither receives tribute any more as royalty." I know Jana well enough to recognize that she is telling the truth. She laughs. "It's an assertion of our closeness to Nature. We threw out Dutch colonizers by reviving our faith in old beliefs and skills. We took military aid from the new imperialists in Moscow and Beijing. It cost us a war which exploded old assumptions that the West had a right to dominate us. But you cannot uproot memories of your past unless you uproot your wilderness." Jana had learned this when she was sent to college in the United States. "I worked for the CIA until disillusion set in." She quotes Albert Einstein: "Imagination is more important than knowledge. Knowledge is limited. Imagination circles the world."

Is that why she wandered as far afield as Afghanistan? There is a small silence, broken by the tut-tutting of geckoes, which look like pale-pink versions of my imaginary dragons. Is this how they look when freed from notional proximity? Such speculation is perhaps only possible in such an odd conversation in such a magical setting. Jana gives another quick laugh. "I saw how another Muslim country like our own, steeped in its own traditions, beat the British only to become a victim of the Russians. I gathered secrets of great powers who told 'backward' countries what to do. I concluded that our survival lies in our own funny old jungle traditions."

# CHAPTER 45

# Two Small Countries Surrounded
# by Big Enemies

FOR INTREPID, I RETRIEVED OLD FORGOTTEN NOTES AND PHOTOGRAPHS of Zanzibar, settled by Arab slave traders who dragged tribal folk across the vast African continent, packing them tight into this one-mile-square island off the East African coast, then selling them to Mideast buyers. While my family lived with me in Kenya, I recognized the reporter for the New China news agency who had been expelled from India as a spy. He was now in Zanzibar. This signaled New China's initial entry into Africa. In 1963, on a trip to London with the ashes of Doug Willis, a BBC correspondent who died in Kenya, I meet the boss of Independent Television News, Geoffrey Cox. I mention this evidence of Beijing's preparations to expand into Africa. Cox phones me the next day. "We just got reports of China's proposal to send its own people to fix parts of East Africa Railways. You'd better come work for us." Cox is a former intelligence officer who was Paris correspondent for the *Daily Mail* before World War II.

My childhood dreams parallel those of the Ninth Rama. I tell Intrepid that the Siamese king warned me, before we began working together in 1987, "This is dangerous both for you and for me." His kingdom was surrounded by enemies who, like Israel, did not share tolerant religious beliefs. The king recalls a book I wrote about the Israeli Air Force, the IAF: *Zanek!* The book's title is the IAF equivalent of the RAF order: "Scramble!" The king knows I flew a Spitfire, kept by Ezer Weizman after he flew as a fighter pilot with the RAF, and commanded the IAF. The king knows a lot about Israel and its improvised weapons. "He may seem remote on the throne, but he is never on a pedestal," I tell Bill Stephenson who, long before he became Intrepid, worked with the Jewish scientist and mathematical genius Charles Proteus Steinmetz, on innovative commercial ventures. "Steiny" is much admired by the king, who loves technical research and writes for US science journals. In 1999, I publish his biography, noting his uncanny memory for historical and personal details. He remembered "Steiny" as a socialist revolutionary who had to leave Germany, even before Hitler's roundup of Jews.

Stephenson wants to know more about the king and Weizman, who later became President of Israel, and how the Ninth Rama knew about the hasty conversion into "flying artillery" of Israel's old warplanes in the Six-Day War that began on June 10, 1967. I left Malaysia between the end of that war and the outbreak of the 1967 war against Israel. Television and my New York publisher threw me into a conflict that revives biblical memories of Maccabee "The Hammer" and the small band of Jews who defied the vast forces of Syria. Israel mobilizes. It has enough weapons to last a week before being overwhelmed by invaders armed with superior arms supplied by the Soviets. Feeling again the heat of battle, I beat other English-speaking TV networks with a sixty-minute Canadian Broadcasting Corporation-TV documentary. I write the book *Strike Zion!* I am reprimanded for "one-sided reporting" and lose my CBC job. I get my satisfaction from letters smuggled out of Russia from Jews still oppressed. They have somehow gained access to my book and the script from the documentary. They need to believe they have a Biblical land, however small, where some day they might start new lives.

Stephenson shares my view that Israel had no choices. It was at the mercy of surrounding hostile Arab states. Its primary goal had been to capture the Sinai and deter Egypt's Gamal Abdel Nasser. Israel had to capture the Golan Heights to stop the constant Syrian shelling of Jewish settlers below. Jordan's King Hussein ignored pleas to stay out of the conflict and the Israelis pushed back, reluctant occupiers of a Jordanian sector. Intrepid is appalled by the refusal of Israel's neighbors to share its technologies, source of Israel's advance from simple farming to inventive modernity. Israel's pragmatic farmers and groundbreaking scientists, given half a chance, could transform life in what the West still calls "backward countries." An Israeli friend, Naomi Dekel, takes me to visit her old school, founded in prewar Palestine by a pioneering German scholar whose classrooms were surrounded by the school's farm. "We studied in company with small animals that we fed and fondled," says Naomi. Tears well up in her eyes. I always considered her a tough young fighter within the armed forces. I wipe away the tears. She returns to the outdoor classrooms of farm animals and says, laughing: "Arithmetic and tortoises."

I fly in IAF aircraft to gather material for more books. The first native-born sabra to command the IAF, Motti Hod, lets me enter his office when I like. I am there when the door flies open and the current Minister of Tourism walks in. It's Ezer Weizman. He throws on Motti's desk a bunch of enlarged photographs of curious mechanical beasts lining the Suez Canal. I get up, saying, "I'd better leave."

Ezer says, "No! I've just flown a Phantom over Cairo and on the way back, spotted these SAM-missile sites." It is the eve of the 1969–71 War of Attrition, an attempt to avenge Egypt's shaming defeat in the 1967 Six-Day War when three major Egyptian cities, Suez, Ismailia, and Port Said, were hit by Israeli bombs. Now some 18,000 Soviets military advisers are in Egypt, courtesy of Gamal Abdel Nasser. They have installed batteries of SAM-2 antiaircraft missiles to cover the 103-mile length of the Suez Canal.

Hosni Mubarak, a leader on his way down in 2011, was on his way up in 1971, after training as a fighter pilot at the Soviet air force academy at Kyrgyzstan. He is chief of staff of the Egyptian air force when his Soviet air force advisers tell him they detect a gap in the Israeli radar screen around the Sinai Peninsula, and this is a golden opportunity to slip through the gap and bomb Israeli-occupied Sharm el-Sheik to boost morale for a dispirited Egyptian population. Five Soviet pilots fly Egypt's MiG-21s to slip through the radar gap. Israeli fighters are waiting for them. Four of the Russians are shot down. One skedaddles back to the Egyptian base. A Russian general is recalled to Moscow. Mubarak is appointed vice president by his friend and mentor, President Anwar Sadat.

The Mubarak legend is established. He is promoted to deputy minister of war and, following the Yom Kippur War in 1973, rises another rung to air chief marshal. Sadat has found a successor.

I recall this for Intrepid when he insists on driving with me in his small, unremarkable car to the Bermuda airport. He is now in his nineties, proud of his hard boxer's handshake. He grips my arm, locks his eyes with mine, and I know he is saying good-bye for the last time. I am flying again to Bangkok, and during a prolonged stopover at Tokyo airport, I am called to a phone. It's Privy Councillor Thawisan Ladawan, the Ninth Rama's Principal Private Secretary. He says the king wants me to know that I need feel no obligation to keep our date for a royal audience, since I doubtless want to go back for the funeral of Sir William. It is the first I know of Intrepid's death. I tell the secretary that it's pointless to return to Bermuda. Intrepid planned to be buried quickly. There's a stunned silence. Siamese funerals are always long, and can last several weeks for a distinguished personage.

And so I keep another date with the king. His mind, behind the mask, bubbles. Even by 2011, he continues to use what he learned about covert operations. Confronted with uprisings funded by a disgraced but immensely wealthy ex-prime minister derided as "Old Money Bags," King Bhumibol withdraws into the hospital he endowed, with money to buy the most advanced medical equipment. It is now one of the largest hospitals in the world. From his hospital room, he directs double agents planted among hostile mobs, in unconventional operations to defang his powerful enemy. His opponent has allies who churn out widely distributed propaganda that the king is the richest man on Earth, adding a great deal of CIA codswallop about Bhumibol as a clever self-promoter with sinister ties to communist China. Not much is said about his billionaire opponent buying weapons and advice on terror tactics from Arab leaders in Saudi Arabia. Muslim terrorists expand their operations against Buddhists in the kingdom's four southern provinces adjoining Malaysia where extremists now control the border.

Intrepid is gone. His student, the king, continues with unorthodox ways to fight evil. He loved to sail small boats single-handedly, and to

Intrepid (Sir Willliam Stephenson) is honored with the OSS Society's William J. Donovan award on board the US carrier *Intrepid* in 1981, in New York. The award is given to individuals who have given distinguished service to the United States of America. The author is in attendance.

map in minute detail every part of whatever part of the world he was in. He painted wild animals and oversaw nature reserves. He carefully copies in his neat handwriting my quote from the 1855 works of Charles Kingsley, who wanted to remain the "perfect naturalist . . . strong in body; able to haul a dredge, climb a rock, turn a boulder, walk all day . . . swim for his life, pull an oar, sail a boat, ride the first horse that comes to hand . . . and if he go far abroad, be able on occasion to fight for his life." I film this king who relishes the *King* in Kingsley's name, and who walks long distances, climbs nimbly over boulders, swims, and sails in the sometimes treacherous waters of the Gulf of Siam a small wooden boat built by himself.

# CHAPTER 46

# "A Little Person" Goes to School
# at the Palace

PAST AND PRESENT ARE CONJOINED WHEN MY YOUNGEST DAUGHTER, Alexandra, follows in the wake of *Anna and the King of Siam*, based on the nineteenth-century memoirs of a British governess. This king, Bhumibol, Rama IX, asks for my help. My other four children now fly solo, and follow their own adventurous careers.

After I married Monika and we settle in Washington, D.C., we have a daughter, Alexandra. She is four years old when she begins six years as a pupil at the palace from 1989 on. She has to speak Thai and is known as "Shasha." She is the only foreigner ever to attend a palace school. The son of the governess in *Anna and the King of Siam* was educated privately, and was not a palace student, as King Bhumibol points out. He calls Alexandra "The Little Person," and she rises to the level of speaking "palace Thai." This delights the king's mother. She hugs The Little Person as "a Thai farang." Praise indeed. Normally a foreigner is always known as a *farang* and never acknowledged as "Thai" or "Siamese," no matter how long that person may live in the kingdom, even if married to a Thai.

Crown Princess Sirindhorn oversees Alexandra's school. We join royally sponsored festivities on the Thai-Malay border, designed by the princess to bring together Muslims and Buddhists from all over Southeast Asia in an effort to ease religious tensions. The king tries to resolve differences between his Buddhist and Muslim subjects. When terrorists blow up the kingdom's railroads, he plays down these and other racial clashes.

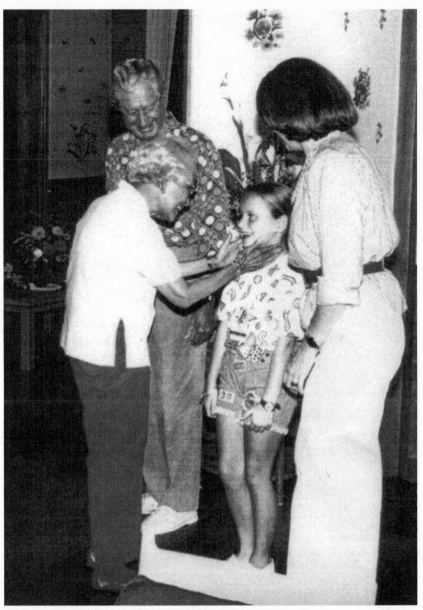

The author's daughter, center, being complimented on her Thai language skills by HRH, the Princess Mother, King Bhumibol's mother.

I see the king frequently when he presides over Buddhist ceremonies. He sits for hours with only the unbroken hum of monks cross-legged on long benches on either side. I ask him, "How can you remain still for such long periods without twitching a muscle?"

"I send my mind upward," he replies. "I detach myself from ugly things, the better to deal with them when I descend." He smiles at some private joke when I say that the Dalai Lama also told me how he levitated into some invisible world of utter calm, returning in better mental shape to handle the physical crises of the day.

The children attending Chitralada spend the first five minutes of every school day meditating. One day, Monika and I find our girl sitting alone under a small spirit-house in a banyan tree. "What are you doing?" we ask. "I'm trying to go UP!" she explains, pressing her hands upward.

Bhumibol has to worry about the several directions taken by neighbors that were once Western colonies. Those that are clients of the Soviet Union and communist China evolve in different directions that are mutually antagonistic. Thailand is unique in having remained free from colonization, drawing upon its long history of playing powerful enemies against each other. Kings kept at bay the British lapping up Asian territories all the way to the western borders, and blocked the French empire from invading from the eastern colonies. Now the country deals with pressures from China, which administers what it calls "tribal minorities" in the north.

"Sasha" is often a source of news after she lunches with canteen workers whose gossip is more fun. Palace school lunches are sedate. The canteens leak information before the local media. She is first to tell us that a Thai general has taken refuge in Sweden when he is thought to be sulking in barracks after failing to grab power. Thai school vacations cover periods when Canadian children are in their classrooms, and we fly with The Little Person to Toronto for a term there. Then she returns to palace studies. Schooling, she assumes, is year-round.

I revisit one of Bhumibol's threatening neighbors, Vietnam. In Ho Chi Minh City, the new name for Saigon, I get the old copy of my Ho profile for the *Sunday Times* of London. The profile is now a fixture in the

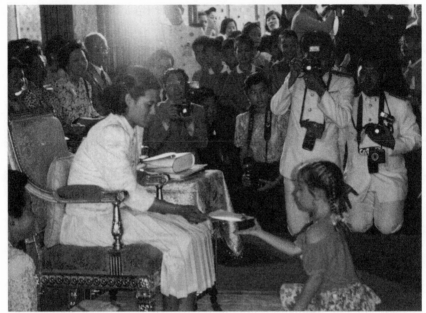

The author's daughter Alexandra receiving an award from HRH Princess Sirind-horn at Chitralada Palace School in Bangkok.

*Literary Gazette,* edited for political correctness. The communist publication has me permanently identified as a Literary Hero.

This is when Bhumibol confides again that after his elder brother was shot dead, although the body was kept in a golden urn for many weeks, the Ninth Rama was leaving the urn for the last time when he heard footsteps, turned, and forgot for a moment Elder Brother was dead. "I said, 'It is for me to walk behind you.' He replied, 'From now on, I walk behind you.'" The king repeats that he has never shared this with anyone until now because I will understand, whereas others might scoff. His enemies once again publish abroad the accusation that he killed his brother. Bhumibol frequently unburdens himself with little-known details of his long life. He publishes his Thai translation of *A Man Called Intrepid.* He is such a revered figure that sales boom, and profits are donated to his Royal Initiatives, the title under which he runs his social reforms.

"Now we are both Literary Heroes," he tells me.

I go with Monika on foot into northern mountains overlooking communist Laos. With the king and Queen Sirikit, we climb a winding stone stairway to a temple carved inside the peak to meet a monk revered by villagers from miles around. The villagers hear through the grapevine of this royal pilgrimage, and in darkest night, thousands tuck themselves into every crevice in that steep climb. They sit in utter silence while their king and queen kneel at the monk's feet and talk for hours about Buddhism and the dangers Thailand is now again confronting.

It is humbling to be in the confidence of the last in line of an ancient Eastern monarchy. After this mountain climb, I no longer dismiss the legend of The Blind Bonze of Luang Prabang in Laos. He is said to have remarkable psychic powers. I visit him with a tough Australian correspondent, Richard (Dick) Hughes, nicknamed The Cardinal. I had known him since the Korean War (he was depicted as a British spy in a novel by John LeCarre.) Dick was determined not to be fooled when he entered the presence of the blind monk. He emerged white-faced and shocked. "The bonze told me things I never disclosed to anybody," he says. "He spoke of my Jewish wife who later died. There is no normal way he could know about such an utterly private tragedy." Dick was once a boxing champion, and usually impossible to fool. Now I understand his mystification, after I climb with my wife and a king and queen into a night of such impenetrable mystery. It is no longer possible to deny the existence of another world of the mind, one I had imagined as a boy.

# CHAPTER 47

# Merry-Go-Round

MY DRAGONS HAVE PORTRAYED OVER THE YEARS A LIFE THAT SEEMS like the merry-go-round defined in my mother's old *Roget's Thesaurus:* a complex, fast-paced series of activities in which the past comes round again and again, always changing form. In 2008, I am in China with Monika. We are visiting Alexandra, who had been studying at Beijing University and is now in Manchuria at the University of Dalian, once the Russian Far East Fleet's Port Arthur. One of her professors invites us to dinner. The question comes up: "Why are there no records of the Great Famine after Mao's Cultural Revolution?"

The young professor says, "Because we are ashamed. My father was jailed as a Wicked Landlord. Even today, he tells us, 'But I *was* a Wicked Landlord.'"

Alexandra speaks Mandarin Chinese, and wherever we go, this instantly prompts the locals to go out of their way to be helpful. They like us because "You are friends of China." It was so different when the Red Army arrested me at The Great Wall for trespassing into Mongolia. I return to that spot with Monika and Alexandra. Everyone pours through that great hole in The Wall. Once you could not even climb on it. Now the winding top is packed, except when Alexandra ran a marathon for twenty-one miles along it, coming in at seventeenth among 2,000 runners who finish.

In 2010, in Palm Beach, Florida, I spot a replica of the ancient temple by the hole in The Wall. This copy is in a luxury store labeled "Rare Antiquities of the World." I ask owner John Beers why and how he got it.

"Rich buyers from China come here all the time," he tells me. "They pay fantastic prices for these antiques, so we can easily afford shopping sprees to China, where such items sell for peanuts. My nouveau-riche Chinese customers come here because high American prices make these things seem more desirable."

Mao's China used force to cure poverty. Now money is the antidote. When I took Ian Fleming to Macau, the Portuguese colony was a den of thieves. Today, it is so enriched by high-rolling mainland Chinese that it is trying to do even better as the world's most lucrative gambling market. American and other foreign operators raise Macau's monthly revenues in 2011 by 33 percent, bettering a surge in the previous year by more than US $23.5 billion. A new US $2.9 billion Galaxy Macau casino-resort offers 450 gambling tables. Prostitutes still make up the larger proportion of workers. The poor look poorer. The future still depends on Beijing's whims.

The more things change, the more they remain the same. Dragons take me back to childhood dreams of running free to satisfy my curiosity about a wider world. How did a boy of yesterday fail to become like so many freshly minted grown-ups of today, raised on sitcoms and news clips. Those who work in cubicles, grow chubby, raise children, must surely wind up wondering what life is all about? Will they have dragons to tie together across the years the wild adventures that the world still can offer?

# Full Circle

I STAND ON ONE OF THE UPPER DECKS OF A MULTISTORIED VESSEL, THE *Mont St. Michelle*, heading out of Portsmouth for Normandy. Monika and our daughter Alexandra, now aged twenty-five, are curious about my days here as a boy sailor. Is that really HMS *Victory*, such a small and fragile wooden ship squeezed between huge aircraft carriers with ski-jumps for rapid jet-fighter launchings? Yes, that really is the man-o'war in which Admiral Lord Horatio Nelson won the greatest victory in British history. Yes, his last sea battle was more than two hundred years ago, yet is everywhere still remembered. Yes, I did walk that quarterdeck where Nelson lay with kerchief over his face to diminish the horror of his men while he took so many hours to die. Yes, we did have to learn about the greatness of the past before we could fly from warships not much bigger than that little wooden ship almost hidden behind such battleships as HMS *Ark Royal*, tied up along a shoreline packed with other modern fighting ships. But today, *Ark Royal* is for sale, to be converted into a passenger liner, or cut up for scrap. Nelson's old ship only survives to remind us of days when Britannia ruled the waves. *Victory* seems so tiny, fragile, a toy ship with rigging that now looks like a network of bits of string. It reminds me of the Japanese model airplane kits Dad brought home from sea. Did I really overcome my vertigo to climb the rigging of a two-stepped mast on that distant warship in order to advance into something more than an Ordinary Seaman, the lowest form of marine life?

Author with Admiral Nelson's famous wooden warship, HMS *Victory,* where he did some of his initial training for the Royal Navy, in the background. He points to a Royal Navy warship with a unique design that is headed for the breakers yard because the Royal Navy is broke.

It is a warm September evening in 2010. Our gigantic ferry moves majestically past my old parade grounds, now looking like little squares on a Monopoly board. The sun sets in a blaze of glory. We retire to our bunks. I turn up the collar of my pajamas.

# Index

D